A. E. HOUSMAN

A DIVIDED LIFE

A. E. Housman, 1911

A. E. HOUSMAN

A DIVIDED LIFE

George L. Watson

RUPERT HART-DAVIS
SOHO SQUARE LONDON
1957

92
H 8424 w

Printed in Great Britain by Butler & Tanner Ltd., Frome and London

FOR EDWARD CUSHING

"But now it matters not"

Contents

7

Illustrations

Foreword

A POPULARITY that would have exhilarated many other poets came to Housman unsought and, it sometimes appeared, against his wishes. Embarrassed by admiration and repelled by curiosity, he persistently averted himself from the consequences of becoming a successful author. Except for the demand that his books should be low-priced, and a fussy concern about the spelling and punctuation of each edition, he lived remote from the literary world and a recluse from his fame. There was almost the mark of anonymity about his work: a voice that could not easily be identified with the outward man. Small in volume and repetitive in theme, his poetry issued from a hidden source and was disciplined into a narrow channel. It had the intensity of a single experience long secreted, which at last forced its way, as if involuntarily, through all the bars of self-restraint. This belated trickle of inspiration, seeping out at the onset of middle age, in defiance of the austere and reticent scholar which Housman had by then become, is the peculiar interest, the unravelled problem, of a life otherwise so firmly and methodically organized. He was a remarkable example, even in the Victorian age, of man's struggle to curb and adapt himself to his environment —a struggle, in Housman's case, discernible only in the bitter lyricism of his poetry.

A boy of six when Swinburne dared to flout the conventions of the period, and a man of thirty-six when Oscar Wilde paid the penalty for such bravado, Housman grew up in that fortress of respectability—the mid-Victorian middle class. It was a society against whose rules of conduct few were tempted to rebel. But whereas conformity was a yoke to which other poets more or less unwillingly submitted themselves, conformity was for Housman the pre-condition of his poetry, the stimulus without which it might never have been written. A prim and decorous personage who "appeared to be descended from a long succession of maiden aunts," as donnish gossip described him, Housman was outwardly indistinguishable from the stiffest model of propriety. With his old-fashioned clothes and meticulous habits, his unbending manner and glacial reserve, he reflected all the typical effects of a rigorous self-abnegation. Among the rare and strange specimens of poetic talent, Housman's belonged to that species which, like a desert plant, thrives in arid isolation. His poetry illustrates the compensations that may spring from loneliness and discontent: a flowering in what seems barren ground. There was nothing in his overt character to imply the presence of, and least of all the audacity to express, a passionate undercurrent; as indeed little biographical evidence remains, outside his poetry, to betray those subterranean emotions for which his life provided no other outlet.

The formidable scholar and ruthless pedant, the emendator of Manilius and the Kennedy Professor of Latin at Cambridge University are not the subject of this book, though behind their impressive classical façade the poet often tends to disappear. Housman devoted the major part of his time and talent to building a reputation in scholarship, and achieved in that dusty enterprise a position more exalted than he will ever occupy in literature. His poetry was an avocation that he professed to regard as the whim of idle moments, an impulse that seized him when in poor health or low spirits. But one accepts this understatement according to the value one assigns to poetry in the scale of things, and to the sombre tolling of Housman's poetry in the midst of his calm and cloistered life. It may be as wrong to ignore as to exaggerate the subjective element in products of the imagination. The poet transcends but never altogether eliminates himself, and the residue of self-exposure is his finger-print, not only visible between the lines, but stamped in the tone and texture of his verse. Even Housman, once he was committed to writing poetry, could no longer suppress the fervencies that, in person, he would never have allowed himself to reveal. Despite the smoke-screen he threw up, which his friends and relatives have loyally conspired not to penetrate, those spurts of flame are biographically unavoidable. At the risk of burning my fingers, therefore, I have chosen to treat the *Collected Poems* as something more than a superior but incidental accomplishment, an exercise irrelevant to the rest of Housman's life. In this study, on the contrary, his poetry becomes the indispensable key to a personality which even those who knew him best always confessed to finding adamantine.

The material with which to construct a factual biography of so reluctant a subject is at best marginal and scanty. A man who discouraged intimacy and practised extreme self-control, whose correspondence was crisp and cursory, who forbade the republication of his occasional writings and who ordered the destruction of his private papers, does not, by careful design, lend himself to documentary discoveries. Only his unyielding mask was turned outward; only bareness and books filled the space around him, in which others would have stored up the tell-tale debris of living. Someone has described Housman's rooms at Trinity as the aesthetic counterpart of a railway station waiting room. Their authentic furniture—mission oak, a hip bath, a green turtle's shell—conveyed nothing but his indifference to comfort and his contempt for fashion. Like one of those literary shrines—the author's cottage preserved for posterity—Housman's external life has an air of desertion as one tries to reanimate it; at its most vivid, the bleakness of a wall topped with broken glass and posted with *No Admittance* signs, beyond which a figure of intimidating silence and unsociability wards off the rash intruder. Posthumously guarded, moreover, by that cult of discretion which has locked so many doors in English literature, Housman is still wrapped in almost inviolate seclusion.

Across this barrier, if one presumes to have surmounted it, the material with which to compose a likeness of the inner man, a biography of the spirit which so obviously underlay those bristling defences, is even more tenuous and speculative—the cryptographic evidence of the poems, with not much else except an assortment of impressions and implications, the scraps, hints, pieces of a puzzle which might be used, alternately, to support one of several interpretations. Housman the monastic scholar; Housman the rejected lover; Housman the forbidding, the mysterious, even the abnormal—all these are familiar and not inconceivable theories, among which the right choice, or proper intermixture, becomes less a matter of reason than of instinct. But if there is no other method by which Housman can be pried from his shell, no method at the same time requires more conscientious manipulation and sharper scrutiny. As a poet, Housman habitually spoke in the first person, but in a solitary discourse that, with a blend of anguish and detachment, ranged over that landscape with figures, the mythical Shropshire into which he transmuted his experience. Wry ballads, brooding elegies, lyrical cries from the heart, they were variations of the same lament, the same unspecified affliction. But in the company of possible witnesses, and even among his most sympathetic friends, Housman did not tap this vein at all. Instead, a growing taciturnity and aloofness repelled those who sought to win his confidence, while professorial quirks more and more engulfed him. The first of many questions that Housman conjures up is the determination of what, among these layers of self, was the order of depth and precedence. Which of them represented the root from which his character drew its strength? Was the poet a true if discrepant image of the man? That such gradations and contradictions undeniably existed in him is enough, I might claim, to justify my title. A divided life, in some sense, Housman's certainly was, in which the force of feeling was diverted and restricted, but never totally submerged by his will and intellect. It is hardly guess-work that, in a man thus torn between mind and emotion, the failure to combine and reconcile them was the source of a life-long conflict.

On this much solid ground, then, I have tried to reassemble the sort of Chinese box in whose compartments Housman contrived to fit himself. It was a habitation different only in degree from the framework of most human lives. Housman sealed off, with an exclusion that came close to asceticism, the sexual and emotional needs that impelled him, no less than other men, towards the ordinary forms of happiness: those approximations with which all but the most indomitable or incurable learn to satisfy themselves, but which, even these, were unattainable for him, except in the sublimation of his poetry. Indomitable he was, in the long climb from his early failure at Oxford to his final eminence in that branch of knowledge in which the examiners had once found him wanting; but unlike one who dedicates himself to a single ambition, Housman did not quench the desires he was driven to renounce. Blighted and imperceptible in his life, they were the very pulse of his poetry, exposed and explicit there in the shadow of his resignation. The qualities of the man were conspicuously reversed in the poet: the one dry, distant, inflexible; the other confiding, sentient, disarmed —a gap that was bridged only in their mutual fatalism. As if released from the irascibilities of his daily life, Housman became, under the poet's mantle, an almost unrecognizably compassionate, commiserating voice. And thus in spite of himself, perhaps, his verse can be turned into a traceable path through the brambles he so diligently planted. His own words, signalling along the hidden passages of his life, may be strung out as the stepping-stones by which, not without hesitation but with some assurance that his footfall may still be heard, one ventures to traverse that dark thicket—his privacy.

What follows, therefore, is an undertaking, against his will but in emulation of his own search for truth, to exhume the pattern, half-obliterated like a Roman pavement, of his buried life. In this self-appointed task I have received no help from the custodian of Housman's memory, his brother, Mr. Laurence Housman, and must regretfully transfer to the reader the handicap of missing letters and other unpublished material from which quotation was forbidden.[1] Such contributions would have made the biographer's work easier and his text more

[1] A diary Housman kept during the nineties, for example, and now in American hands, but of which no further intimations can be given until the ban is lifted.

abundant. By good fortune, however, Housman's notebooks—the valuable if no longer pristine record of his poetic composition—now repose in the Library of Congress, to which I am indebted for the advantage of examining, at first hand, all that remains of those original work-sheets.

To Mr. Noel V. H. Symons, Housman's nephew, I am grateful for access to the material with which his mother had planned to write a family history, including her notes about Housman's childhood; for the photographs of Housman's mother and father which he has allowed me to reproduce; and not least for his friendliness to a project whose outcome he could not foresee. To Dr. Gerald C. A. Jackson, Housman's godson, I owe much of my information, though none of my deductions, about his father's relationship with Housman; and the further assistance of his own recollections of his godfather. I wish also to thank (and exonerate) Mr. Andrew Gow for his counsel and hospitality; Professor Basil Willey for his kindness in opening Cambridge doors; Mr. John Bryson for the same service in Oxford; Mr. S. C. Roberts and Professor H. W. Garrod for the benefit of their conversation; Mr. John Carter for his expert guidance; Professor Gilbert Highet for a reference to one of Housman's classical papers that I might have missed; Mr. David Breslove for enlarging my grasp of Greek and Latin; Mr. D. J. Walters, Headmaster of Bromsgrove School, for his warm and unflagging co-operation; Mr. George Penny, Housman's servant at Cambridge, for his willingness to reminisce; Mr. C. H. Roberts, the Librarian at St. John's College, Oxford, for his aid in tracking down, and Mr. P. I. Clemow, the tutelary Captain of Boats, for his permission to copy the photograph of the St. John's crew of 1880; and Mr. Martin Secker and Mr. E. O. Hoppe for their joint efforts in recovering the portrait which Mr. Hoppe made of Housman about 1910.

Bibliophily, I have learned, is more than a form of manic acquisitiveness, and from the collectors of Housman I have gathered both more ample material and a wider knowledge. To Mr. Houston Martin, for his generosity in sharing not only the fruit of his own research but the various well-chosen relics in his possession, I am particularly indebted. To Mr. H. B. Collamore, Mr. Seymour Adelman, Mr. David Randall and Mr. I. R. Brussel, for similar favours, I am equally grateful.

Among the innumerable students and scholars who have helped to elucidate Housman's poetry, I have profited especially from the advice of Professor Tom Burns Haber and Mr. William White.

For the rest, all books of this kind are written with a reliance on friends, and an exploitation of strangers, that no memory can fully recall or acknowledgments repay; and are published in large part by consent of the many copyright owners (the Administrators of the Estate of the late A. E. Housman; Jonathan Cape; Oxford University Press; Cambridge University Press; etc.), without whose courtesy this or any public discussion of recent literature would be impracticable.

G. L. W.

CHAPTER ONE

To south the headstones cluster

WHILE Englishmen were invading France in that marathon of combat, the Hundred Years' War, a Flemish family crossed peacefully to England, not later than the fourteenth century, and established itself in Yorkshire. Weavers by trade, they prospered and multiplied until, by 1500, some of their descendants had already migrated into Lancashire, and the name had been anglicized from Haussman to Houseman. About 1530, John and Thomas Houseman, as tenants of the manor of Skerton, complained with a native boldness against the Abbot of Furness, whose fishery in the river Lune infringed upon what they conceived to be their own privileges. Clearly, they were by then loyal subjects of Henry VIII, though the outcome of their case is unknown.

From these distant and stubborn forebears, the Lancashire branch of the family soon grew strong and independent, producing more Johns and Thomases, with a scattering of Roberts and Richards, Alices and Marys (though not until 1859 an Alfred Edward). Their history was recorded in lawsuits and title-deeds: a younger Thomas, in 1564, contested, and won, the rights of tenancy over some 258 acres of land in the neighbourhood of Skerton; and in 1618, a Richard could afford to buy the house in Skerton which, in 1693, was sold to a John for the "full and just sum of 120 pounds of lawful money of England." Housman House, as it was called, with the soundless "e" disappearing about this time, raised the ex-immigrants into that yeoman class which administered the farms and villages, and whose red faces glistened from the inns and marketplaces, of agrarian England. Plain, persevering country people, who were quick to grasp the opportunities of rural society, they now abandoned farming and launched into the chief local industries—brewing and cotton-spinning. The John who at the end of the seventeenth century acquired Housman House was a brewer of substantial means, but perhaps from lack of education or excess of caution, left no written will. His son Robert inherited the family homestead, which he enlarged and renamed Lune Bank, inserting over the front door, with a patriarchal gesture, a round stone on which his initials would catch the eye of coming generations.

The next Robert carried on the brewing business and lived in placid eighteenth-century style at Lune Bank, where a numerous family, subject to the prevailing rate of infant mortality, was delivered from his marriage to Miss Alice Gunson. When the first-born John died early, the name was passed along to a subsequent arrival. Thus of ten children, two were duplicates, and only four lived to middle age or longer. Nevertheless, the prolific father could count, among his children's children, a vast progeny, and was said to have assumed a deportment befitting his responsibilities. Solemn-mannered and fastidious in dress, he strove to inculcate, in his namesake above all, those rational principles, that sedate temper and balanced view in which the age excelled. A homespun yet stately figure, Mr. Housman was determined to hand down, like Lord Chesterfield, his knowledge of the world.

About the future of his handsome daughters, Alice and Mary, renowned in Skerton circles as the "Stars of the North," he had no cause to worry; they could, and did, look after themselves, marrying respectively a Unitarian minister and the governor of Lancaster Castle. As for the younger sons, they were expected to make their own way, and those who survived—the second John and Miles, the late-born but not least lively William—followed the conventional course into a business or profession. John was a merchant whose leisure was occupied in admiring the adjacent scenery, and who wrote, before his heart failed at the age of thirty-six, a *Descriptive Tour of the English Lakes.* Miles plied the ancestral trade as a mercer in the booming industrialism of Lancaster, and with higher hopes sent his son to

Cambridge; while the infant William became a solicitor and convivial citizen, whose popularity served to offset, in his father's eyes, a sometimes undignified exuberance. Always shrewd and sensible nonetheless, William had a long and prosperous life, inheriting Lune Bank and transmitting to his own children those solid if unliterary qualities which, in a separate offshoot of the family, can still be found in distant relatives today.

But the junior Robert, a studious boy with a propensity to write verse, gave his father some uneasiness from the beginning. On the verge of his graduation from the Lancaster Free Grammar School, he showed promise—but for what, exactly, it was difficult to decide. The Church was the obvious career for a country-bred youth of modest station and impractical tendencies. But Mr. Housman had observed the fate of too many eighteenth-century clergymen: a run-down vicarage where poverty waged a grubby fight with gentility. No, he was looking for something that would combine intellectual *with* material advancement, and from a small expenditure would yield quick results. Fortuitously, as he surveyed the possibilities, a solution appeared on his own doorstep just in time; and thus, at the quivering age of fourteen, Robert was apprenticed to the village surgeon, Dr. Barrow, a half-trained Scotsman whose limited knowledge and profitable practice it should prove easy for a precocious schoolboy to absorb.

Nothing, as it turned out, could have been better calculated to inflame the sensitiveness and focus the religiosity of adolescence. In 1773 medicine was a primitive science requiring stronger nerves than Robert's. Bleedings and amputations surrounded him by day; the shrieks of the victims echoed in his dreams. Dutifully, for a year or two, he went his rounds and concealed his thoughts, shrinking inwardly from that brutal exhibition of mortality, while in self-defence his troubled conscience groped for some means of spiritual solace. What else could relieve the pain he was helpless to prevent, or reconcile his patients to their agonies? The Sunday sermon conveyed a new message, the priestly function exuded a fresh balm, as he desperately prayed for deliverance from his bondage. The first tremors of conversion had already seized him, and were soon to reach a climax during an Easter holiday at Halton where, on Good Friday, a self-searching meditation on the river bank led him once and for all to renounce the surgical knife in favour of the divine calling.

The conversion of Mr. Housman was another matter which progressed more slowly. But while the parental anger cooled, influential advocates sprang to Robert's defence. Not only the grammar school staff, abetted by the local vicar, loudly championed their protégé; but even in the family circle, by more dulcet methods, Alice and Mary entreated and finally won their father's consent to the resumption of Robert's studies on a theological basis. An interval of harmony followed, during which Robert composed several poems, regrettably never published and now lost, but reputed to have shown "a considerable elegance of mind." Until his coming of age, nevertheless, Robert was detained at Skerton, maturing but not weakening his resolve, which even Mr. Housman could no longer fail to recognize as a deep-seated and incurable vocation. Reluctantly he must consign his favourite son to a realm of thought and experience which he could not enter. And so at last, with a wave of the hand and the provision of pocket money, he saw Robert off for St. John's College, Cambridge, in the autumn of 1780.

The moment of departure marked a turning point in the family history. Behind the reckless student of divinity stretched a line of stolid, practical forefathers—"that endless line," as Robert's great-grandson would phrase it a century later, "of men whose thoughts are not as mine"; while invisible but not far ahead opened a new era to which the Housmans, now rising above the mundane struggle, would contribute a preponderance of clergymen—at least five in the nineteenth century—and one nostalgic scholar-poet. But their heyday of rustic simplicity and earthy enterprise would not recur. It was as if, in man's development, a state of natural adaptation could not survive the awakening of his intellect.

In the mellow October light, however, Robert's immediate prospects seemed more cheerful as he proceeded, on horseback, by post-chaise and on foot, across the Midlands to Cambridge, a devious and disconnected journey that took six days. To his "honoured parents," after having his hair done and presenting himself to his college tutor, he addressed a long epistle retailing the adventures of the trip and the savings he had already effected. "A gown (when new) costs £4. 10. I have got a very good one for ten shillings. The cost of a surplice is £1. 10. I have got one, bands and all, for sixteen shillings." Promising to send "a more exact account of every particular" with the quarterly bills, he installed himself in the clammy Gothic chambers of St. John's, where within a year he had demonstrated sufficient qualifications to be admitted to deacon's orders, and was forthwith appointed curate to the Rev. Mr. Croft, Vicar of Gargrave in Yorkshire.

There, on the moorlands not far from the Lancashire border, in a setting that resembled nearby Haworth, but in a blander atmosphere which the young Brontës, a generation later, would have envied, Robert for the first time performed the Anglican rites and observed, from behind the scenes, a skilful and sophisticated minister in action. The Rev. Mr. Croft had been coached by David Garrick, and on abandoning a theatrical career, had applied the deft methods of the stage to the sober tasks of the pulpit. He was considered one of the best readers in England, and his elegant sermons, delivered with the gamut of dramatic expression, against the howling wind, must have been a popular and impressive entertainment. The novice stayed more than a year, learning to be eloquent but in danger of losing some of his zeal.

Ostensibly to receive priest's orders, but subconsciously to recapture that mood which had first possessed him on the river bank at Halton, he returned to Cambridge in 1783 and soon fell, as if by magnetic attraction, into the orbit of the Rev. Charles

Simeon, a devout and energetic dissenter in search of converts.[1] The recent frivolities of Gargrave had weakened Robert's resistance to this evangelical campaign. Under the Rev. Mr. Simeon's fiery attack, he succumbed not only to that upsurge of religious independence which at the time offered and demanded a more vigorous faith than the Established Church, but also to the charms of Miss Audley, who was herself imbued with staunch Wesleyan principles. By these joint forces and in this frenzied circle Robert's fate was quickly sealed. The old mood came back with such renewed, such overwhelming conviction that he rushed to preach, in Trinity Church, a precipitate and challenging sermon, of which the doctrinal irregularities now disbarred him from not only a fellowship at St. John's but any imminent hope of a career in the Church of England. On the eve of his marriage to Miss Audley, moral courage ran high but the outlook for a secure future was dim.

Undeterred, the militant couple set forth, after the wedding, armed only with the Bible and their stout missionary purpose. From one brick chapel to another, among those minorities of the population who found in the transports of revivalism what they lacked in the rewards of this world, the outcast wandered for the next ten years, enthusiastically spreading the gospel. A more powerful opposition now goaded and strengthened him, as his father's had done once before. Even early sorrow did not shatter his invincible religion. For within a year Mrs. Housman, ardent in spirit but frail in body, died after the birth of her first child. Yet with unabated vehemence, her husband continued to preach and pray, exhorting others to bow down and be granted those consolations which so visibly transfused his own grief.

Among the material blessings which further eased the widower's plight was Miss Jane Adams, whom destiny led one evening to St. Mary's Church in Leicester where, in Robert

---

[1] Samuel Butler has confirmed, in Chapter XLVII of *The Way of All Flesh*, the influence which the Simeonites still exerted at Cambridge, more than a half-century later, in the days of Ernest Pontifex.

Housman's glowing countenance, the man for whom she had been searching confronted her at last. Once in a girlhood dream she had envisioned him, this very knight in clerical garb, with an intimation, which she then confided to a friend, that he would some day become her husband. And now there he was, romantically personified in a young curate reading the lesson with a fine tremolo, and as she quickly discovered, not only eligible but bereft. It was both a suitable and a prophetic match. For Miss Adams could remember sitting on John Wesley's knee; her father was a distinguished renegade to Methodism; her mother had been persecuted for her beliefs; and Jane herself had already gained a certain celebrity as the author of *The History of Susan Ward*, a best-seller of the Religious Tract Society. They were married in Leicester on September 24, 1788, just before the Rev. Mr. Housman moved on to fresh pastures at Markfield.

Four years later, on his return to Leicester, another episode of mysterious import occurred, and with its sequel was preserved in the annals of the family—a subject that was like a parody, long beforehand, of the Housmanesque ballad. Having duties both in Leicester and at Foston, seven miles away, the busy curate was in the habit of going in the morning to Foston, sometimes on foot, but on this occasion in a gig, whose reins he held as Mrs. Housman gave him a last-minute embrace. Shortly after he had driven off she noticed that her wedding ring was missing; looked everywhere in vain, and at length spread the alarm via the town crier. But only after several months did the precious symbol turn up at Foston, having evidently been carried there in the gig and dropped out. Years passed, and the point of the story was finally revealed, at a Lancaster tea party, when Mrs. Housman retold it. Then weirdly, as she raised her hand to display the ring, it fell off in two pieces.

Whatever its significance, the anecdote did not imply the estrangement of Mr. and Mrs. Housman, who not only fulfilled their vows of matrimony, but clung together through all the slings and arrows that hurtled down upon the missionary's head. No less among his own people, when he reappeared in Lancaster, this bombardment greeted him and accompanied his efforts to rescue the unconverted souls who were flocking to work in the factories. Tired of his itinerant life, and prompted by the want of a refuge for dissenters on his native ground, he had begged permission, from the Bishop of the Diocese and the Vicar of Lancaster, to build a chapel in their midst. They grudgingly consented, in December 1794, and the project was announced on the 19th. A protest meeting of the town fathers was convened in January, but did not seriously delay the plan which, as subscriptions poured in, grew brick by brick into the unadorned, steepleless Church of St. Anne. William Wilberforce, Esquire, paused long enough in his labours for abolition to donate £20, and annually thereafter sent Mrs. Housman £5 for the Sunday school. But while the network of an embattled brotherhood rallied to the support of St. Anne's, it was sadly outnumbered on the spot by those who scorned the upstart parish, and reviled its unwelcome minister.

Once again, adversity merely stiffened the back of Robert Housman and fired his determination. Deceptively shy and unassertive in manner, he could be stalwart in defence of his freedom to believe what his conscience dictated; a gentle individualist who was always loath but never afraid to challenge his ubiquitous opponents. "The character of a man in the sight of God," he mildly suggested, "is not formed by his creeds and notions, but by his dispositions; by the state of his heart." In 1795, however, it was a provocation for which he was soon made to suffer.

During his early years at St. Anne's, the Lancastrians did not scruple to conceal their antipathy for his person, while slanderous gossip and insinuations attacked his name. To one who avoided even polite society, and was at ease only in the company of his friends, such treatment inflicted the extremity of mental torture. A thin-skinned and involuntary martyr, Mr. Housman fortified himself every morning by rising early to read the Bible and conduct family prayers before breakfast; and each evening at eight o'clock he would assuage his wounds by another domestic service. They were among his few periods of respite and hours of gratification, as the difficulties and discouragements thickened around him. With a wife and eight children to support the financial deficit did not improve, and was met only by regular gratuities from his congregation. Even at the end of his working life, when by a different course he might have reached opulent bishophood, it was estimated that Mr. Housman's income had never exceeded £200 a year.

Worst of all, his afflictions not only sprang from a hostile and unrepentant world, but were harboured in the very bosom of his family. For among so many children, some were bound to stray from a path so narrow. His first-born son, the motherless Robert Audley, grew into an incorrigible scapegrace who, after pawning his grandfather's silver cup and even the family Bible, mercifully absconded. Whereupon Miss Mary Housman, fanning the scandal, gave further distress to her parents, and ammunition to their enemies, by distributing her favours among the neighbourhood rakes. She, too, pursued a downward course and disappeared; but there remained Mr. Housman's own brother, the effervescent William, whose conduct always left something to be desired. When duty called this incongruous pair, as magistrates of Lancaster, to punish the misdeeds of other sons and daughters, William would smile maliciously at Robert's discomfiture. When they met informally on Sunday mornings, crossing Skerton bridge, Robert in turn would sigh, "You're going the wrong way, William," as one brother headed for a day's sport on the moors, while the other marched resolutely onwards to his chapel in Moor Lane.

But in spite of so many thorns in the flesh, Mr. Housman never allowed himself to doubt that "all who diligently seek will assuredly find; and that they who do not seek will perish." Even at the dawn of the Industrial Revolution, this simple faith had the power to soothe and sustain him, as if shedding a golden haze over the smoke-stacks of Lancaster. The cotton mills clattered within earshot but did not interrupt the flow of his sermons, or disturb his contemplations at Skerton, where he could still breathe the Arcadian atmosphere of his youth, and begin to enjoy, with the indefatigable assistance of Mrs. Housman, a more tranquil domestic life. Having few opportunities to travel, and no intercourse with the intellectual world of his time, he kept his mind, like his religion, in a state of aggressive innocence, sedulously guarding it against the encroachment of new ideas, in particular those "of a merely scientific character." The old defiant spirit still flared amid the veritable fleshpots of materialism. But more often his work at St. Anne's involved a tedious preoccupation with the kind of incident which, as late as 1820, Mr. Housman was moved to describe with inordinate enthusiasm:

> One of my good people had abundant evidence of the infidelity of her husband. . . . But the consolations which she has received from God within the last three days, seem so to leave behind all her former experience of his mercy, as if it had only been "the hearing of the ear." Her meekness towards her husband, and her concern for his soul, have been astonishing. They have won upon him, he has frankly acknowledged his *persevering* baseness, and he has begun to pray; and she is this day rejoicing in a trembling hope. . . .

On this humdrum level, but with saintly forbearance, his energies were expended in a tireless social service, while in growing numbers the tearful wives and fickle husbands now deposited their burdens in his lap. Shepherding his unruly flock towards eternity, Mr. Housman patiently heard their confessions, ministered to their frailties and continued to bestow on each of them, until his own strength gave out, the same tender solicitude.

By then, at seventy-nine, he was nearing the close of a Bunyanesque saga which had brought him not only hardship and humiliation, but in his old age a modest fame. No longer ostracized, he was granted the rare boon of witnessing, before it was too late, his own vindication. The town fathers now saluted him respectfully, even some of his arch-antagonists, those churchmen of a more rigid doctrine, had relented and were pleased to honour him with their acquaintance; while his reputation spread from Moor Lane to the highest ecclesiastical circles, though without benefit to his income, which still depended on the generosity of his congregation. But the flatteries and successes of this world did not change that earnest and benign expression which a steel engraving has preserved for posterity: the likeness of a dignified evangelist and true Protestant, grappling with sinners to the end. Thus in 1838, a year after the death of Mrs. Housman had left him stricken and inactive at last, the founder of St. Anne's confidently awaited the hour he had so long proclaimed; a man fixed on heaven, yet happily commemorated, after his departure, by a paragraph in the *Dictionary of National Biography*.

Not even his most obedient children could have hoped to emulate so virtuous a father, but among them, two daughters married well, Elizabeth choosing a high sheriff of Anglesey and Jane the Vicar of Tarvin; while Thomas followed almost step by step his father's early path, being admitted a sizar at St. John's College, Cambridge, in 1814, and ordained a priest at Chester in 1820. But at this juncture, pausing to consider, he had diverged from that rocky road by espousing not only the Anglican faith but also, within a few years, the daughter of a propertied Worcestershire family. His in-laws-to-be, the Brettells and the Holdens, were old landowners in the district of Bromsgrove, with an array of escutcheons, ancestral portraits and solid assets that must have dazzled the impecunious clergyman so unused to anything but frugality and abstinence. The Holdens' lineage dated from the twelfth century and their library from the age of Caxton; the Brettells were local worthies and patrons of Bromsgrove School, a multifarious family to which, by some intricate and remote cousinship, even Herbert Spencer was related. The Brettells had lived originally at Finstall House and the Holdens at the Clock House; but, having been united, a generation ago, through the marriage of Joseph Brettell to Ann Holden, the attractions of both houses were now embodied in the person of Miss Anne Brettell, who could provide for Thomas, at the outset of his career, those favours and amenities which had always eluded Robert Housman.

A sharp-featured version of his father, Thomas felt no pangs of regret as he strayed into the green fields of the gentry; on the contrary, knowing at first hand the discomforts of a spiritual crusade, he had gained a deeper respect for material things. The early years of his marriage were spent at Kinver in Staffordshire—a temporary exile from which he was recalled, in 1846, to the curacy of St. John's Church in Bromsgrove, and thence soon promoted to the first incumbency of Christ Church in the adjoining parish of Catshill. Here, according to well-laid plans, he could settle into a pleasant country benefice newly created for his convenience. It was a parish where his relations formed the dominant group among which he enjoyed all the privileges of social and financial equality. The small church and perfunctory duties of Catshill, the intimate company of country squires, exactly suited his ambition, which desired the welfare of others at no sacrifice to himself, but valued most of all the facilities for rearing his family in the security his own boyhood had so sorely lacked. Twelve children romped through the big house at Fockbury which his widowed father-in-law had, in lieu of an available vicarage, invited him to share, and where he was content to remain, administering his wife's affairs on week-days, and delivering a severe Sunday sermon to his parishioners, most of whom still wore the quaint smocks and beaver hats of a subservient peasantry. Between this domestic bower and the convenient pulpit of Catshill, for the rest of an uneventful life, Thomas sauntered back and forth like some placid figure in the purlieus of Barchester, until death overtook him, when his grandson was eleven years old, in 1870. He was buried in the churchyard of Catshill where his obelisk monument, near the spot soon to be occupied by his daughter-in-law, marked the final admission of the Housmans to good county society.

The children Thomas left behind him were already dissociated from his humble past. Reduced to eight by the hazards of the Victorian nursery, they had been conscious from the cradle of those nuances which tend to arise in unequal marriages, and were prompt to recognize the source of their advantages. Mere proximity, if not self-interest, would have led them to cultivate grandfather Brettell and to neglect grandfather Housman. Even their names—Joseph, George, Edward—belonged to their new background, as their lives now drifted still further from their Lancashire origins. Joseph Brettell Housman, the first Oxford alumnus with that surname, pursued a clerical career as far as the Rectory of Cheriton Bishop near Exeter, where he lapsed, like his father, into pious retirement. George met an untimely death, on an unexplained voyage to the colonies, in the wreck of the *Canadian* in 1861. While Edward, a dreamy but unadventurous youth, stayed at home and, in deference to grandfather Brettell's profession, studied law. The last scion of this rapidly crumbling alliance, it was Edward who in the end scooped up not only what was left of the property and the heirlooms (a few of which descended to his eldest son), but those remnants of pride and prestige to which the childhood of Alfred Edward would shortly be exposed.

By Edward's time (he was born in 1831) the Housman pedigree resembled one of those gnarled and ancient fruit trees that flourish so persistently in the English landscape. Deep-rooted in the common soil, it was a good country stock which had produced men of homely and durable character, but from which brilliant minds and creative talents were hardly to be expected. For nearly five centuries the majority of the Housmans had been content to remain indistinguishable from their neighbours. But as in every family, strange aberrancies could occur, like the prodigal Robert Audley and the scarlet Mary, now suddenly joined by their brother William (a crown of thorns held in reserve for his father's old age). After years of staid marriage and quiet conformity, with ten children and all the respectable virtues, the latest reprobate was one of those model citizens who, in middle life, kick up their heels and decamp, as he did outrageously, with an actress. The guilty pair fled to America and some undivulged fate, from which William never returned and the family but slowly recovered. Echoes of the disgrace rumbled from Lancaster to Fockbury, where Edward could not have missed hearing them in his youth, and even in Alfred's childhood the skeleton still faintly rattled in the closet—one note of wildness in the pervading gentility.

From this average mixture heredity was now about to select, according to its own obscure laws, the paternal endowment of A. E. Housman. It was the kind of inheritance that seemed to promise, in mathematical succession, a sound body, a conventional mind, a placid temperament and a simple life. But though ill equipped to deal with more complex offspring, such parentage could at least provide, as it did for Alfred, the benefits of a sheltered home and gentle nurture, with exemption from social or economic handicaps. Having risen into the middle class without a struggle, the Housmans were untouched by the cruder phases of getting on, and not yet quite severed from their pastoral background. They had become, when Alfred was growing up, typical denizens of that provincial society which moved between the vicarage and the manor house. Thomas still lived at Fockbury, indulging his healthy appetite with a stern air of fasting; while Edward, as a young solicitor, had attached himself to the no longer outcast mercantile community of Bromsgrove. Both were amiable, comfort-loving, unambitious men who did nothing to hamper, if little to encourage Alfred's intellectual development. Nevertheless, certain hereditary traits—the doggedness and determination which lay dormant in his father and grandfather—reasserted themselves in Alfred's character. Always circumspect and outwardly submissive, he was not unlike those shrewd and tenacious progenitors who had ploughed their fields, sued their landlords and accumulated their property. With his grimly stoical demeanour, Housman often recalled some ancestral farmer, glowering at the inclement weather.

Not merely the Housman family, of course, but equally his mother's helped to form his heritage; and in the good judgment of his sister Katharine (afterwards Mrs. E. W. Symons), Alfred's superiority was credited to the maternal side. "Mentally," Mrs. Symons believed, "his great abilities were probably derived from his mother. Her father, John Williams, D.D., was an accomplished tutor as well as a parish priest." But even Mrs. Symons' memory could not restore the faded outline of this other grandfather whom his grandchildren never saw, except as a portrait in the Housman parlour.

The Williamses were a Devonshire family claiming descent from Sir Francis Drake, though sharing, apparently, none of his Elizabethan loot. Around the turn of the nineteenth century John Williams had come out of the West Country, from what was probably a rustic setting similar to Lune Bank and matriculated at St. Edmund's Hall, Oxford. Besides a religious training, he studied to acquire, with better results than Thomas Housman achieved at Cambridge a decade later, some wider education; but less successfully, after taking orders, he wandered from one curacy to another, meeting and marrying, somewhere along the way, Miss Elizabeth Cooke of Gloucestershire. In that county he was finally rewarded, at the age of fifty-four, with the modest living at Woodchester, a secluded Cotswold village where the rest of his life was immersed in parochial duties, family anxieties and pertinacious efforts to keep in touch with literature and learning. Occasional pupils from the neighbouring gentry sharpened his Latin and supplemented his income; while his leisure was spent in translating the works of early Christian bishops or in reviving and composing hymns to enliven the Anglican service. But as time wore on, the chills and dampness of the Woodchester Rectory lowered his spirits and ravaged his thirteen children, of whom only two had the hardiness to survive; his own career was ending in what seemed a forlorn struggle; and in 1857 he was buried in the churchyard, among the shards of a Roman villa, two years before the birth of his grandson.

Indirectly, through his daughter Sarah Jane, the Rev. Dr. Williams may have communicated his literary aspirations, his antiquarian interests and gift for prosody to some of her children. A clergyman who took seriously, as the Church intended, his civilizing mission, he laboured to raise not only the moral tone but the cultural level of his parish; and would certainly have imparted a sound education to his own children. It can therefore be assumed that, on becoming Mrs. Edward Housman, Sarah Jane would in turn have upheld her father's standards in the laxer mental climate of Bromsgrove; as it was no doubt Mrs. Housman who guided her children's reading and directed their play, suggesting, for example, those poetic games which planted the seed of literature in the receptive minds of Alfred, Clemence and Laurence Housman. Thus at second hand the Rector of Woodchester continued to give his salutary lessons and to shed his intellectual light. But simultaneously, it should be noted, a cousin of Edward's on the Housman side displayed talents of the same order, as a lecturer in Greek and Divinity at Chichester College; and was moreover an ex-resident of Woodchester, an authority on its natural history, and a relative whose influence might have contributed something to Alfred's aptitude for scholarship and appreciation of the countryside.

As much as hereditary factors, perhaps, Woodchester itself conveyed, to Alfred in particular, the spirit of his grandfather Williams. For within the stone walls of that tiny hill-town brooded an atmosphere which Alfred often savoured on boyhood visits, and was later to distil in his poetry. Like a sleepy evocation of the past (". . . so many Roman remains have scarcely been found in an equal space in any part of England . . .") Woodchester captured and enriched his imagination; while among his mother's friends there he found a refuge filled with reminders of her girlhood. This early connection, cherished and maintained throughout his life, held an obviously important place in Housman's heart, linking two of his strongest attachments—for his mother and that scene of "hanging woods and hamlets" where her shadow lingered. Woodchester was the spring at which, from childhood, he refreshed himself: the landscape he loved and the memories he clung to. But in spite of his predilection for her home, Housman never bothered to explore his mother's genealogy; and with her death, the Williams family, or that branch of it, flickered out and was forgotten.

A steely mood of acceptance was to be, even in Housman's youth, his predominant response to the transiency of human life; while as a pastime he preferred the study of astrology to that of family history. But he was not, as Mrs. Symons remarked, "insensible to the charm of an ancient lineage"; and when the family possessions were divided, he carried off, with an unprecedented show of sentiment, one of the Holden portraits to adorn his rooms at Cambridge. This silky Caroline gentleman in a peruke was, he might have argued, at any rate more companionable than the melancholy gaze of grandfather Williams or the rapt expression of Robert Housman. For those closer but less colourful antecedents, in fact, Housman manifested neither curiosity nor distaste; they simply failed to interest him, least of all that unquenchable minister whose biography must have been familiar to, but was never mentioned by his great-grandson. The Anglican faith, Housman once conceded, was "much the best religion I ever came across," and to that extent he paid tribute to Dr. Williams. But for the more jubilant forms of proselytism he had only this to say:

> There is Hallelujah Hannah
>   Walking backwards down the lane,
> And I hear the loud hosannah
>   Of regenerated Jane.

It was, of course, a young and irresponsible statement which intended no disrespect to his great-grandfather, but which probably gives some clue to what his serious thoughts on the subject might have been.

In certain odd ways, nevertheless, Housman's experience was to repeat, across the gap of a century, that of Dr. Barrow's unhappy apprentice. Both were studious and sensitive boys who confronted dilemmas beyond their years; both underwent a period of adolescent storm and stress; both developed a quiet, unflinching fortitude; and both retained, in the most disparate circumstances, some of the same idiosyncrasies of character. "He had a strong dislike of being entrapped into the company of those with whom he was unacquainted"; but "though a naturally timid and retiring man . . . nothing could daunt him when he felt that he was right . . ."—those traits of Robert Housman's were transplanted, unmistakably, to his great-grandson's shy yet caustic temper. They alone, moreover, shared now and then a raw-nerved awareness of the human condition, a sense of pity and terror to which the rest of that huge clan had never shown themselves acutely susceptible.

> Undone with misery, all they can
> Is to hate their fellow man.

It was a reflection that must often have crossed the lonely clergyman's mind, as he traversed the hostile streets of Lancaster. But Housman himself never found occasion to visit the cemetery at Skerton or to indulge these idle speculations. Such matters he dismissed with a customary and perhaps commendable brevity: "My father's family was Lancashire. . . ."

CHAPTER TWO

My mother and my father

THE town of Bromsgrove was, in 1859, a small slow-changing community of some ten thousand inhabitants mainly occupied with the manufacture of nails. Not yet lapped by the suburbs of Birmingham, it was one of those wayside stations which travellers failed to notice in the hubbub of approaching a metropolis. Trains skirted the site at a respectful distance, coming from Droitwich and proceeding to climb, as early editions of Baedeker pointed out, "one of the steepest railway-inclines in England." But Bromsgrove itself rested where the downward slope merged into flat meadowland. Lacking the grimmer aspects of Midland industrialism, it produced the effect of a place which belonged neither to one age nor another. Along the high street a few half-timbered houses, like stray woodcuts, broke the expanse of prosaic brick; while aloof on two mounds, confronting each other and commanding the mundane traffic below, stood the Church of St. John and Bromsgrove School.

A sizable edifice of reddish stone and post-Reformation style, with steepled tower and surrounding graveyard, the parish church had an air of massive aplomb that would have pleased Thomas Housman as he first ascended the long flight of steps up which, like a penance, generations of worshippers had scaled the hillside. Here the dignified composure so wanting in Moor Lane was securely embedded in the thick Gothic walls; the hysterics of evangelism would be unthinkable in this lofty structure which derived its tone more from a rich endowment than from spiritual need. Charmless but impressive, the building suggested its conservative and practical donors, those early Holdens and Brettells, whose property in fact spread possessively over the tableland at its feet: there in the foreground lay the Clock House where Joseph Brettell had resided, and nearby the Valley House in which A. E. Housman was shortly to be born, dots on a checkerboard of fields and lanes; while beyond to the west rose a blue rampart, terminating the valley of the Severn in which the county of Worcestershire fans out between the Malvern Hills and the Cotswolds.

A year before, in the summer of 1858, Edward Housman and Sarah Jane Williams had been married at Woodchester. It was the traditional June wedding of the middle classes, a ritual heavy-laden with moral commitments and social overtones, attended by that phalanx of parents, uncles, aunts and cousins who conspired to draw the bonds even tighter. The ghost of the Rev. John Williams, hovering in the churchyard, might have wished for a more brilliant son, as the Rev. Thomas Housman, knowing the benefits conferred by Miss Holden's dowry, would have liked a wealthier daughter. But on the whole, having inspected each other with critical approval, the friends and relatives were bound to consider it a most felicitous occasion. Above all, Miss Lucy Housman, who had long been scheming, with the matrimonial zest of spinsterhood, to unite her favourite cousin and her dearest friend.

Edward was twenty-seven—a sad-eyed young man who inherited from his father those indolent habits allied with a taste for luxury, both of which Thomas Housman had so adroitly managed to indulge. But Edward already wore (in a photograph of the period) the anxious expression of one shadowed by some foreboding of disaster against which it would be useless to struggle; though his actual circumstances, at the time of his marriage, were not at all unpromising. A comfortable home awaited him at the Valley House, close to the Clock House where he had grown up, and the country sports to which he was still (too fondly, some of his children came to think) addicted. A sufficient source of income was provided also, in the person of Captain John Adams, an old Bromsgrovian who, as it happened, was related to Mrs. Robert Housman *née* Adams. Then turning ninety but still actively engaged in the affairs of a local office-holder and man of business, Captain Adams had, by employing Edward as a solicitor, given him both a present job and a budding reputation in the town. The sort of life he chose to lead opened out invitingly—a suitable but not too exacting occupation that would leave ample time for the pursuits of a country gentleman. Thus braving a friendly and familiar world from which only support and encouragement were to be expected, Edward commuted between Perry Hall, the Captain's residence in Bromsgrove, and the Valley House two miles away. Certainly no one, least of all Edward himself, could have found a cause for his vague but congenital malaise, that recurrent self-distrust which his wife, as they settled into domesticity at Fockbury, now discovered for the first time.

Sarah Jane was then thirty—older than her husband not only in years but in philosophy; an equable, disciplined young woman who had been taught to accept the vicissitudes of life with Christian forbearance. Having witnessed so many deaths in her own family, and so often observed in her parents the capacity to suffer and endure, she had acquired a precocious wisdom. On the threshold of the Valley House, she would have told herself, stern duties and solemn responsibilities awaited her, quite apart from happiness, which one did not hope for except as a posthumous reward. All the marks of strain were sponged from that smooth brow and those pensive eyes, as the desires she could not gratify were automatically locked within her. Inclined to plumpness, with her dark hair drawn tightly over her ears, and her body enveloped in voluminous crinolines, she rustled from room to room of her new home, organizing her household with the diligence of those vanished ladies who had no other ambition, and only pausing at intervals (as in her photograph) to rest her hands gently in her lap. With the same careful supervision that she gave to her parlour, Mrs. Housman supplied her husband's needs and disguised his imperfections, restoring his stamina as regularly as she watered the plants. United as much by dependence on his side as by protectiveness on hers, they were one of those outwardly immaculate Victorian couples whose problems were unsuspected by their neighbours, and while Mrs. Housman lived, barely admitted even to themselves.

The Valley House was a modest example of Georgian brickwork which, though standing near the road and surrounded by outbuildings, assumed a manorial pose, with its formal gateway and walled courtyard in front of its gabled porch, and which commanded from its upper windows a rolling rural prospect. No longer redolent of dairy and stable, the premises had become, as the practice of agriculture declined while the cult of landed property increased, one of those gentlemanly farmhouses which made the English countryside at once so cultivated and so unproductive. Not yet quite at home in these unfamiliar lowlands, and perhaps discomfited by the neighbourly surveillance of her mother-in-law, Mrs. Housman often pined for the friendlier atmosphere of Gloucestershire. All the more nostalgically, that autumn and winter of her first pregnancy, she must have watched the wind bending the tree-tops and swirling the snow outside her bedroom. "Yon flakes that fret the eastern sky," as her son afterwards gloomily adverted to the event, "lead back my day of birth." But as the time of her confinement approached, the gusty phase of early spring had come —a sequence of rain squalls and bright interludes which, towards the end of March, accompanied the onset of her labour. Then while the Bromsgrove physician, shaking his head, advised a consultation with Birmingham, Mrs. Housman lay helpless in the grip of obstetrical complications; until at her insistence, a telegram summoned instead her old Woodchester doctor who, after painful and prolonged delay, delivered her of a son at four o'clock on the afternoon of the 26th of March, under the sign of Aries, in the year 1859.

It was the year of *Adam Bede*, *The Rubáiyát*, *Idylls of the King*, and *The Origin of Species*—a confluence of the main currents of nineteenth-century culture; while in astrological terms, as the child was not destined to learn until he was past seventy, his birthdate augured a character replete with "energy, passion and emotion, combined with an equal degree of refinement . . .

Mrs. Edward Housman

great critical powers and splendid intuitive judgment." The belated horoscope went on to unfold not only those safe generalizations in which the fortune-teller deals, but certain rashly specific details: "You are capable of very faithful attachment and of waiting a long time; but some kind of secret and irregular union is more likely than an ordinary marriage. . . . You are somewhat liable to illnesses which arise from excess or indiscretion in diet or habits of living," and "You are pretty certain to benefit from a legacy." Weaving a tissue of promise around his old age, this document must have entertained Housman as a mode of ancient divination applied, when it no longer mattered, to his own life and personality—a subject that still held, under the cloak of his indifference, a lurking fascination for him.

More earthly influences, however, impinged upon his consciousness from the start. The infant was, like so many firstborn sons, his mother's favourite, and enjoyed among her children the priority of the eldest and most devoted. Living among strangers with whom she had not much in common, and often languishing at home while Edward roamed the countryside, Mrs. Housman naturally bestowed, on the child whose temperament so much resembled her own, a special attention. But even the restrained intimacy of a Victorian mother had, in Alfred's case, the usual psychological aftermath. Timorous and introspective, he drew apart more and more into that inner world he shared with her, sensing too soon the complexities of adult experience. The process served to awaken his mind and deepen his emotions, but with a premature development that already furrowed his brow at the age of two, and continued to impose a look of undue solemnity on his early photographs. This intensity of perception was first manifested at his christening, on April 24, 1859, when he was four weeks old: an occurrence he afterwards claimed dimly to remember. But as if already prone to scepticism, his growing faculties quickly turned from religious ceremonies to the childish study of astronomy which "a little book we had in the house" had stimulated.

The house was then no longer the Valley House but Perry Hall, to which Edward had removed his family, sometime in 1860, after the death of Captain Adams. As ponderous as its name, Perry Hall stood smothered in ivy and encircled by lawns, in the middle of Bromsgrove. A solid if ungraceful building which the Captain had erected on the site of an older house, it was designed to be at once residence and office, with an ingenious system of locks, shutters, chains and alarm bells invented by the late controller of stamps, which at night gave the inmates a truly inviolable privacy; but less forbiddingly, by daylight, tall Gothic windows opened across the plain brick façade, and the lawn receded into beds of flowers, screens of shrubbery, an orchard and a vegetable patch. All of which, with the Captain's blessing, now became the fixed home of the Housmans, and the birthplace of their remaining children, each of whom was celebrated upon arrival by the planting of a chestnut tree in the garden.

Inside, a congestion of Victoriana filled the rooms, interspersed with occasional relics of earlier periods—a cabinet of tortoise-shell or an inlaid chest, unfashionable objects that were presently consigned to the attic. Elephantine cupboards crowded the halls and bedrooms; water pipes and oleographs decorated the nursery; and in the parlour, amid the horsehair and mahogany, globular lamps cast their glow upon the bric-à-brac. Bedecked with the first products of industrial art, it was a setting calculated to numb, as it did forever, Alfred's aesthetic sensibilities. But in the garden where he played, nature trained his eye to observe other forms of beauty, and there his imagination took root among the flowers and fruit, already constructing a paradise that was menaced now and then, for the diversion of his brothers, by aerial torpedoes which he improvised out of wooden stumps; while overhead, from its tower visibly vibrating just beyond the trees, the bells of St. John's spaced out the carefree hours of his childhood.

There was, in those impressionable years, no evidence of strain or insecurity at Perry Hall. Edward's affairs seemed to prosper, without interrupting his pastimes; new hobbies competed with the old, in a breathless round of hunting and horticulture, photography and metal work. Often absent and always forgetful, he was a mild and casual father who imposed no tighter curbs on his children than on himself. Sitting with a look of distraction at the head of the table, he represented Victorian authority in its least threatening aspects, and was never that image of tyranny to which his children could attribute any future neurosis. But with the help of nurses and governesses, Mrs. Housman managed, as the chestnut trees multiplied, to preserve order and command obedience by the same legerdemain with which Edward paid the bills. To the passer-by, glancing at the well-tended lawn across which parents strolled and children scampered, it was an exemplary domestic picture; while from within, as it appeared to Laurence Housman, "there was a delicious hour before bedtime; dim gaslight burned on the landing, and . . . when late dinner was at six, we would go down to the dining room for dessert, be given a biscuit or a fruit, and half a glass of wine, before bidding our parents goodnight." The pleasures of wine-tasting were to become for Alfred a lasting consolation, as the code of manners under which he grew up would have its permanent effect on his afterlife. Governing the old and young alike, Victorian behaviour was so formalized that even trips to the W.C., as his brother remembered them, were veiled in furtiveness and fraught with anxiety; while sexual questions remained, as year after year new babies screamed behind closed doors, ubiquitous yet unmentionable.

A second son named Robert was born that first summer at Perry Hall, followed in quick succession by Clemence and Katharine; then at longer intervals by Basil, Laurence and last of all, when Mrs. Housman was forty, by George Herbert. In this populous nursery, Alfred's childhood was anything but lonely, though his shyness and reserve were already evident in a photograph that shows him, at the age of seven, standing stiff and embarrassed, with a sword dangling from his limp hand, beside Robert's small but nonchalant figure leaning on the barrel of a gun—Two Huntsmen, as Edward must playfully have posed them, shouting directions from under the black cloth of his camera. Robert was, in spite of delicate health and angry moods that once or twice provoked Alfred to retaliation, the most companionable of his brothers, and a constant play-mate in the garden. The others were, in his early years, too infantile and, later on, too different, both Basil and George turning into athletic boys who shared their father's love of sport, and whose marksmanship often dented the weather-vane atop the steeple of St. John's; while Laurence soon developed a streak of emotionalism that always somewhat disturbed his elder brother. Yet over them all, as Mrs. Symons has recalled, Alfred maintained the ascendancy of a trusted leader who could persuade even George and Basil to compose sonnets as a form of entertainment.

Taught to read by one of his grandmothers (probably the former Ann Brettell who still lived at the Clock House), under the supervision of his mother (who was herself too preoccupied for the task), Alfred advanced from toys to books even before his first lessons with a governess. What he read in those years was unrecorded, except for the "little book" on astronomy, the erudite pages of Lemprière's *Classical Dictionary*, and a hint from Mrs. Symons that the influence of Lewis Carroll and Edward Lear might explain his early addiction to nonsense verse. The appearance of *Alice in Wonderland*, when Housman was six years old, set the fashion for whimsical humour and the fantasies of childhood. From Windsor Castle to Perry Hall, that masterpiece of topsy-turvydom invaded every home, en-rapturing an audience that seldom permitted itself to be amused. Therapeutically, by the simple device of ignoring the laws of common sense, Alice had eased the tensions of an all too sensible world, and taught even her most sober readers, in laughing at the Dodo and the Duchess, to ridicule their own portentousness. Lisping his way through this ambiguous litera-ture, Alfred soon learned not only to enjoy the mockery but to grasp the method, and "at eight or earlier," had already begun to compose that juvenilia which reflected, in the odd form of Mother Goose, his first poetic inspiration. Mrs. Symons has transcribed an early version of *Little Miss Muffet*, whose mouth, in Housman's graphic treatment, "opened very wide . . . and the spider ran down her inside." Equally adept were the imitations of Carroll and Lear with which he used to regale the nursery. Not unlike the frustrated Mr. Dodgson, Housman was even as a child in need of some escape from his reticence, and in these verbal pranks found a convenient approach to social relations. They served then to make him popular, and continued for many years to add a peal of merriment to his family correspondence. Long unsuspected by the world at large, it was a talent that displayed, only through a forgotten peep-hole, the skill and effort he had once devoted to the art of being funny. With its twists of facetiousness and its knack for parody, Housman's light verse revealed the private jokes of an amiable brother, the gay interludes of a young man's struggle to overcome his shyness, but perhaps most of all the defensive antics of one who was guarding his inner life.

At the age of ten or eleven, however, Alfred had few other ways of ingratiating himself. A small silent boy of whom no one could afterwards remember much, if only because no one except his mother had been able to unlock his thoughts, he slipped almost unnoticed into the background of a large and boisterous family. But now, in addition to that sense of loneliness in a crowded room which afflicts every timid child, he began to suffer the first guilty twinges of puberty. It was a period of natural self-torment, probably exacerbated, as Mrs. Symons confided in her notes, by the inhibitions which a strict course of Victorian hygiene imposed on the Housman boys. Like most fathers, no doubt, Edward Housman took refuge from his own embarrassment in hasty lectures which only served to invest the subject with a darker mystery. In Alfred's case, Mrs. Symons appeared to imply, the result may have been to enforce habits of chastity and repression which in later life he could never overcome; and certainly Edward's clumsiness had some part in destroying the confidence which from now on Alfred withheld from his father. What he denied to one parent, of course, he gave in excess to the other, lavishing on his mother all the child's capacity to adore and identify himself with his beloved. Already in quest of "friends to die for," Alfred drew closer to his mother and strained to emulate her character, just when Mrs. Housman was exerting her utmost powers of discipline and restraint.

A buxom woman whose calm expression still, at the age of forty, concealed any sign of inner distress, Mrs. Housman had long ago turned back to religion for the spiritual support which her marriage failed to provide. The care of an exigent husband and seven small children had drained her strength without replenishing her faith. Exhausted by childbirth and oppressed by vague premonitions, she was in fact entering the first stage of illness and the last phase of her life. But in the midst of a clamorous household, no one detected the early symptoms of physical pain and mental stress which passed now and then across her soft and passive features. Imperturbably, Mrs. Housman waged a lonely battle with the onset of disease, as she wrestled in private with those delicate shades of belief and fine-spun theological distinctions which, in the wake of Darwin's theories, grew so agonizing for the Victorian conscience. The fever of speculation drove her, about this time, even to the brink of Catholicism, from which her brother (then Dean of St. John's, Cambridge and a staunch Anglican) narrowly rescued her on his deathbed. Obediently, Mrs. Housman promised never to approach that pitfall again, but the problem continued, as her own health declined, to plague her thoughts and to increase her concern for the proper religious indoctrination of her children.

In a family still professionally connected with the church, religious observances were not, of course, neglected, but had already lost for its younger members the power to uplift or intimidate. Each Sunday morning, after a skirmish of last-minute scrubbing and combing, the Housmans set out in decorous formation to climb the steps of St. John's. And every week-day, peremptorily summoned by the breakfast bell, they assembled in the dining room for prayers. Edward presided on these occasions with a sleepy air, sometimes absent-mindedly repeating the Lord's Prayer twice over, while on their knees his children impatiently waited for their porridge. Outmoded yet compulsory, the performance punctuated Housman's childhood with a ritual that, in his great-grandfather's domestic circle, had once been "beautiful and affecting," but which no longer moved Edward's victims to more than a fidgety submission. It had become, like church-going, one of those conventions that demand only lip-service; indeed, too much devoutness would have been frowned upon. For even when religious feeling was genuine, as in Mrs. Housman's case, its outward expression proved unbearably awkward in the etiquette of Victorian society. The bare soul was almost as indecent as the naked body.

But for a thoughtful boy striving to conform to his environment, the process of adjustment was not eased by such intricate do's and don'ts. Even at school the curriculum was often arbitrary and the pedagogy ruthless; a system of education which had made few concessions to the modern world, and none at all to the sensitive child. Housman fared, nevertheless, surprisingly well. Studious by nature and always disposed, as Mrs. Symons put it, "to avoid troubles," he gave his teachers no excuse for harsh treatment. Having acquired the rudiments from a governess, he first attended, in Robert's company, one of those small elementary schools which in every town provided a tormented livelihood for some impoverished spinster. Wielding a punitive slipper, Miss Johnson offered a choice of edification or chastisement to the youth of Bromsgrove; but within a year or so her tutelage had already equipped Housman to win a scholarship at Bromsgrove School, which he entered as a shyly expectant day pupil in the autumn of 1870. Nearly two centuries before, a rich patron had established a fund for "the clothing, education and apprenticeship of twelve poor scholars of the town." Garbed in long blue coats and peculiar knobbed caps, they had suffered ever since the indignity of wearing a costume that denoted their inferior status. But luckily for Housman, a more humane headmaster and a new regulation had abolished these accoutrements just before his admission to the school, and he was among the first group of Foundation scholars privileged to appear, like the other students, in contemporary dress, topped by that universal badge of learning— the mortar-board.

Bromsgrove School was, at the time of Housman's enrolment, an old and reputable if not famous public school. Sprung from an original endowment of £7 per annum, on which its early masters somehow contrived to subsist in the sixteenth century, it had weathered the ups and downs of economic history to emerge, after Waterloo, as a small but prosperous boarding school. Its affiliations with Worcester College, Oxford, held out the promise of future fellowships, and attracted students from all parts of England. Profiting from that general revival of the public school spirit which the methods of Dr. Arnold had begun at Rugby, and which a disciple of Arnold's had carried on at Bromsgrove, it had become, in Housman's day, one of those muscular yet high-minded institutions where Tom Brown would have felt quite at home. The headmastership of Dr. Blore, ending in Housman's third year, was chiefly notable for his enlightened policy towards the Blue Coat Boys; but under his successor, Mr. Millington, whose reign lasted until 1901, the school rapidly expanded both in material equipment and intellectual capacity. As Housman knew it, however, the advantages of a gymnasium and a cricket field were missing; while its principal building (and still its finest ornament) was the old School House constructed in the period of Sir Christopher Wren, a graceful benefaction whose dormer windows high above Bromsgrove surveyed the route by which the diminutive scholar, at the age of eleven, now made his daily pilgrimage.

It was a short walk from Perry Hall, but no longer accom-

panied by Robert, who had been removed about this time, because of asthma, to the more salubrious climate of a school in
Bath. Lacking other playmates of his own age, Alfred applied
himself with still greater intentness to the mastery of Greek and
Latin grammar—a form of drudgery in which, even though his
lessons stretched from seven in the morning until six at night,
he seemed already to find some congenial element. As a timid
day boy of poor physique, he was nicknamed "Mouse" or, by
less polite fellow-students, "Stinky"; but except for occasional
scuffles, he was left to himself, and when athletic games were
played, could usually be found at home, conjugating verbs or
memorizing, with the same studious exactitude, the names of
trees and flowers in the garden. It was here, too, that a new
friendship burgeoned with the boy who lived next door. Edwin
Grey was the son of a carpenter whose workshop stood, just
beyond the shrubbery, on the other side of Perry Lane. A substitute for the absent Robert, he became in this period a welcome and habitual visitor, providing the first taste of that spontaneous comradeship which Housman so rarely encountered
and which circumstances so invariably destroyed. For with
Edwin Grey, who did not attend the Bromsgrove School, and
who stayed in Hanover Street for the rest of his life, time
quickly erased this interlude of a childish attachment.

Between the activities of school and garden, there was the
gas-lit hour before bedtime and the precious, but now often
limited, enjoyment of his mother's company. With a noticeable
waning of strength, Mrs. Housman could no longer hide the
marks of advancing illness, and was confined more and more
to her bed. But as if planning even there to insure Alfred's
happiness, she summoned energy enough to enlist the help of
old Woodchester friends, to whom, should the emergency arise,
she could safely entrust her son. Under the care of the Wise
family, she knew, he would be shielded from whatever might
happen; and by the autumn of 1870, Mrs. Housman had already
begun to contemplate the possibility of death. "She used to talk
to me as if I were a grown-up person," Housman recalled at the

end of his own life; discussions during which his mother would escape from the realities of Perry Hall into reveries of her youth, baring to his meticulous observation glimpses of that mortal struggle which now took possession of the sick-room. In those bedside colloquies, as he sat writing letters at her dictation to Mrs. Wise and Miss Lucy Housman, or listening to the stream of Woodchester memories, Housman's close yet still immature feeling for his mother deepened, preternaturally, into a stark love-lorn response. It was an experience which, at so tender an age, abruptly terminated his childhood; while for Mrs. Housman, his growing look of comprehension added one more to the spectres that, from then on, would haunt her long nights of pain.

In all subsequent accounts of this crisis, the role of Edward Housman was mysteriously neglected by that large and literate family. Perhaps its chief mourner, he was at the same time its most obscure member. Having lost his father less than a year before, he was already shaken and depressed when, at his most vulnerable moment, Mrs. Housman collapsed. As the props fell one after another, Edward himself sank into a helpless state of despondency. Ill-fitted by temperament to bear not only the strain of such an ordeal but the weight of new responsibilities, he was the sort of man apt to show, when his deepest feelings were engaged, only his weakest side. A distraught and sometimes intoxicated figure, stumbling along the passage-ways of Perry Hall, Edward must have appeared to his eldest son a negligent father and demoralized husband who, in the face of his wife's suffering, merely indulged in the vice of self-pity. Alfred's devotion to his mother had already produced, as its usual counterpart, a certain latent antagonism to his father, which now easily turned into a pent-up and festering aversion. With his sympathies drawn irresistibly to his mother, and his resentments heaped accusingly on Edward's head, the pattern of Housman's future relations with his father was foreshadowed by this early but irreparable misunderstanding— a conflict destined fatally to warp his emotional development.

The unhappy household was still held together, in those first months of 1871, by the hushed presence of Mrs. Housman, around whom the zone of silence and inaccessibility widened day by day. Once again the wind and snow swirled outside the windows of her bedroom—a reminder that when the time came, Alfred should be sent away. But not yet, if only because the studies in which he was beginning to excel must on no account be interrupted. The winning of his scholarship a year before, his evident seriousness of purpose and love of reading, had given her the conviction that he would some day fulfil that intellectual ideal to which her father had so long aspired. It was one of the few half-certainties that consoled her, as she tried to project the lives of her children, all so unpredictably young and some of whom she hardly knew. Among the oldest, Robert might turn out well if his health permitted; and Clemence was said to be, at the age of nine, extremely bright. But only Alfred had yet emerged as a definite if not quite fathomable personality, with something in his character on which she could pin her hopes; a lonely sad-faced boy who had always melted her heart and to whom she now felt herself clinging, with a final grasp of maternal love.

The winter days grew darker, and Perry Hall more comfortless, as the condition of its mistress steadily declined; until at length Lucy Housman was called from Woodchester to assume the domestic burdens with which Edward could no longer cope. Crisply efficient, she managed at once to restore the smooth administration of servants and to segregate the inhabitants of the nursery. Calmness and order prevailed again, the gloomy atmosphere lifted slightly, and as the Easter holidays approached, it was decided that Alfred should accept the pressingly repeated invitation of Mrs. Wise, and go to stay at Woodchester House. In spite of its implications, the arrangement pleased his mother —it was a journey of which she could follow every step, and of whose beneficent effects she felt assured. So with ordinary good-byes and fond messages to Mrs. Wise, he set out, on the verge of being twelve years old, travelling by the still adventurous railway, via Gloucester and Stroud, to enjoy a short respite from the toil and tension of Bromsgrove.

At his destination stood the gate-posts of Woodchester House, beyond which a driveway ran across the hill-top to what seemed in the distance hardly more than a stone wall. But on its far side, the grey bulk of Woodchester House materialized, dozing in its courtyard, with its façade fronting an open valley. Secluded even from the secluded village at its back, it might have been designed to suit the retiring disposition of its young visitor, as its occupants knew intuitively how to make him feel at ease. Mrs. Wise had not only her own matronly warmth of heart, but long and intimate friendship with his mother; her daughter Edith, five years older than Alfred, was mature enough to respect his bashful solemnity; while a younger son and daughter, in the firm control of their German governess Miss Becker, completed the family group which had assembled to greet him. It was a scene his mother had so often described that now, indoors and out, it seemed all friendly and familiar. There, just as he had pictured it, stretched the green panoramic landscape of Gloucestershire; and not far off lay the huddled village of Woodchester, like an outcropping of the stony soil. In every direction some inviting vista beckoned; but one of his first expeditions was to inspect the churchyard where, under the disinterred bones, his grandfather's predecessor had unearthed the remains of a Roman villa. Even Latin grammar came to life as he trod this archaeological site, now bursting into early spring.

Amid such pleasures Alfred received, soon after his arrival at Woodchester, word of his mother's death. Not unexpected by Mrs. Wise, it was for him a blow delivered unsparingly in the presence of strangers, and with no chance to bolster his defences. A letter from his father brought the cold details and precise instructions (she had died on his birthday; and he was to remain temporarily at Woodchester) along with her last wish that was forwarded now, across the void, in Edward's lachrymose phrases. Alfred must not, she had implored, lose his faith —a contingency that, with clear motherly insight, Mrs. Housman had foreseen, but which her death-bed invocation only served to precipitate. Already, as he read and reread the letter in which her last words echoed, the frail bonds of his mid-Victorian religion began to snap. Watchfully, Mrs. Wise must have counselled him to pray, and herself administered all the proper spiritual guidance. But alone in his room, those first days and nights, Housman's mind was free to face death as he felt it to be, invested with that exact imagery of the grave ("hearse and spade" and "the bed of mould") in which later on his poetry abounded. Conducting a private burial service in his imagination, the bereaved schoolboy laid his mother to rest; and within a year, as Housman afterwards revealed, cast off those beliefs to which he could no longer subscribe, and at thirteen precociously "became a deist."

The kind ladies of Woodchester House played a valuable part, nonetheless, in surrounding him with tactful sympathy. Each of them in turn, at the right moment, had been able to offer just that touch of gentleness, understanding and refreshment which carried him step by step towards recovery. Like the instruments of a trio, Mrs. Wise, Miss Becker and Edith performed together in delicate harmony; and from andante to allegretto Alfred's mood responded. Delight in Woodchester, they seemed to say, was itself a kind of loyalty to his mother, and the company of her friends a way of remembering her. So too, Miss Becker might have lectured, poetry should be read and studies resumed, as his mother would have been the first to insist. Thus a chat with Mrs. Wise, a walk with Edith and a lesson with Miss Becker began to work their healing effect, as the initial stage of mourning passed; while the gratitude they inspired was already, before Alfred left Woodchester, great enough to endure until, in his old age, the last link with that foster family was cut by the death of Theodore Wise. The cheerful comfortable household possessed all those attractions with which unhappy children are apt to invest a home that is not their own; and certainly without this refuge, then and in future years, Housman's life would have been less patiently borne.

CHAPTER THREE

When I would muse in boyhood

THE years in which Housman was growing up have been labelled, in economic text-books, the "golden age" of British capitalism, a period of mounting prosperity abruptly terminated, in the middle seventies, by a sharp cyclical decline. But already, in the spring of 1871, a sense of desolation had fallen on Perry Hall, darkening the sunlit days and rendering its older occupants impervious to the still cheerful bustle of Bromsgrove. Edward Housman faced the future not only bereft of that undivided loyalty and attendance which Victorian wives gave their husbands, but further dismayed by the seven-fold obligation, the heavy and immediate burdens of rearing a motherless family. At forty, his life was suddenly bleak and shattered, with a long prospect of domestic servitude stretching ahead of him, from which all avenues of escape would now be rigorously cut off. The cares of business and the responsibilities of fatherhood began to press down at last on his bowed shoulders, intensifying a plight which only his children, or at least his eldest son, could presently share and perhaps somewhat relieve.

Alfred did share, but could do nothing to mitigate, his father's grief and dejection. The furtive appeal for sympathy, the fumbling gesture of affection with which Edward tried to overcome his son's reticence were designed to produce, in a boy overwrought by his own sorrow, exactly the opposite effect. Having hardened himself against the slightest display of emotion, Alfred recoiled from these signs of sentiment and moments of weakness, which merely confirmed his unfavourable opinion of his father's character. Deprived of the only person in whom he was able to confide, and who could release his capacity to love, he was himself struggling to dissimulate, after his mother's death, the degree of his feeling and the extremity of his loss, but not without certain irrepressible physical manifestations which, in its ignorance of psychology, the family teasingly miscalled "pulling faces." A nervous tic that plainly denoted some acute reaction, this intermittent spasm began to sweep across Housman's features from now on, and as Mrs. Symons has recorded, "never entirely left him." At its mildest a look of "inner intensity," as his sister remembered it, the affliction grew within the next few years into habitual seizures of such violence that Mr. Millington, observing Alfred's facial contortions in the schoolroom, ascribed them to St. Vitus's dance; and though in later life the phenomenon was rarely visible, it might still incongruously reappear in the course of the most impersonal lecture, as he read aloud one of the odes of Horace, leaving his astonished students "afraid the old fellow was going to cry."

By making it impossible to discuss, even with his father, the event which had so deeply shaken both their lives, Housman not only widened the breach between them, but adopted at too early an age the most severe and unrelenting self-discipline. Small, frail and taut-nerved, in his thirteenth year, the lonely schoolboy imposed on his slender body and straining mind an excessive determination to control his natural impulses and conceal his private thoughts. That precautionary defensiveness into which mature people withdraw from the blows of experience had overtaken Housman at the threshold of adolescence; and in the phase when youth normally flings itself at new objects of enjoyment, he held aloof and grew more introspective. The drudgery of school-work was, for such a boy, a stimulus rather than a deterrent to the regimen he chose to follow. Greater knowledge, he could persuade himself, might dispel the fog-bank of apprehension, and a well-trained intelligence help to resolve the quandaries, that beset him. So each morning, as if to join the Spartan but conforting ritual of some monastic order, he hurried away with eager diligence from Perry Hall to Bromsgrove School.

The younger Housmans were still confined to the nursery

and their upbringing entrusted to a governess, while Edward sat all day in his office transacting business or debating, as their shrill voices and stamping feet now and then penetrated through the walls, how to administer his unruly household. Distracted by this domestic quandary, he managed to keep, nevertheless, an unruffled temper—"easy and good-natured," as Laurence Housman remembered him, with an inclination, "if he heard an outcry," to dash upstairs and "put sugar on our bread and butter." But spurts of kindliness could not regulate a growing family; nor was it probable that an unwealthy widower with seven children would again find both a loving wife and dutiful mother. Edward postponed the inevitable for two years, during which the circumstances demanded but his instincts rebelled against a marriage of convenience; until at last he resignedly proposed to his cousin Lucy Housman, who had personified from the beginning the obvious practical solution.

In the hope of reducing the difficulties that usually confront a step-mother, and perhaps to preserve undiluted his memories of the mistress of Perry Hall, Edward seized the opportunity that presented itself, early in 1873, of installing his family in the former Clock House at Fockbury, where he had spent his own childhood and where Thomas Housman had continued to reside until a few years ago. There, among fresh surroundings and removed from the indelible associations of Bromsgrove, they would all, he planned, begin new lives and entertain brighter prospects. Renamed Fockbury House, the gabled Victorian exterior which had superimposed itself on the original seventeenth-century farmhouse was the centre of what had once been the extensive Holden estate; and the neighbouring countrymen still referred to it as "The Clockus," although its titular clock tower had long since disappeared. Lacking the comforts of gaslight and indoor plumbing, this abode challenged the domestic abilities of the second Mrs. Housman; but with its own fields, orchards and vestigial farm buildings, set among rural environs, it provided for the town-bred children an inexhaustible playground. Like some bird's-eye view of the English countryside, patched with woodland, crisscrossed by hedges and threaded by meandering brooks, the Fockbury district spread its green tapestry around the ancestral house, in whose attic old books and emblazoned pedigrees gathered the dust.

Here, in the intervals which his hours of study and the daily trips to Bromsgrove allowed him, Alfred began to recover some of that elation he had felt at Woodchester. Instead of the circumscribed garden at Perry Hall, miles of unexplored country and the wild haunts of nature now lay within his reach; a landscape whose peculiar features—the wide valley of the Severn over which, from occasional vantage points, the Shropshire hills loomed at sunset—corresponded to his own expanding mental horizon. That "western brookland" was to be, in the most susceptible years of adolescence, the background of his thoughts and the source of his greatest happiness, though he still preferred to wander off by himself, separating family life and social activity from these sessions of silent communion.

At the age of fifteen, nevertheless, Housman had achieved an exceptional equilibrium which gave him, in relation to other people, the freedom to pursue his own way unmolested. Towards his father he discharged his filial duty by undertaking to supervise, with more patience than Edward could command, the leisure of his brothers and sisters; to his step-mother, even before she had entered Fockbury House, he declared his intention of lending every assistance; while at school, under the new headmaster's stern hand, he continued to fulfil the most exacting requirements of the classical curriculum. Among those who wielded authority over him, none could find any pretext to curb or reform this industrious student and submissive son. The resulting liberty, which he took care never to abuse, left him in solitary possession of his soul and unhampered, except by his own discretion, in what he chose to read or think. Already, with a first step into maturity, he had won the privilege of independence as a reward for the self-control he had practised since his mother's death; and now, on those lonely walks which were to become a life-long habit, his mind roamed at large over the flowering meadows and along the pensive streams of the Worcestershire countryside.

Insofar as the inception of poetry can be traced back to a simple origin, it was, in Housman's case as in that of so many English poets, the influence exerted by the local landscape upon a responsive temperament. From *The Faery Queen* to *Four Quartets*, some native scene has pervaded the poems of every period; and in the formation of poetic sensibility, geographical factors have played a more than subordinate part. In the nineteenth century, above all, the charming and benign aspects of nature provided not only the daily environment of most young men, but a solvent to their intellectual perplexities. They were accustomed, from early childhood, to an intimate awareness and constant observation of the countryside; and for those gifted with imagination, as for Mark Pattison, "a delight in rural objects grew within me, and passed insensibly into the more abstract poetic emotion." All over England the same process had occurred wherever a rambling boy encountered, at the turn of his path, something which pierced his consciousness—a blossoming tree, a sweeping view or simply, as Quiller-Couch recorded from his own experience, "sunlight slanting down a broad glade." By such tokens literary talent was acclimatized and its themes interlaced with the terrain.

Housman's impressions of the country around Fockbury differed, however, to the extent that he was more reticent and reflective than other boys of comparable discernment. Living so much within himself, he was a little detached, as if he had already discovered that one's identification with any part of nature was only a momentary illusion; while his intelligence, of a kind that led the retired Dr. Blore to describe him as always on the verge of asking some unanswerable question, tended to analyse and undermine even his own pleasures. Like an ominous cloud in the most radiant sky, the memory of his mother and the shadow of her death still overcast his mind.

Summer! and after Summer what?

. . . . .

Only to us its tones seem sighs,
Only to us it prophesies
Of coming Autumn, coming death.

Written at Fockbury, as Mrs. Symons recalled, probably in the
summer of 1875, these exclamatory yet dispirited lines have
embalmed the earnest schoolboy attitude and inward melancholy with which, at the age of sixteen, Alfred contemplated
the "brooding lands" and waving beech-trees: a mood com-
pounded of his gravity and introspection, his probing thoughts
and stifled feelings, along with the faint stir of poetic ambition.

As the studious and exemplary head of the Fourth Form,
Housman had won, a year before, the prize for a composition
in English verse on the subject of *The Death of Socrates*. Delivered on Commencement Speech Day by the proud if palpi-
tating author, and published in the *Bromsgrove Messenger* on
August 8, 1874, in whose yellowing files it can still be found,
the poem marked Housman's first involuntary appearance in
print, and was typical of those rhetorical productions with
which he competed for and twice captured a doubtful literary
honour. Neither better nor worse than it should be, *The Death
of Socrates* was an exercise whose negative requirements Housman contrived to meet only too well. The musty air of text-
book antiquity emanated from its orthodox couplets, while all
the platitudes of the subject unrolled as if the model boy were
making an almost calculated effort to win over his audience.
Plainly, among his betters, Housman liked to create a good
effect and was even susceptible, on such occasions, to the
temptation of professing those popular sentiments which in
private he had already outgrown. No wonder that he would
not allow the republication of these embarrassing juvenilia, or
that the only record of a work entitled *Paul on Mars Hill*, which
enjoyed a similar success the next year, has mysteriously vanished
from the archives of the *Messenger*.

At home, under less exacting conditions, Housman continued to write the kind of verse that took the place, in educated

Victorian families, of today's cross-word puzzle; a test both of wit and vocabulary, to which in the Housman circle Alfred was always the most energetic contributor. Lacking this verbal facility, Edward gladly relinquished the role of cultural guide to his eldest son; and with an early bent for pedagogy, Alfred quickly transformed the parlour game into a writing course, the country walk into a botanical lesson for his brothers and sisters. Plays, poems, stories and even a family magazine were executed on a communal basis, each member of this unlettered kindergarten being coerced to submit his reflections on such Housmanesque topics as "Death" or "Spring Flowers." A parody of *Hamlet* and other impromptu dramas were performed, before a stunned parental audience, on holiday evenings; while on the long summer days, by combining his own interests with an educational purpose, Alfred disseminated his knowledge of trees, architecture and astronomy. But as Mrs. Symons fondly remembered it, "we found great fun in all this," and in fact Alfred's enterprise helped not only to reunite the broken and disconsolate family but to soften the abrasive quality of his step-mother's disposition.

Eight years older than her husband, the second Mrs. Housman had to bridge an almost impassable distance between middle age and her younger step-children. As an unloved and childless woman of fifty, she had accepted Edward's hand in marriage and undertaken the direction of his household in a spirit of altruism and self-sacrifice, both out of pity for her cousin and devotion to the memory of Sarah Jane Williams. But her own years of self-denial and spinsterhood, her disappointments and renunciations had made her, as Mrs. Symons privately observed, "not a woman of tenderness but of rather rigid discipline." However willing and conscientious, she could not impersonate an affectionate mother, or diffuse an atmosphere of grace and warmth in Fockbury House. For this somewhat intrusive and unsympathetic figure, nevertheless, Alfred showed from the beginning a determination to be especially considerate of her trials and serenely oblivious of her asperities, without ever betraying the resentment he might have been expected to feel towards any woman in her position. Perhaps because he detected that Lucy Housman had really cared for his mother, Alfred could transfer some of his loyalty, if almost none of his love, to an ill-favoured substitute; and thus once again he was moved to ally himself, not with his father, but with the person who must bear the brunt of Edward's unheeding masculine egotism. By what proved to be a further mischance, Alfred was exposed in his youth, and seemed chiefly attracted, to women of strong character but slight physical allure—to his angular and ageing step-mother, to the maternal Mrs. Wise, and above all to Miss Sophie Becker, the plain-faced but quick-witted German governess with whom he had formed an acquaintance at Woodchester. This, as Laurence Housman has expressed it, "was one of his most comfortable friendships": a connection that was now renewed by Miss Becker's occasional visits to Fockbury and which continued, unimpaired though with diminishing points of contact, until she died, after years of repatriation, in Hitlerian Germany.

No scrap of Housman's correspondence with or from Miss Becker has been recovered, and therefore no gauge of the mutual attraction, the strange bond that in spite of so many disparities held them together, but the letters written to his step-mother, and long preserved by their grateful recipient, not only still attest to the nature of their relationship but provide a glimpse of Alfred's outward manner, his air of resolute composure and his already piquant sense of humour at the age of sixteen. His first trip to London, in the Christmas holidays of 1874, was the earliest opportunity for a report to "My dear Mamma," covering his itinerary and listing his impressions with the feigned nonchalance of a worldly tourist. He wrote about the Chapel Royal and the British Museum ("What delighted me most was the Farnese Mercury"); St. Paul's and the Abbey where "Service was at three with an anthem by Greene which was like a boa-constrictor—very long and very ugly";

the populous vistas from Trafalgar Square and Westminster Bridge; "but I think of all I have seen, what has impressed me most is—the Guards. This may be barbarian, but it is true." To such a preference, among the conventional sights and numerous temptations of the capital, one can hardly help attaching a particular significance. In an unguarded moment, it seems, Housman cast off his superior pose and became an awe-struck schoolboy, transfixed with admiration in the presence of those life-size toy-soldiers who stand, blank and immobile, outside their sentry-boxes, or march and strike their heels in mock ferocity on the parade ground. Chosen for their statuesque tallness and trained to a machine-like precision, the guardsmen in their red coats and towering bearskins represented then as now a colourful but inhuman military symbolism. In their daily performance of superfluous tasks they suggested, not the glory of the battlefield, but the discipline of the drill-master; they were not so much heroes as automatons. Yet for these handsome effigies Housman conceived at first glance an irresistible attraction, to which the only clue lay in his use of the word "barbarian": a term that usually connotes either some brutal assault upon the life of reason and restraint, or a yielding on the part of civilized people to their baser instincts. Apparently half-conscious that his enthusiasm for the Guards partook of both meanings, Housman revealed and even underlined, in this passing remark to his step-mother, not only his discovery that young men of flesh and blood existed inside the uniforms, but that to feel about them as he did was obscurely reprehensible. It was, in fact, the beginning of a long vicarious romance.

This emotional excitement produced by the stimulations of London helped to colour, on Housman's return to Bromsgrove, the dull things and familiar people at home, now further dramatized by an outbreak of scarlet fever which had quarantined Fockbury House in his absence, and obliged him to live at school for several weeks. Writing again to his step-mother, Alfred described himself as lingering "from 2 o'clock till 3" in the churchyard, from which he could obtain a distant aerial view of Fockbury and watch "especially the window of your room." Overcast by illness, the house recalled that wintry and besieged atmosphere of four years ago; but now, scanning the area over which, within a short radius of St. John's, his whole experience was mapped out, he felt still more isolated and in need of some reciprocal companionship. Among those with whom he came close to intimacy—his step-mother, Miss Becker, Mrs. Wise and Edith—all were more or less adequate replacements for his mother, but none could serve, for a young man approaching sixteen, as the repository of his full confidence. Even though surrounded by men and boys at school, or by his father and brothers at home, Alfred suffered from the want of a congenial masculine friendship, and was emotionally too dependent on those decorous older women, whose influence merely fostered his natural tendency to over-sensitiveness and withdrawal. The solitary figure in the churchyard, still somewhat undersized and always a punctilious example of good deportment, must have seemed anything but inviting to his own generation; while to Alfred in turn, his school-mates were not the sort with whom he could discuss the poetry of Swinburne, much less his private thoughts. Nor were his step-mother and Miss Becker beyond a certain delicate point which now became the habitual limit of Housman's ability to disburden himself. But even if deleterious, their maternal ministrations sufficed to explain Alfred's early penchant for feminine society, and in particular his recurrent visits to Woodchester House, which were converted about this time, amidst howls of laughter, into what Mrs. Symons called one of the "silly childish jokes" that used to circulate at his expense in the family circle:

> Alfred Edward solemn and wise
> Opens his mouth and rolls his eyes,
> But when chasing Selsley slopes
> Opes his eyes and eyes his 'opes.

The object of this ocular pursuit was Edith Wise, now a young lady of twenty-one and already engaged to be married. Like an older sister, she had been for Alfred, ever since his mother's death, the nearest equivalent to a friend of his own age; a Renoir girl (as she appeared in a beribboned photograph) whose five extra years made it possible to enjoy, without the risk of blushing embarrassment, a larger freedom of inter-course. Both could safely confess, as to the most trustworthy but unconcerned listener, something of those secret desires which are so hard to divulge in adolescence. Chasing Selsley slopes, they were apt to speak less about their relation to each other than of their distress in relation to other people. Having advanced further than Alfred into the intricacies of the heart, Edith played the role, not of some romantic schoolboy heroine, but of a love-sick maiden exhibiting for his benefit the ardours and agonies of her condition. For eventually her en-gagement was broken off, "owing," in the words of Mrs. Symons, "to financial difficulties." Thus again prematurely and with a special insight, Housman witnessed as a youth of sixteen the kind of unhappiness usually reserved for adult experience. On every side those with whom he was most in sympathy—his struggling step-mother, the loveless Miss Becker, and now Edith—had been reduced to a state of bitter resignation.

The effect of such early morbidities was only displayed, on Housman's part, in a slight restlessness and occasional inatten-tion to the curriculum of Bromsgrove School. After the summer vacation of 1875, the Grade Book recorded that

> Housman has been working well, but I must warn him and Cochrane, but more especially the latter, not to think that, because their lessons are somewhat shortened for the sake of the new boys, they may be less carefully prepared.

A week later, however, with renewed application to the sub-jects of the Fifth Form, "Housman is working very well," as he continued to do until, during the week of October 23, "Mr. Bozwadowski complains of Housman as often coming to him with his lessons unprepared." The slump prolonged itself for a fortnight, sinking to the nadir when, in the examination on November 20, "Housman broke down in his Sallust, which was inaccurate and careless." In Horace, Plato, Euripides,

Grammar, Divinity, French and Mathematics, however, he maintained a respectable standard, with high marks in Horace and Mathematics; and by Christmas, in a final test of his eligibility for promotion, he achieved the rising score of 1,098 out of a possible 1,593, with the further commendation that "Housman's grammar paper, and Ellis', were both very good." In the New Year, therefore, Alfred passed into the Sixth Form and under the personal tuition of Mr. Millington, who from then on did not require himself to keep any written record of his students' progress.

The Headmaster's opinion of Housman's abilities was favourable, nonetheless—"May all my boys be like him," was the accolade he conferred, a year later, on his best pupil; while his own forceful character and rigorous but stirring instruction had a lasting effect on the quiet, docile boy of seventeen who now encountered at close range this paragon of the masculine virtues. Still a young man of thirty-five when Housman entered his last year at Bromsgrove School, Mr. Millington had all the attributes of those massive Victorians who combined superabundant physical energy with phenomenal intellectual equipment. A devotee of horse-racing and a hearty advocate of cricket, he was at the same time an inspired teacher, a meticulous scholar, a successful administrator, an impeccable model and merciless judge of conduct, yet withal the kind of dynamic personality that could overawe the most diverse and refractory elements of a boarding school. Outside the classroom, as an ex-student remembered him, the terrifying disciplinarian gave way to a handsome, courteous, imperial figure bearing some resemblance to "certain portraits of Matthew Arnold." Such a man, then at the peak of his powers and with so many of the gifts and qualities that Alfred was prone to admire, inevitably held a fatal fascination for the wistful acolyte at his feet, a fascination all the more compelling, perhaps, because the idol would tolerate no approach to familiarity. But as it was, Alfred's hero-worship expressed itself merely in redoubled efforts to win the praise and satisfy the most gruelling demands of this attractive tyrant, whose methods were "excellent," Housman laconically recalled in later years, "for clever boys with a taste for the classics."

The iron hand of Mr. Millington now quickly dispelled that fretful boredom which, in the presence of a less commanding teacher, Alfred had sometimes succumbed to; while the Headmaster's brilliant exposition "of a difficult passage in Thucydides" or "the beauties of a poem of Catullus" awakened to the full Housman's susceptibility and response to classical literature. The cloudy veils of a dead language were slowly parting to reveal, under the laborious conjugations and declensions, the hidden palpitant work of art. It was a discovery akin to those chance meetings with some person or fateful readings of some book destined to influence the rest of one's life. Unrealized at the time and afterwards even forgotten, they are the vague decisive moments when youth begins to lean, as Housman was doing at the age of seventeen, in a direction that will become at every turning-point harder to reverse and easier to follow. The instrument that originally focussed his mind on classical studies, he later alleged, was one of those volumes that used to rain down upon him each Prize Day—in this case *Sabrinae Corolla*, a miscellaneous collection of English poems rendered into Greek and Latin by the best scholars and most industrious fellows of Cambridge and Oxford. First published in 1850, it had already reached a third edition in 1867, and was emblematic of a period when education still largely consisted of such linguistic exercises. But by giving an equal place to English poetry, the editor of *Sabrinae Corolla* had struck a happy compromise between the exigencies of metrical translation and a generous anthology of native verse; while its insidious effect, for any schoolboy, was to link the values of scholarship more closely with those of literature.

Like the hieroglyphic pages of a musical score, however, Horace and Catullus and even *Sabrinae Corolla* required some interpreter to bring out their latent properties, and it was this function (always invested with excessive glamour) that Mr.

Millington so well performed. With his "austerely handsome features" and his "sanguine, strenuous, somewhat emotional outlook on life," no one was better fitted to stir the imagination and personify the ideals of a bookish and precocious student who had missed having a father to revere or until now any leader to follow. The opportune person, in fact the only available mentor at hand, was that severe yet scintillating taskmaster, whose adamant Victorian code left its visible mark on Housman's character. Mr. Millington brought his influence to bear not only as the arbiter in major scholastic decisions, advising against Cambridge, for example, and grooming his favourite for classical honours, but even more potently as that symbol of authority and mirror of perfection, before which young men of a romantic tendency are impelled to prostrate themselves. Above all, in the world of lonely women, uninteresting men and grubby schoolboys which Housman inhabited, this exuberant figure who not merely taught the language but in himself relayed the burning torch of Athenian education must have had the impact of a god-like protagonist astride the Bromsgrove stage.

Alfred's romanticism could now be seen, faintly smudged around the averted eyes, in a photograph of 1877. It was a gentle beardless face of which one could predict the vulnerability, but not yet the pinched look and hostile stare of later days. With his arms gracefully folded and his head turned as if to contemplate some ephemeral object or inward vision, the modest head of the Sixth Form exposed to the camera's lens his neatly dressed, freshly combed, well-mannered surface in a polite effort to please without attracting attention. If not quite the "pleasant open countenance" that Mrs. Symons professed to find in it, the picture conveyed, nevertheless, the semblance of a relative contentment, and registered something of that self-assurance and maturity of mind to which Housman had attained in his eighteenth year. Though often marred by fits of melancholy and still haunted by loneliness, this chapter of his life yielded more pleasures and rewards, especially at school, than he had ever known. Flaunting the purple tassel with which upper classmen were privileged to trim their mortarboards, and holding a secure intellectual eminence among his fellow-students, Housman outdid himself, under the baton of Mr. Millington, in good work and the capture of prizes. With the vigour of an athlete, he pursued, instead of the goal-post and the silver cup, the laurels conferred by Lord Lyttelton for Latin verse, the honorarium for Greek verse and the Senior Wattell prize, in addition to the crucial Oxford scholarship. But even before the ceremonies of Prize Day, his elation would have reached a zenith on that June night when a party of masters and friends, accompanied by Mr. and Mrs. Millington, strolled from Fockbury House to a near-by hill-top whence they could observe the joyful beacons flaring up in a vast ring round the horizon. It was a view Housman often stopped to admire on his solitary walks, and the setting, Mrs. Symons thought, which he "must have had in mind when he wrote the Jubilee poem that opens *A Shropshire Lad*." Engraving itself on his memory, as he stood there with a sense of his own imminent triumph, amid the flickering fires of a national celebration, it was to become, in fact, symbolic of those evanescent glories which he would some day, in a darker mood, attribute to the sacrificial and anonymous "Lads of the Fifty-third."

From necessity as well as zeal, Alfred had exerted himself to win the academic prestige and financial emolument of a scholarship, without which he would have been unable, in the present state of his father's affairs, to continue his education. That sudden economic collapse of the middle seventies had lately overtaken Bromsgrove, and in combination with Edward's inefficiencies, had imposed what Mrs. Symons called "an increasing restriction of means" upon the family establishment. Apathetic and disheartened in his personal life, Edward had resumed all those costly hobbies and idle distractions—the horticultural experiments and the country sports—to which Fockbury House provided the daily temptation, but which he could now so ill afford. An expert shot, an avid hunter and tireless fisherman, he reverted more and more to the pastimes of his boyhood as the knocks of adversity grew louder; and in order to maintain the illusion of being driven beyond endurance, he sought frequent refuge in the bottle. Once again, as it must have seemed to Alfred, his father had failed to meet the test of an emergency and deserved nothing but contempt; while for the last time, before his son left home, Edward tried to impart his advice and shoulder some at least of his parental duties. But by interposing an objection to Balliol, because of Dr. Jowett's unorthodox religion, and on the other hand by refusing to consider any Cambridge prospect but St. John's, he may simply have prevented Alfred from gaining admission to some college better suited to his abilities.

Just as Edward took the spiritual state of his model son for granted, so lesser issues were probably never raised between them; and the quiescent atmosphere of Fockbury House remained unruffled, even as its fortunes declined and its shabbiness began to show through. On Sundays the family now walked sedately to church at Catshill, where the seven chestnut trees had been transplanted along the graveyard wall, and where Alfred could not escape, as he sang the hymns and echoed the prayers, a surge of hopeless regret for his mother. But if only out of respect for her religious faith, he submissively pretended to share these weekly devotions, and would sometimes consent to read the lesson in his father's absence. With the same amenability, he helped to keep up appearances at home, still organizing the parlour games and assuming, between his bouts of depression, a festive spirit of the kind commemorated in *A Morning with the Royal Family*—that secret literary prank which one of his brothers "nefariously passed on" to the *Bromsgrovian*, where it has preserved, in the almost unobtainable early issues of a school magazine, Housman's only work of prose fiction. A whimsical caper not unworthy of Lewis Carroll, it reflected the happier side of which his brothers and sisters "saw a great deal more," Mrs. Symons has testified, "than of the troubled depths"; and being most of them too young to win his confidence, they merely failed to detect his "occasional moodiness." But to plumb the depths, there has survived the "commonplace book" in which, on ruled lines and with his already careful penmanship, Housman was in the habit of copying out the poems and passages that in the course of his reading made some particular appeal to him. Dating perhaps from as early as 1875, when he was sixteen, this youthful anthology retraces not only the development of his taste but the trend of his thoughts, and in its first entry—a triad of verses entitled *The Progress of Poesy*, by Matthew Arnold—strikes the note that was to become his own peculiar trademark:

> Youth rambles on life's arid mount,
> And strikes the rock, and finds the vein,
> And brings the water from the fount,
> The fount which shall not flow again.

What could so nearly approximate, twenty years in advance, his favourite theme, or define so well the object of his nervous adolescent quest?

If Housman was then dimly conscious, at sixteen or seventeen, of such golden but fleeting opportunities, he would have reached, by the following year, yet a further stage of apprehension; and it must have been in this anxious, anticipatory mood that he received, as the climactic award of Prize Day, the best of the available scholarships, with a munificent annual stipend of £100, to St. John's College, Oxford. Relief flooded like sunlight over the worn carpets of Fockbury House, making that summer of 1877 a season of bright promise for Alfred and of renewed hope for his family. They were much in need of some practical encouragement, but to Edward's credit, it was never remotely suggested that his able-bodied son might have gone to work, or still less that he should regard the university as a source of material advantages. The purpose of a gentleman's education was not linked, even by improvident families, with a choice of career; and whatever its other drawbacks, this tradition gave their sons the means of enjoying, on the doorstep of maturity, a long speculative pause. For young men of Housman's quality in particular, it was a system ideally designed to foster their talents and extend their scope; a utopia in which they could ignore, temporarily, the limitations and encumbrances of the real world. As a pent-up, introspective student, moreover, oppressed by the difficulties at home, he would have looked forward all the more to some romantic fulfilment of his expectations, some miraculous escape from the confines of his past experience. But Housman's character was already hardening into its stubborn mould. Formed in solitude and bristling with those "eccentric little habits" to which Mrs. Symons referred—"punctuality, industry, fixed routine, daily walking, love of flowers and trees, woods and hills"—he presented at the age of eighteen a mild youthful version of that granite personality which would in later life so firmly resist the inroads of change. Like the Professor of Latin, he "drank beer daily" and splashed each morning in his "shallow sponge bath"; like the man-to-be, under his protective aloofness, he responded vibrantly to a poem or a landscape and knew the measure of his capacities, if not yet, as he dreamed of Oxford, what the future held in store for him.

CHAPTER FOUR

Leave your home behind you

THE towers of Oxford dominated a scene of comparative tranquillity when Housman went up to matriculate in the autumn of 1877. In spite of that "base and brickish skirt" by which Gerard Manley Hopkins had been repelled a decade before, it was still closer to the town Shelley knew than to the industrial city of today; an almost exclusive academic grove where the colleges were like small independent kingdoms and their bells smote the air in unchallenged supremacy. In the wake of the Oxford Movement and the period of Blue China, the intellectual currents flowed as gently as the Cherwell; in his rooms at Christ Church Mr. Dodgson puttered amidst his photographic equipment, and at Brasenose Mr. Pater might have been composing the first pages of *Marius*; while in the streets and courtyards, on that early October day, the neophytes loitered in awkward and awe-struck expectancy.

Housman occupied rooms in the second quad at St. John's, on the same "stair" with A. W. Pollard, with whom he quickly struck up an acquaintance; both were solemn and friendless young men adrift in a sea of strangeness. But in writing to his step-mother, Housman adopted the tone of amused condescension with which, as a bored schoolboy, he had viewed the wonders of London. After a tutor had summoned the twenty-two freshmen of St. John's, "at a quarter to five on the Saturday afternoon," for a lesson in how to sign the University register:

Then he marched us off to New College, where we found the Vice-Chancellor seated in dim religious light at the top of the hall. Another college was just concluding the ceremony, and when they had finished, we one by one inscribed our names in a large book, in this wise. "Alfredus Edwardus Housman, e Coll. Di. Joh. Bapt. Gen. Fil. Natu max." which is, being interpreted, "A. E. Hous-

man, of the College of St. John the Baptist, eldest son of a gentleman." Sons of Clergymen write "Cler. Fil." and sons of officers
write "Arm. Fil." Then I wrote my name in English in a smaller
and less dignified book, and then paid £2. 10s. to a man at the table.
. . . Then an attendant brought in twenty-two copies of the Statutes
of the University, bound in violet, and piled them on the table,
hiding the Vice-Chancellor from the eye. Presently his head appeared over the top, and we got up and stood in a sort of semi-circle
in front of him. Then he called up each of us by name and presented each with a copy of the Statutes. . . . Then he settled his
gown over his shoulders and . . . said, in Latin, "Allow me to inform you that you have this day been enrolled in the register of the
University, and that you are bound to keep all the Statutes contained in this book," (with the violet cover) "as far as they may concern you." Then we went. As to keeping the statutes, you may
judge what a farce that is, when I tell you that you are forbidden to
wear any coat save a black one, or to use fire-arms, or to trundle a
hoop, among other things.

Impressionable and observant, as this letter shows him to be,
Housman must also have noticed, among the twenty-two freshmen, a tall, sturdy, dark-haired young man with a somewhat
defiant manner; but neither at the time nor in later reports did
he confess a growing attraction to this fellow-undergraduate
who was finally to become his "greatest friend," and except for
whom, Housman afterwards maintained, "Oxford had not
much effect on me."

The young man was Moses John Jackson, the son and namesake of a schoolmaster who, in spite of his Biblical appellation,
had no claim to Jewish blood. Born at Ramsgate in 1859, and
educated at the local Academy over which his father presided,
Jackson was the Victorian equivalent of the all-round boy—
an effortless honours student, a natural athlete, an estimable
manly character. Yet under his father's sedulous training and
the burden of his own accomplishments, he had not lost the
spontaneity of youth; in fact, an air of self-conscious rectitude
merely enhanced his appeal. With his good looks and his
upright bearing, this ideal freshman combined the high principles of Mr. Millington with the physical attributes of a guardsman; and even though his interests were more scientific than

classical, he embodied all those qualities which for Housman rendered life at that age so promising, so perilous and so poetic. But to one who had received few overtures of friendship, it seemed hardly possible in the beginning that a Jackson could be more than distantly polite to a Housman; and it was all the more wonderful, therefore, when that alluring but inaccessible figure voluntarily chose to cultivate his shy and speechless admirer. On Jackson's part, some faint perception of the feelings he inspired, as well as a generous impulse, must have drawn him towards the quiet lonely resident of the second quad; while for the first time, in the excess of his desire, Housman lowered the bars of his restraint and freely responded to these preliminary advances. Coming from the same social background and with the same strict standards of conduct, they had more than enough in common to offset their differences and inequalities. Jackson's unromantic temper and distaste for literature only served to add something more to the enticement of the unknown, as no doubt Housman's intensity and introspection had a peculiar charm for his debonair friend. But above all, by one of those chance encounters, two people had met and, without reasons or motives, simply liked each other.

The advent of Jackson gave not only a new zest to Housman's social life, but further impetus to the studies into which, "from the very beginning," as his tutor at St. John's later testified, "he threw himself . . . with the most remarkable vigour and ardour, and in mature and original ways." His weekly schedule included nine lectures in college, and three private lessons with Mr. Warren at Magdalen, who had the same "strong impression" of Housman's exceptional talents. "He was certainly to me one of the most interesting and attractive pupils I can temember. He had even then, as quite a young student, a combination of force, acumen and taste which I shall never forget." The atmosphere of Oxford did have, obviously, a stimulating effect in those eager days when, against a backdrop of Gothic spires and in the company of

Jackson or Pollard, both Housman's mind and his emotions were beginning to expand. In a world where young men wore bowler hats and carried walking sticks, where they decorously invited each other to breakfast or tea, where they gathered seriously to read Sunday-night essays and where intellectual pursuits were taken as a matter of course, Housman was almost at ease and sometimes even the blushing centre of attention. "When he was in the mood," Pollard recalled with a smile, "Housman would go so far as to recite to very restricted audiences humorous stories of his own making, which were made doubly humorous by his prim method of telling them." And of course he continued those punctual walks, but no longer invariably alone, into a countryside already familiar to him in the poetry of Matthew Arnold, and which may have been, in retrospect, the setting for his own happiest lyrical compositions.

Such a spirit of contentment possessed him that even the rousing protests of Mr. Ruskin could only seem extravagant and slightly absurd:

This afternoon (of 29 Nov. 1877) Ruskin gave us a great outburst against modern times. He had got a picture of Turner's, framed, and glassed, representing Leicester and the Abbey in the distance at Sunset, over a river. He read the account of Wolsey's death out of Henry VIII. Then he pointed to the picture as representing Leicester when Turner had drawn it. Then he said "You, if you like, may go to Leicester to see what it is like now. I never shall. But I can make a pretty good guess." Then he caught up a paintbrush. "These stepping-stones of course have been done away with, and are replaced by a be-au-ti-ful iron bridge." Then he dashed in the iron bridge on the glass of the picture. "The colour of the stream is supplied on one side by the indigo factory." Forthwith one side of the stream became indigo. "On the other side by the soap factory." Soap dashed in. "They mix in the middle—like curds," he said, working them together with a sort of malicious deliberation. "This field, over which you see the sun setting behind the abbey, is now occupied in a *proper* manner." Then there went a flame of scarlet across the picture, which developed itself into windows and roofs and red brick, and rushed up into a chimney. "The atmosphere is supplied—thus!" A puff and cloud of smoke all over Turner's sky: and then the brush thrown down, and Ruskin confronting modern civilization amidst a tempest of applause, which he always elicits now, as he has this term become immensely popular, his lectures being crowded, whereas of old he used to prophesy to empty benches.

Querulous, intractable and on the verge of breakdown, at the age of fifty-eight, Ruskin was nevertheless at the height of his fame and, as Housman deigned to note, still in effective command of his powers. A brilliant writer, an impassioned speaker, a glowing personality—but he was not the sort of man for whose ideas an undergraduate imbued with Victorian sobriety and devoted to exact scholarship could feel much enthusiasm. Always deficient in his response to the non-literary arts, Housman caught only the shrillness of Ruskin's fulmination but was himself not disturbed by these familiar sore-spots of the cultural scene; and though his enjoyment of architecture grew keener, it derived more from the historical aspects of the subject than from the aesthetic values of a beautiful building. Ruskin's obsession with the conflict between life and art was, moreover, immaterial to Housman's view; and at eighteen he was already opinionated enough to ridicule and reject whatever seemed extraneous to his own process of thought. This headstrong tendency now began to assert itself in the first mild signs of intellectual intransigence.

The prevailing tradition to which Housman found himself exposed at Oxford gave more importance to the background of scholarship than to scholarship itself; variety of knowledge was cultivated at the expense of precision; and the chief protagonist of this educational theory was Dr. Benjamin Jowett, then Regius Professor of Greek, who had been for more than forty years a dominant influence and leading light among the Oxford intelligentsia. But even Dr. Jowett was still dissatisfied: "The present teaching," he complained in 1878, "is—1. Utterly bad for the students; 2. Mere reading to students." He had practically ceased, however, to lecture on those classical subjects to which his Chair obligated him, and was more apt to discourse at random on Philosophy, Logic, Divinity or Political

74

Economy; while he took pains to attack the "futility of conjectural emendation" and in particular its foremost English
exemplar, that long-extinct curmudgeon, Dr. Richard Bentley, "of whom he had a great dislike." Jowett was at this
period a cherubic, silver-haired figure capable of investing his
thoughts with "literary grace and charm," but also addicted to
sharp dogmatic statements which his position made it dangerous to contradict. A reformer who did not always foresee the
outcome of his efforts, he was one of the unconscious pioneers
in that movement which has led to the progressive school and
the decline of classical studies. Such a man, profoundly at odds
not only with Housman's natural bent but with the standards
so firmly implanted by Mr. Millington, could merely provoke his scornful opposition; and "from the single lecture of
Jowett's which he attended," as he told a trusted colleague in
later years, "Housman came away disgusted by the Professor's
disregard for the niceties of scholarship."

Likewise, among the rest of his Oxford tutors and teachers,
Housman could find none to compel his deference, still less to
admire, and even ungenerously refused, when he had left them
behind, to reciprocate their compliments; but having displayed
his abilities and won their approval, he now began to follow his
own independent course of study, and in a mood of passive
resistance to the conventional curriculum, applied himself much
more energetically to the text of Propertius than to the prescribed philosophy of Plato. It was certainly a decisive, and
may have been a revealing, choice of subject on which to
expend the best years of his youth. For Propertius was not
simply a Latin author whose garbled works invited extensive
editorial revision, but a poet of the most powerful and passionate order. Contagiously emotional and erotic, his verse could
hardly fail to stir the blood of any young scholar; and Housman's scholarship, it has been generally agreed, was of a kind
that excelled in sensitive perception. With this inflammatory
material, then, he was mainly engaged in his working hours;
while at leisure he continued to enjoy the friendship of Moses

Jackson and to fill the "commonplace book" with excerpts from English romantic poetry.

The solid Jacobean walls of the second quad where Housman lived for three years, the vaulted library where he often studied, the emerald gardens where he strolled and even sometimes played what Pollard judiciously called "elementary lawn tennis"—all the surroundings of his Oxford life have remained visibly changeless and intact. But that life itself has ebbed into a few letters, the faint reverberations of the "commonplace book," and the fragmentary reminiscences of Pollard, from which it must be largely deduced and reconstructed. The central figure had now reached a height of five feet nine inches, but was still slender, small-boned and nervously constrained. The gentle expression and contemplative eyes of the schoolboy occasionally hardened into a scoffing look of critical impatience—doubtless the look which prompted the Senior Tutor to proclaim that Housman "was *not* a genius." But his intellectual pride reflected something more than heady conceit; it flashed a beam also into those dark corners which had oppressed his boyhood. The secret writhings of sexuality were laid bare as he read Propertius, while in the presence of Jackson's vigorous and magnetic youth the cold intimations of death began to dissolve. Besides which, the pretensions of learned men were neatly deflated when one of his teachers mispronounced a Greek word, and the frailties of great men betrayed, as he thought, in such performances as Ruskin's lecture. With the unsparing judgment of his limited years, Housman was derisively amused by those who professed to instruct him; and yet "I think," as Pollard described that early Oxford phase, "he was quietly happy."

The second entry in the "commonplace book" was a passage from *In Memoriam*—the hundred and twenty-third verse which ends:

> But in my spirit will I dwell
> And dream my dream, and hold it true;
> For tho' my lips may breathe adieu,
> I cannot think the thing farewell.

76

Leaving the reader in no doubt, at this stage of the poem, that "the thing" was death, Tennyson had tried to convey, with something less than his usual felicity, the same kind of desperate resolution to which Housman was clinging when, at sixteen or seventeen, he had copied it down. Mute and friendless in those days, he too could only dream and dwell perforce in his lonely and afflicted spirit, unaware that other parts of the poem would shortly acquire more literal significance for him. The background of *In Memoriam* would strikingly correspond, in fact, to the experience which awaited him at Oxford. Like Tennyson, he was a despondent self-conscious young man brought up in the depths of the country, and now thrust into a bewildering social microcosm where, like Arthur Hallam at Cambridge, Jackson in turn had appeared, with the sudden effulgence of a meteor, to streak through the Oxford sky; and as in that earlier friendship, one man's relation to another constituted the major event, the absorbing memory of his life. Like a golden anniversary, moreover, Housman's first encounter with Jackson occurred just short of fifty years after the historic meeting, in 1828, between Tennyson and his "much-beloved."

The shadings and overtones of these duplicate affairs were as different, however, as Tennyson's poetry from Housman's. Not only was the first Alfred more temperamental and less ratiocinative than Housman, but the dazzling Hallam had greater advantages and richer potentialities than his successor could pretend to. Heralded by his precociously brilliant reputation and already the centre of an adoring coterie when he descended on Cambridge, Hallam had worn the air of a messenger from some Parnassus; an Ariel or a Mercury sent to rescue Tennyson from his unhappiness and obscurity. By taking the forlorn young poet under his wing, Hallam lifted him to new heights of inspiration; and for "four sweet years" Tennyson did indeed enjoy a blissful interlude, from which Hallam's death plunged him into a despair all the more crushing and irrevocable. But while it lasted, Tennyson's affection was given openly and fully returned, his innermost thoughts and feelings were poured out in headlong profusion.

The nature of Housman's friendship with Jackson was, by contrast, apparently casual, colourless, unemotional and yet thickly strewn with ambiguities. If only because of the character of the participants, there could be no clear and meaningful avowals, but merely on one side a guarded dissimulation and on the other a stolid innocence. Housman did not presume to be a poet, and in any case would have never dared to adopt, with the husky, unimaginative "Mo," such an effete posture; while Jackson assumed the role of a strict but amiable prefect towards one who needed his manly guidance and support. The extent to which they somehow communed, across these walls of prevarication, was a feat of tacit understanding on which, many years later, Housman's poetry would throw an oblique and inferential light. But the reality behind those posthumously published lines

> Because I liked you better
> Than suits a man to say,
> It irked you, and I promised
> To throw the thought away.

must have been a diffident and groping approach to the intimacy that Housman was at last able to offer, but which Jackson was now embarrassed or warily indisposed to accept. Instead of that responsive "pressure of thine hand" which Tennyson remembered, Housman received only a startled look, an evasive laugh, a gentle but firm rebuff. For as in most relationships, there was more urgency on one side than the other; an urgency intensified, in Housman's case, by his inchoate, half-understood feeling, his agonizing hesitation, his sense of the unsayable. Impelled to clutch at any small favours which Jackson would grant, yet paralysed by the fear of losing them altogether, Housman's emotional life was at the same time arrested by and focused on a single person. And thus hovering in a state of exquisite indecision, of suspended and inarticulate excitement, he spent his hours of study with Propertius and his hours of recreation with Jackson, teased by that strange and provocative combination, perhaps only to be found in English universities during the late nineteenth century, of amatory verse and pints of beer, sombre reflections and exuberant country walks.

The prosaic tone which Jackson imposed on their intercourse may have been an act of instinctive wisdom as well as the application of rude common sense to a delicate experiment. Apparently one of those people, themselves inveterately brisk, normal and uncomplicated, who possess a surprising warmth of sympathy for their less happily endowed fellow-men, Jackson knew how to be sane without becoming unhelpful. Sharing none of Housman's thwarted impulses or introspective analytical temper, and therefore unable to attach the same crucial importance to their friendship, Jackson contrived to stabilize and preserve it, nevertheless, with a kind of extra-sensory perception that won Housman's eternal gratitude. The young man who could muster, from the callow experience of his nineteen years, so much sound judgment and kindness of heart was an object worthy of esteem; and whatever he may have failed to give Housman, in terms of romantic ardour and emotional release, he more than compensated for in plain honesty and firmness of character, in simply continuing an association from which he might have been expected abruptly to withdraw. The embodiment of those sterling Victorian principles that were beginning to die out in his generation, Jackson helped to strengthen and confirm, among his friend's conflicting desires, the tendency to invoke lofty and strenuous rules of conduct. With his athletic prowess, his lucid practical mind and his ignorance of temptation, this resolute moral giant effectively blocked what may have been Housman's first incentive if not his only chance to rebel against the demands of "a world I never made."

The sable-hued contents of the "commonplace book" were now and then relieved, during Housman's early years at Oxford and under Jackson's infectious influence, by passages of a more cheerful tenor, ranging from the sonnet *On First Looking Into Chapman's Homer* to Shelley's *Hymn of Pan*—poems that must have echoed Housman's delight in some opaque Latin text, or conjured the "sweet pipings" and "moist river-lawns" of his own college garden. But these brighter notes struck fitfully through the pervading gloom and sepulchral shadows, the "Dirges" and "Laments" which even at this period were evidently Housman's favourite quotations. Unerringly, from poets as high-spirited as Burns and Byron, he selected only the most dismal lines; while in Shelley, Beddoes, Tennyson, and Christina Rossetti he found an abundance of depressing material whose monotonous and invariable theme was death. This funereal compulsion may have reflected, however, not so much his predominant Oxford mood as the despondency which overcame him at home, whenever he revisited the haunted rooms of Perry Hall, in which his hard-pressed family had been forced to take up residence again. It was there, certainly, that Housman would have been more inclined to search for and copy out the sad Stygian entries of the "commonplace book"—a collection of all the melancholy sentiments which the memory of his mother still induced; and in the absence of other proof, I would assign this lugubrious catalogue mostly to his vacations in Bromsgrove when, as Mrs. Symons observed, he fell prey to a growing "taciturnity."

The poem for which, according to Pollard's recollection, Housman then reserved his most lavish praise was *Empedocles on Etna*—a work that contained, he used to say, "all the law and the prophets," but of which no part was confided to his scrapbook. Though written when Matthew Arnold was himself comparatively young, this invocation to despair and argument for suicide expressed an attitude more suitable to middle age, but which, in the Victorian intellectual world, often tinged the minds of younger men, and none more deeply than Housman's. With almost unbounded freedom of thought but a rigid curtailment of action, and trained to rationalize their problems but to subdue their feelings, these enlightened yet imprisoned spirits were brought quickly to the point of frustration and that conundrum which Empedocles propounded on the crater's edge:

> Baffled for ever; and still thought and mind
> Will hurry us with them on their homeless march,
>
> . . . . .
> . . . .
>
> Back to this meadow of calamity,
> This uncongenial place, this human life;
> And in our individual human state
> Go through the sad probation all again,
> To see if we will poise our life at last,
> To see if we will now at last be true
> To our own only true, deep-buried selves.

Perhaps not without the ulterior aim of shocking Pollard, Housman liked to extol the bottomless disillusionment of Empedocles; but his cries of admiration also signified that, beyond the mere commentary of unhappiness, he had by this time penetrated to its substrata and philosophical root, even if at eighteen or nineteen he was hardly more capable than Matthew Arnold of resolving his personal difficulties and of being true at last to his only true self.

The other contemporary author with whom Housman was quick to feel an affinity was Thomas Hardy, then just beginning to enjoy, with the publication of *The Return of the Native* in 1878, a wider recognition. Still unknown as a poet, Hardy's work so far consisted only of those early novels—*A Pair of Blue Eyes, The Hand of Ethelberta, Far from the Madding Crowd*—in which, alongside the conventional elements of Victorian fiction, his sombre ironies made their first tentative appearance. "It requires," as one of his characters remarked, "a judicious omission of your real thoughts to make a novel popular"; but like the more discerning of Hardy's readers, Housman soon found traces of the reflective poet and stoic philosopher lurking behind the scenes; and in Hardy's predilection for the grave-yard, his Attic sense of an implacable destiny, and his dramatic, almost participant landscapes Housman could not mistake a kindred spirit. Images of himself were mirrored back from those analogies and parallels which gave him a sense of uncanny identification with Hardy's fore-doomed victims of circumstance. Again and again, he must have felt, his own experience had verified Hardy's observation that "There are disappointments which wring us, and there are those which inflict a wound whose mark we bear to our graves," or that—a passage to which he would have just then given special heed—our dearest friend "is really somebody we got to know by mere physical juxtaposition long maintained, and was taken into our confidence, and even heart, as a makeshift."

Irreparably saddened by his mother's death, and even after more than six years so prone to grief and dejection that he had bought, as the only adornment for his college rooms, prints of Durer's "Melancholia" and "The Knight, Death and the Devil," Housman was already equipped to understand every dark hint of Hardy's pessimism. But no repining mood could sustain itself, at the age of eighteen or nineteen, in total despair, or consistently hold that all prospects lead to failure. Jackson was the best antidote to such forebodings; the always present refutation of his friend's sicklied thoughts. With the confidence of a sober and sensible Hercules for whom the future seemed to pose no unconquerable difficulties, Jackson personified the expansiveness, the innate resources and calm outlook of a period that possessed every advantage except the certitude of its ultimate destination. Death without religion was the private Victorian nightmare, the devouring spiritual problem which had so early lodged itself in Housman's mind, and there, with the help of his natural propensities, gained a rapid strangle-hold. But now, as if to challenge that ineluctable fate, Jackson rose up in all his vigour and vitality—the likeness of some eternally poised-to-win athlete of the golden age. Anything but pagan in his habits or disposition, Jackson brought to life, nevertheless, a figment of that remote Roman world whose passions throbbed in the *Elegies* of Propertius. It was a world into which, as he pushed further each day, Housman could easily project some of his own anxiety and self-torment. For at the same phase of development Propertius had written his first poems; and he, too, was a pallid, nervous young man haunted by the shadow of mortality. But already, in that *Cynthia Monobiblos* which appeared before he was twenty, Propertius had exchanged one form of anguish for another:

> No more now, my Cynthia, fear I the sad world of death; I care not for the doom that at the last must feed the funeral fires; this fear alone is bitterer than death itself, that I should go down to the grave unloved by thee.

The consciousness of love had not yet administered the final twist to Housman's personal dilemma, and in the early Oxford years at least, he pursued the normal activities of a studious undergraduate, reading diligently if not often in conformity with the syllabus, and competing in 1879 for the Hertford classical scholarship and the Newdigate prize for English verse, though without success in either. But with a comfortable First Class in Moderations, Housman seemed quite content—an obviously less concentrated and more easy-going aspirant than he had been, two years ago, at Bromsgrove School. For the first time, however, some deeper interest had replaced the narrow ambition and bookish confinement of a scholar's life; he had tasted the drowsy syrup of Jackson's friendship, the complex fascinations of human intercourse. With Jackson and to some extent with Pollard, he had formed the kind of daily, almost domestic intimacy which flourishes among students, soldiers and wherever men are isolated from women; an intimacy reinforced by their febrile state and detachment from the outside world. Each member of this adolescent brotherhood was the son of a middle-class family, the holder of a scholarship and the product of a society which valued moral standards no less than intellectual distinction. Whatever pitfalls Oxford may have provided in the late seventies did not seduce these young men of serious purpose; they were indifferent to the pleasures they could not afford, and easily reconciled to their own modest scale of entertainment. Even

Jackson, whose athletic triumphs must have brought him more exciting invitations, did not desert his old friends, but continued to prefer their quiet company; while this compact trio, in which Pollard habitually took a minor part, only served to increase Housman's dependence on its attractive leader, in whom alone he found a substitute for all those beguilements to which young men are naturally drawn.

The letters that came regularly from Bromsgrove did nothing to enlarge the appeal of a place that for many reasons Housman could only wish to forget, and from which even in vacations he was not sorry to escape. A visit to London in the spring of 1879, Pollard remembered, was the occasion for attendance "on four successive evenings" at the Lyceum, where they must have seen not only *Hamlet* but *The Lady of Lyons*, in that compendious Victorian repertoire, and "I think Housman was the most absorbed member of the audience." Pollard in turn came to relieve the tedium of the summer holidays at Perry Hall, and perhaps also to give the rest of the family a closer look at one of Alfred's Oxford friends; but as if he belonged to a higher sphere, Jackson was apparently never exposed to this inquisitive circle. The younger Housmans were now old enough to speculate about their brother's life—a curiosity which he repaid with fresh outbursts of nonsense verse and an access of what Laurence called "social affability." The parlour still resounded with those exuberant literary games in which, once again, Housman became the most vigorous and inventive participant, even though he might retire at midnight to transcribe some doleful passage in the "commonplace book." It must have been about this time that he was moved to copy down, from *The Cenci*, one of those frenetic soliloquies in which Shelley had probed the depths of filial antagonism, magnifying the harshness of Field Place into the horrors of the castle at Petrella. But if only a slender thread connected Sir Timothy Shelley with Count Cenci, no possible relation existed between Edward Housman and that monstrous prototype of the unkind father; yet apparently Housman did harbour, in the interstices of his

84

subconscious mind, some of Shelley's resentments and re-criminations:

Ha! tis the blood
Which fed these veins that ebbs till all is cold:
It is the form that moulded mine that sinks
Into the white and yellow spasms of death.

Like Pope Clement VIII, however, Housman preserved "at least blameless neutrality" and outward respect towards poor Edward, who was now approaching the point of both financial and physical collapse.

Weak, careless and all but irresponsible, Edward Housman had allowed himself to drift, ever since the death of his first wife, in what seemed a steady current of adversity bearing him further away from the safe anchorage of his youth. Reared in the deceptive stability of a small country town and accepting good fortune as his birthright, he had neither conserved nor replenished his resources but merely continued to live in the manner to which he was accustomed. Pride and credulity kept him from realizing, before it was too late, that his inheritance had spent itself; and he was then nearly fifty, with a wife and still growing children whom he could barely support. The younger boys had, one after another, obtained their scholarships at Bromsgrove School, but were so ill-clothed that, on one occasion, Laurence Housman's shabbiness provoked the headmaster to public criticism; while at home, Edward refilled his decanter and the tradespeople called in vain to collect their bills. The strains of such a household could not always be concealed under the mask of genteel impoverishment, and as Mrs. Symons suspected, "Probably A. E. H. knew more than we did," though assuming like the rest an air of forced gaiety and haughty indifference. Something of that compulsive desire for privacy which from now on began to afflict Housman's character must have sprung in part from these family reverses which he wanted naturally to hide but which only became, in such a conspiracy of silence, more oppressive and inescapable. The target of so many unspoken thoughts, Edward himself was both the guilty cause and the pathetic result, a figure of drooping dignity and tortured conscience, whose further struggles now simply invited a stronger condemnation. His father was already a premature example, in Housman's eyes, of that abjectness to which human life eventually succumbs.

A single incomplete and impersonal letter has been retrieved for publication from those which Housman may have written to Edward, either during the Oxford years or afterwards. A lengthy account of a raucous Union debate, in February 1878, it implied that politics was one of the few subjects about which father and son could wholeheartedly agree. With an exceptional display of partisan spirit, Housman had joined the Oxford Union and was, though inactive, an avowed member and staunch champion of the Conservative faction. By one of those inconsistencies to which even the best minds are liable, he endorsed the very party whose militant foreign policy, under the suave leadership of Lord Beaconsfield, would arouse the most jingoistic sentiments and lead inexorably to some "field afar." Not only that, but Housman showed himself perversely unsympathetic to Mr. Gladstone and those Liberal reforms which had brought, just a decade before, religious freedom to the Universities. He remained, nevertheless, an unregenerate Tory and was still animated by vociferous feeling in the by-election of 1880, which he reported in lively detail to his step-mother. But perhaps the chief significance of these forays into the political arena was that, until the end of his third year at least, Housman was taking a zestful interest and some small part in the extra-curricular affairs of Oxford. The undergraduate who "kept shouting out of the front windows Hurrah for Hall, at which the crowd looked up and made the scathing rejoinder—'Yah! yer ain't got no votes!' " was emphatically not yet overwhelmed by problems of a more private nature.

In their last year Jackson, Pollard and Housman "took five rooms together in a picturesque old house in St. Giles', nearly opposite the college," and thus installed in a domestic setting even more conducive to close intimacy, Housman began what was to be the most perturbed and momentous period of his life. Characteristically, it was also the most obscure and elusive —a phase of indeterminate duration, of unfathomable relationships and uncertain meaning, on which no letters, diaries or recollections have survived to throw any helpful light. Pollard himself, the single corroborative witness, confessed to an almost total bafflement. "What had he been doing?" Pollard still somewhat plaintively inquired, more than fifty years after that delightful but disastrous season in the picturesque old house in St. Giles', where the elements of bright promise and happy culmination had turned, so mystifyingly, into stark and inexplicable failure. Perhaps "he had occupied himself too much with the text of Propertius"; or he had found it "psychologically impossible to make the best of his knowledge on subjects in which he had lost interest"; but in fact, during this critical time when Housman lived under his direct observation, Pollard "mostly retired to work by myself in the lower sitting room, leaving the other two on the first floor," and was therefore reduced, when events themselves had overtaken him, to the groping speculation of a relative outsider. One of those friends who never quite reach the deeper levels of intimacy, Pollard had been from the beginning a congenial but dispensable attendant whose rather myopic gaze did not perceive the complexities around him. An earnest bookish young man destined to become an eminent bibliographer, he was already a better judge of the printed page than of human character; and especially in his own last year at Oxford, Pollard was immersed in those serious preparations which, he would have innocently assumed, also to some extent engaged his friends upstairs, though inasmuch as Jackson "was an absolutely safe first in science" and "I took it for granted that Housman would do well in Greats," he did not stop to question the seeming abundance of their leisure.

Jackson, on the contrary, was glad to lounge in the evenings, after an energetic day of rowing and running. A candidate for both athletic and scholastic honours, he contrived to have at the same time a sense of relaxation and an air of success; and indeed to win, as it turned out, not only a "first" but a "Blue." With the confidence that comes from steady nerves and multiple talents, Jackson could be indifferent to the ordeal of a test (the examination for Greats) which has driven many less equable undergraduates to suicide. But perhaps he was not unmindful, too, of that nostalgic regret which hangs over every senior class, and hence welcomed all the more, in those idle conversations with Housman, the comradeship of one who attached a supreme value to this efflorescent yet perishable hour of youth. Basking in Housman's frank admiration, Jackson must have looked very much as he appeared in a photograph of the St. John's crew—a stocky, self-assured figure perched on the arm of the sofa and confronting the camera with a fixed unflinching gaze under his hooded eyelids. The crew of 1880 conferred no great distinction on St. John's, having been "bumped" by Corpus, Oriel, Worcester and two other colleges in the Torpids of that year; but the crew's photograph continued to have a treasured though incongruous place among Housman's possessions, reminding him obviously not of an outstanding group or a memorable victory, but of the friend whose youthful features it accidentally preserved. For Jackson had literally become, soon after the picture was taken, Housman's consuming interest at Oxford.

Like the last weeks of a long and glorious holiday, the autumn of 1880 signified for Housman the coming-to-an-end of experiences he would never repeat and a freedom he might never regain. From the gathering clouds of that summer in Bromsgrove, he escaped back to Oxford as to the opposite of penury and discouragement. The plight of his family made it clear not only that he must now provide for himself, but also that others were depending on his efforts. Thrifty by nature he had managed to resist any form of extravagance and to "pass through Oxford," as Mrs. Symons noted, "without debts or follies"; but neither his background nor his education had prepared him to cope with the harsh necessities of a financial

The St. John's Crew, 1880

crisis. From his father's example as from his Victorian school-
ing, Housman had learnt simply to ignore such mercenary con-
cerns, and in effect that was the bland air of disbelief that he
adopted towards the practical "troubles" which were beginning
to converge in his last year at Oxford. He had not yet outgrown the age when hope springs up automatically, and at
twenty-two had been elaborately trained to think of himself as
a scholar and a gentleman, one of that favoured minority
whose intellectual gifts and code of manners used to be granted
a certain measure of economic support. With some justification, moreover, Housman could regard himself as endowed
with abilities that equalled or surpassed those of his mentors,
and that would assure him of at least a fellowship as the step-
ping stone to academic preferment. By this vague but plausible
course he must have expected to circumvent the difficulties
that loomed ahead, and in the meantime to snatch from the
boredom of Oxford's classical requirements those evenings
of pleasure in Jackson's company.

The self-imposed study of Propertius continued to distract
his attention—a task that involved not only the most delicate
tools of scholarship but a searching analysis of the heart.
Already, before his experience could quite match his knowledge, Housman was embarking on those problems of conjectural emendation which are the acme of classical learning,
and to which some of his early solutions would emerge, eight
years later, in the pages of the *Journal of Philology*. But like Propertius, he could not remain always chained to these labours:

> I was as one who seeks whether a fish may live on the dry sands,
> or a fierce wild boar in the midst of unfamiliar waves, when I tried
> to pass the night in sterner studies. Love is put off, but never
> extinguished.

Housman must have paused, in scanning that prophetic statement—*numquam tollitur ullus amor*—to ask himself what applicable truth it contained and how to diagnose a phenomenon
that, under the name of *amor*, could imply so many variations.

For certainly his own grasp of the subject did not include a sleepless passion for an unfaithful mistress; and yet, in whatever context, Propertius was disturbingly right. That Housman gave as much thought to the human as to the technical aspects of the material he worked with was evident from his subsequent commentaries, in which, for example, he did not hesitate to inform the most erudite audience that Propertius was "a man desperately in love." All the more, therefore, in the ripe and yearning phase of his youth, Housman must have pondered that sultry text from which, in a kind of learned infatuation, he could not tear himself away.

By his own account, the person to whom Housman had been most warmly responsive and most deeply attached, ever since their first encounter, was Moses Jackson. It was heretofore a friendship in the best tradition of English university life, a masculine intimacy that partook, on Housman's side, of those sentiments which Milton, Tennyson and Matthew Arnold had already celebrated in poems more fulsome than he would ever bring himself to write. But while he may have been reminded of such precedents, and even influenced by them, Housman did not deceive himself that Jackson corresponded in reality to Edward King or Arthur Clough or the beloved Hallam, much less that his own feelings were largely abstract and poetic. Jackson represented, not a form of literary inspiration or a memory bathed in roseate colours, but something which, as their day of parting drew nearer, Housman must have been goaded more frantically to define; and in fact, during his last year at Oxford, Housman's erratic behaviour was exactly that of a person inwardly distraught and preoccupied. Hitherto always sensible, methodical and conscientious, he allowed himself, on the very brink of an easy success, to neglect his proper studies and deliberately to cast away his future prospects. No one was more likely to know just what the examiners would ask for; and no one, when the time came, could have appeared to care less—he simply "showed up no answers to many of the questions set." But even before that climactic breakdown,

Housman had not only written but exposed to view, in an
Oxford magazine, two salient verses that fleetingly sounded a
note commensurate with his agony of mind and which still hold
their place in his *Collected Poems*. Standing apart from everything he had previously written and forecasting by more than
ten years the lyrical despair which produced *A Shropshire Lad*,
these twelve lines are the solid evidence that, sometime in 1881
but preceding the examination for Greats, Housman had undergone some other shock of an equally violent character:

> Good night; ensured release,
> Imperishable peace,
> Have these for yours,
> While sea abides, and land,
> And earth's foundations stand,
> And heaven endures.
>
> When earth's foundations flee,
> Nor sky nor land nor sea
> At all is found,
> Content you, let them burn:
> It is not your concern;
> Sleep on, sleep sound.

In the light of this exquisite threnody, spilling from the heart
of a young man of twenty-two, what *had* Housman been doing?
What could precipitate, in the midst of enjoyable studies and
sympathetic friends, so dark a lament? The news (if he was
notified) of his father's grave decline would hardly provoke
such repercussions; and there was no shadow of a reason why,
after twelve healing years, his thoughts should abruptly revert
to his mother's death. But in connection with Jackson, and
indeed with no one else, might Housman have been driven to
this emotional pitch, in the event of some misunderstanding
or estrangement. Yet from all outward signs the course of
their friendship ran smoothly and Jackson did not cease to be,
then or afterwards, the object of Housman's implicit and un-
shakable devotion. Since a grievous change had occurred,
nevertheless, it must have arisen, not on Jackson's side, but in
Housman himself, and was marked certainly not by a dearth

but rather an excess of feeling; an acute disorder, moreover, which temporarily disrupted his life and yet was incommunicable except in poetry. Manifestly, by these immemorial symptoms, Housman was "a man desperately in love," but as he had discovered to his shame and horror, with one who was incapable of reciprocating or even of tolerating it, and from whom every flicker of a culpable passion must be scrupulously concealed. For to Housman quite as much as to Jackson the betrayal, not to say the very existence, of such impulses could only be regarded, in the frost-bound climate of Victorian morality, as a hideous revelation. From the moment when he began to suspect the nature of his attachment to Jackson, Housman would have been overcome by the sense of a disaster for which he was criminally at fault, while the long jovial evenings turned into nightmares of duplicity, and the once pleasurable days stretched into a nerve-wracking interminable tightrope. But if the strain of this imposture did not disclose itself even to Jackson, its internal effects must have been all the more corrosive in those penultimate months at Oxford, during which Housman first gleaned the knowledge that he could neither hope for any abatement of his misery nor dare to confess its origin; and impaled on the horns of this dilemma, he was led, as a single, short poem testified, not only to contemplate the interception of death but to welcome at last its abysmal finality. His failure in Greats was, after this, the next step and minor consequence.

CHAPTER FIVE

Here I lie down in London

THE ensuing yet unpredictable failure of such a serious and superior student mystified the examiners as much as his friends. In the Oxford vernacular, Housman had been "ploughed"—a term that literally expressed the kind of upheaval which had overtaken his long-cherished hopes, as if some engine of destruction had swept across a field ripe and ready to be harvested. The authorities "had no option," he later admitted, in withholding not only the expected honours but even a pass degree; while "the bewilderment of the examiners," as Pollard learned soon after the event, "had caused enquiries to be made, which were now passed on to me, as to how it had come about that on some of the papers Housman had hardly attempted to offer any answers." One of the college tutors remembered "one paper being marked E" and "that his answers on the philosophy papers were short and scrappy"; but no lack of interest in History and Philosophy, no extenuating circumstances could any longer ameliorate this woeful ignorance or reverse the fatal outcome. By his own apparently deliberate omissions, Housman had disbarred himself from the only career for which either his training or his inclinations had so far equipped him; and in fact, on leaving Oxford in the summer of 1881, he retired from academic life in a voluntary and prolonged banishment.

The family to which he returned in disgrace had already been cast down, within recent weeks, by Edward Housman's physical collapse—an elusive but persistent illness about which the doctor was not reassuring. At the age of fifty, Edward had succumbed to one of those indispositions which in middle life attack both the mind and the body; a sapping weariness from which, at certain moments, the spirit can muster no impulse to recover. In this battered condition he could only serve to emphasize, for his son's special benefit, the penalties of self-indulgence; and from Edward's prostration, if other inducements were needed, Housman now drew the grimmest warning and the sharpest admonition to pull himself together. "He met no word of reproach at home," Mrs. Symons has recalled, "but his own self-reproach was deep and lasting," as well as more tortuous than his younger sister could have realized. The material problems which closed around him in Bromsgrove were merely the counterpart of those inner tensions which had overwhelmed him at Oxford. Without present employment or future prospects, and even deprived of his small allowance by a disgruntled relative, Housman was confronted by crude necessities in the very thick of an unresolved emotional conflict, and trailed by inquisitive eyes just when he wanted most of all to be left in solitary seclusion. "A stricken and petrified brother," as Mrs. Symons so perceptively described him, "who, from that time, was withdrawn from all of us behind a barrier of reserve," Housman dragged himself through the first ignominious days of his homecoming with the tenacity of a wounded animal, from whose impenetrable look every trace of personal feeling had been drained away.

Having outgrown the "commonplace book," Housman did not choose to keep any further record even of his reading, and left no other clue, in the form of diaries or letters, to his private thoughts in that umbrageous period. He had gone back to Oxford for a single term, in the fall of 1881, to qualify for the humble but perhaps useful pass degree; he had obtained, from the still sympathetic Mr. Millington, occasional work as a tutor in Greek and Latin at Bromsgrove School; and he was preparing himself, behind a barricade of text-books, to meet the entrance requirements of the Civil Service. Forced to study, that winter, in the dining room of Perry Hall, where the entire family used to congregate around one economical fire, Housman would sit apart like some stony anchorite—"an amazing example," his brother remarked, "of his power of concentration." But in spite of this almost flagellant determination to redeem himself, Housman did not appear to gain any comfort from his progress or even momentarily to relax, as the months passed, his intemperate mood. The fountain of nonsense verse abruptly ceased to flow and all means of approach were blocked off so effectively that no one tried or dared to breach his defences. Such a morose figure, alongside the gaunt and sagging presence of Edward Housman, could have scarcely pretended to relieve the burden of anxiety which oppressed his family, if that were the ruling motive and sole provocation of Housman's behaviour; but while his brothers and sisters meekly or naïvely brought themselves to interpret it in that light, he was free to struggle with a more desperate and devious, a truly unmentionable problem.

The enforced intimacies of Perry Hall must have been, as Laurence Housman observed, "an exasperating strain," to which the shabby atmosphere of his old home gave an extra twist. The familiar rooms and childhood garden now bore those marks of hardship and neglect which can disfigure the physiognomy of places no less than of people. At best a severely utilitarian house, it possessed no faded charms which could offset its air of stolid decline, and by the winter of 1882 it had become for Housman a scene inseparable from the past, a barren stage on which the same domestic drama seemed drearily to repeat itself. His father's illness echoed, with a sour and sordid note, that of his mother thirteen years before; each day, once again, he trudged back and forth to Bromsgrove School; while from the churchyard of St. John's, on clear afternoons, he could survey all those landmarks—the gables of Fockbury House, the cemetery at Catshill, the still glowing battlements of Shropshire—with which his early youth was identified. But if not cheering in themselves, these memories were, by comparison with his present thoughts, already wrapped in the pathos of distance. For they recalled and renewed, especially when he could escape into the country, a sense of pristine simplicity, a time when his desires were guiltless and his future undefined. The first days of spring filled him with nostalgic pangs for those pellucid streams which had reflected, so recently, the face of a dreaming schoolboy. More than ever, the landscape was a refuge from the grating trivialities of Bromsgrove, and a walk to Fockbury yielded the only refreshment to his spirit.

Housman was then just twenty-three, but prematurely, as usual, he had reached another milestone and was able to look back, as if from the perspective of later years, on the closed chapter of his past life. The shy but amiable young master who had been, not long ago, a rambling figure in the fields and lanes now reappeared like a surly ghost whose path the country lads must have trembled to cross. Sombre and unresponsive, his frigid manner and hostile glance discouraged the most casual greeting, not to say the boon companionship of the bar-room. But if in reality Housman had no rustic friends and knew little at first hand of their "jesting, dancing, drinking," he was all the more conscious of the sociable pleasures from which he was cut off. Every peal of laughter and burst of song, as he passed the village tavern, ridiculed his lonely predicament; every market day offered a distracting glimpse of those faces "I wish one could know"; while every flowery mead was a background devised by Nature for some pastoral romance. With his sensibilities alert to all these incitements of the season, Housman paced the shadowy woods and hidden retreats where he was driven to slake, "among the bluebells of the listless plain," his thirsty passion, but "washed his hands in innocence in vain." Still gnawed by his remorseful conscience, he felt himself at the mercy of some malign fate which threatened even this festival of the earth, and spelled the doom of all young lovers. The bitterness of his heart beclouded his vision; the world seemed radiant yet ominous; and though his experience hardly yet justified his foreboding, Housman could no longer dispel these impressions whose value stemmed, not from their verisimilitude, but from their subjective intensity.

It was an occasion expressly designed to provoke the muse, but if at this time Housman ever had recourse to poetry he did not, contrary to his later habit, preserve the results. The note-books in which he first set down and afterwards hoarded nearly all his compositions in verse contained, according to his brother, nothing earlier than 1890; and in fact, when he was laying plans eight years before then, Housman quite clearly had given no serious thought to a literary career. Unlike the major-ity of poets, he showed in his youth neither a strong inclination nor a special aptitude for writing poetry. The nonsense rhymes with which he largely occupied himself sprang from a different order of inspiration; he had made only a dilatory effort to com-pete for the Newdigate Prize; and except for that isolated poem, wrung from the experience of his last year at Oxford, he had betrayed no signs of poetic talent. Among his family and friends no one could have suspected a gift of which he was himself apparently so neglectful, and at twenty-three, whatever medium he might have promised to excel in, the least probable was poetry. But like a few great writers and many lesser ones, Housman required a long spell of dormancy and preparation in which to overcome those impediments which can retard, with the persistence of a stutter, even the most articulate voices. Often constricted by some obscure psychological obstacle, such authors have dawdled like Gibbon or Proust in what seemed a permanent state of dilettantism, though seldom, like Housman, without a trace of literary ambition and while osten-sibly cultivating another kind of intellectual discipline. An oddly distinguished example of the writer who cannot bring himself to write, Housman did not manifest even the desire to conquer this paradoxical inhibition.

Perhaps uppermost in his thoughts, as the months dragged along in Bromsgrove, was the craving to escape from his family and to re-establish his independence. After four years at Ox-ford, he could bear no more than other young men who have tasted freedom the suffocation of being once again at home, even though he would be driven for economic reasons to desert the countryside which he loved, and go to work in London. But anything seemed preferable to the prison bonds of Perry

Hall, and in such a mood the roaring capital itself had a transient appeal. By nature Housman belonged in, and now especially must have wanted, the studious seclusion of some grey-toned cloister where he could both repent and repair his misdeeds, but from which *A Shropshire Lad* might never have emerged. As it would shortly transpire, the price of freedom was both less congenial and more tempting—an appointment, if he was lucky, at the Patent Office where Jackson was already employed.

Their friendship had not lapsed and its old fraternal character had not outwardly changed in the interval of separation; in fact, Housman must have sought, and Jackson must have helped, to bring about a reunion as soon as it could be arranged. For in spite of his "first" in science and his "blue" for racing and rowing, Jackson found himself stranded, also, in one of the duller branches of the Civil Service and with only the narrowest bureaucratic prospects. From the grimness of Bromsgrove, however, the Patent Office held out not only a respectable occupation and a modest income but the irresistible lure of Jackson's company; and it was obviously in the pursuit of such a post that Housman used to labour, with so furious a concentration, amid the chatter of the dining room. During those eighteen months which he spent at home, moreover, there had been time enough to overlay if not absolve his sense of guilt, and even for new tendrils to spring out of his buried attachment. To condemn a feeling was not, he learned, to uproot it, but merely to divert its growth, like that of some tenacious vine, in other directions; and by the end of his sojourn in Bromsgrove, Housman's struggle to renounce had become an eagerness to resume, on the convenient pragmatic basis which now presented itself, his relations with Jackson. Safe from emotional disturbance, he had passed the Civil Service examination sometime in the autumn, and perhaps not without Jackson's connivance, had been offered an almost immediate appointment at the Patent Office, which he hastened to accept in December 1882. It was a low-paid subordinate position, but as Jackson reassured him, he would have abundant leisure and could live quite comfortably, by sharing rooms, on his beginner's salary of £100 per annum.

Towards the relief of his family's chronic financial distress, Housman had already contributed his share of a legacy which had brought each of the seven children, in the previous June, a windfall of £200. This small but opportune inheritance was sufficient, in the case of Robert and Basil, to defray the expense of completing their education; while Alfred's portion served to pay the mortgage interest and thereby hold together for a few more years the disintegrating household. Edward had also rallied to some extent, but could no longer hope to repair the wreckage of his affairs, or do much more indeed than avert his haggard eyes from the domestic trials of which his wife and daughters had to bear the daily burden. Endowed with the "gift of taking things more easily than others could," he "would drift away," as Laurence Housman phrased it, "absorbed in his own thoughts—a habit which increased as he grew older." Lost in these bibulous reveries (for Edward's weakness was now an open secret in Bromsgrove), he gave an even more desultory attention to matters of business and lived on, for his remaining years, in a befuddled detachment from reality. Inspiring neither gratitude nor respect in his children, Edward played the thankless role of a parent whose qualities they were anxious not to emulate; and it was perhaps in part his father's irresponsibility that imbued Alfred with such a stern sense of duty, just as Edward's incompetence forced his elder daughter to drudge, far into the night, on "all the income tax calculations for the County of Worcestershire."

A source of embarrassment and an object of disapproval, Edward exerted, nevertheless, that deeper influence which, like the ghost in *Hamlet*, every father wields over the lives of his children; though in Housman's case it was an influence of which he appeared to be unaware and that he acknowledged only by the extremity of his indifference. But the marks of an often hostile and always negative relation between father and

son were already visible in Housman's disposition to feel no
sympathy for Edward and yet to give it freely to other men; a
mechanism by which he could invest any passing member of
the male sex, from a guardsman to Mr. Millington, with those
attributes which his father lacked. Having failed not by deliberate unkindness but from ineptitude and inadvertence to win
his son's affection, Edward had contrived to be, ever since
Housman's boyhood, simply an obstruction in the path of his
emotional development. As a father to obey and a man to
admire, Edward was a figure made too compactly of clay, whose
faults Housman had discovered long before he was old enough
to excuse them; as the husband of Sarah Jane Housman, moreover, Edward had stirred the instinctive antagonism of her
jealous devotee; while as the head of a family, Edward's record
of delinquencies merely added fuel to his son's resentment.
But in spite of all these mishaps and vagaries, Edward had
committed no real offence except that of being forever inadequate—a small crime that becomes at a certain distance rather
pathetic than culpable, but which may have on its more sensitive victims, as it did on Housman, a disproportionate effect.
The misfortune of a father he could not love had created a
dangerous blank in Housman's life.

The shattered patriarch to whom, on that December day, his
son bade an impatient farewell was beginning already to assume
the harrowed and desolate look of his last photograph. Bearded,
puffy-eyed and unkempt, with the drinker's inflamed and
swollen nose, Edward could rouse himself only at intervals to
contemplate the harsh and alien world. It was the face of a man
too easily overwhelmed by suffering, who had become at the
age of fifty-one almost a spiritual derelict and who now bore,
imprinted on his features, all the ravages to which he had so
passively submitted. With the bold yet defenceless expression
of those who are reduced to beggary, Edward displayed, instead of rags and sores, the tragic countenance of a storm-
swept King Lear. But if Edward may have occasionally cast
himself in that heroic part, he could deceive no one else in the

Edward Housman

family circle, least of all the cold judgment of his eldest son. To the harassed inmates of Perry Hall, struggling to keep up appearances, even a genuine Lear would have been something less than tolerable; and Edward's foibles had no dramatic import or sublimity of tone, but were merely the wasteful habits of a lifetime, now degenerating into the helpless infirmities of old age. That his children could see all his microscopic imperfections, however, did not rob him of a last residual dignity which, in his sober moments, still flickered behind his heavy gaze. It was this dying ember that Housman could hardly have ignored and in which he might have found the message of which he was then so much in need. For Edward's fitful glance seemed to convey, with a sweeping application, the fellowship of unhappiness and despair.

Though he could give them nothing else, Edward did provide his children, in this forlorn human quality, with more than a conventional reason to pardon him, and troublesome as he must have been, they conspired to surround him with a thick protective screen. Living somewhat apart from local society in consequence, and more dependent on themselves, they had become, according to Laurence Housman, "a curiously mixed family" to which it was "a liberal, if not an easy education" to belong. Under the prohibitions which its mistress still wishfully tried to impose, the household found an equilibrium that rested somewhere between conformity and intransigence. Goaded by her husband's more frequent lapses, Mrs. Housman grew more fanatically strict, as Edward sank into his daily cups and the now almost grown-up children pursued their own inclinations with an outward docility. As if guided by their brother's early training, Clemence at twenty-one and Laurence at seventeen had already begun to cultivate a surreptitious taste for the arts and to plot their escape from Perry Hall; while Robert at twenty-two and Basil at eighteen were both attending a science college in Birmingham where they could equip themselves, better than at Oxford or Cambridge, to recover their station in Midland society. Only Katharine at twenty and

Herbert at fourteen had not yet formed a plan for the future, though all were destined within a few years to gain their freedom. Restless, eager and determined, with their talents equally divided between the practical and the imaginative, they composed an outspoken and discordant group over which Alfred could no longer assert unquestioned authority and from which, on the eve of a Christmas reunion, he was not sorry to be delivered. "Was there ever," he was reported once to have wondered, in a mood of unusually mellow retrospection, "was there ever such an interesting family as we were?" But during those last months at home he was by all accounts indifferent to its attractions and only anxious to get away; just as his brothers and sisters, enviously watching his preparations for departure, must have resolved to follow him at the first opportunity.

The journey to London was to be, more than ten years later, the subject or at least the germ of that poem which catches, in its opening lines, the uprooted feeling that assailed Housman:

> As through the wild green hills of Wyre
> The train ran, changing sky and shire,
> And far behind, a fading crest
> Low in the forsaken west.

By the most direct route from Birmingham, the Great Western railway did not in fact traverse a landscape of "wild green hills"; but whether Housman travelled across the merely undulant terrain of Warwickshire or roundabout through Worcester and the Cotswolds, he would have made in those days a slow and thoughtful progress towards his destination. Riding backwards, he could watch the sunset irradiate for a moment that horizon to which he had always been so inexplicably drawn, and which seemed to hold, as the distance widened, something "honest," "clean " and "true" that he was now in danger of losing. With the awkward circumlocutions of a young man who was still searching for a device by which to open his heart, Housman had already begun to attach a romantic virtue to the countryside, even though he could have no illusions about life in Bromsgrove; while he feared and condemned the city to which, nevertheless, he was voluntarily and irrepressibly hastening through the night. But in this imaginary contest between good and evil, as in a dialogue between the body and the soul, he could project his inner struggle and try to repossess some of those unsullied ideals which were for him inseparable from the fields and woods around Fockbury, the hills and valleys of Woodchester. Out of nostalgia for that receding world of his boyhood, Housman produced the "hands that gave a grasp to" his present dislocation—hands certainly without a physical counterpart, but simply the immaterial bonds that united him to the composite place and the sustaining spirit which he called, eventually if not yet, by the name of Shropshire.

Thus torn between anticipation and reluctance, Housman arrived in London, probably at Paddington, on one of those chilling December nights when the stranger feels even more homeless amid the holiday crowds and the gargantuan pulsations of a great city. It was, in 1882, the most violent contrast with rural communities, a veritable "City of Dreadful Night" in which the sulphurous flare of gas-lamps and the density of coal-smoke enveloped, as in some infernal region, the populace condemned to jostle through its streets on winter evenings. But like Dante's universe, London had its circles and gradations of punishment through which, in a hansom cab, one could pass quickly from the lowest levels to those of comparative ease. Not far from Paddington and stretching westwards for miles lay such a comfortable purgatory—the vast uniform domain of Bayswater and Kensington where the Victorian middle class had established itself in solid rows of brick and stucco, along innumerable roads, avenues, terraces and crescents. Here the occasional hoof-beats of a single cab-horse rang out and no unseemly visitors disturbed the decorous residential atmosphere; though behind these façades of wealth and refinement lurked many lodging houses and small private hotels, the abodes of less prosperous but equally respectable people who were accommodated, in that sometimes humane social system, without any loss of their perquisites and prestige. To such an address, at 82 Talbot Road, W.11, Housman went straight from the station.

Now bomb-scarred and dilapidated, the house and neighbourhood have lost whatever pretensions to spotless gentility they once possessed; but on that earlier occasion No. 82 must have appeared to Housman an admirable temporary lodging of the sort that most young men, at the beginning of their careers in London, were then glad to occupy. Doubtless under the care of some aproned landlady and with its windows screened by lace curtains, it was one of the narrow porticoed houses, four stories high, that merged into the long grey vista of Talbot Road, a minor thoroughfare running between the Harrow Road and Ladbrooke Grove. Easily accessible and yet fairly quiet, it had all the inexpensive advantages of the West End, including both Kensington Gardens and Regent's Park within its reach. But foremost among its attractions was of course the welcoming hand of Moses Jackson, with whom it would have been a compensatory pleasure to share rooms almost anywhere; while to lend it still more charm and liveliness, Jackson's younger brother had also joined this bachelor menage. A classics student at University College, Adalbert Jackson was graced not only with his brother's good looks and sterling character, but in addition with a taste for literature and scholarship that immediately won Housman's heart. From the outset, therefore, the intimate domestic circle of the little house at Oxford was re-created in Talbot Road; and if "Mo" was not always there, Adalbert could serve as a thoroughly congenial substitute in the generous hours of leisure and study which the Patent Office allowed.

Even at work, however, during the slow-paced six-hour day which Victorian efficiency required, Housman had the consolation of Jackson's presence. Himself a mere clerk engaged in the perfunctory task of registering trademarks, Housman was proud once again to enjoy the favour of one who bore the impressive title of Examiner of Electrical Specifications.

Travelling to and from the office together, often meeting for lunch and now exchanging the same shop-talk as well, they were soon back on the old terms of steady friendship, and perhaps still more socially interdependent than they had been at Oxford. Except for Pollard, Housman's range of acquaintance in London was limited to a few distant family connections, and at first the Jacksons were almost equally alone, so that on small salaries and restrictive budgets, their lives were largely centred in the communal pastimes of Talbot Road. For who could immerse himself in the somnolent routine of the Patent Office, where Housman was already beginning to think of some serious alternative occupation, while his colleagues played a furtive game of cricket in the corridors (improvising their bats out of the morning *Times*).

In spite of the distraction of Jackson's company, Housman could not let himself surrender to it again or this time disregard the consequences; and if he was ever tempted, the prodding memory of Perry Hall, the still smarting humiliation of his failure in "Greats," and the underpaid drudgery at the Patent Office all combined to strengthen his resolution. Luckily, too, "Ad" was there not only to refocus Housman's attention on classical studies, but to stem the natural flow of Oxford reminiscence. On those first long winter evenings, nevertheless, the mere sound of Jackson's voice made it hard to concentrate, and the bitter-sweet mood of two years ago must have occasionally revived. But once more, whether by sheer accident or conscious design, Jackson played his part with a masterly sense of what not to do. Direct and unsuspecting in a situation fraught with subtle possibilities and dangerous cross-currents, he struck the very note of innocent composure that Housman was himself trying to assume. How to prolong their relationship and yet not to betray his feelings was the problem that Housman, on accepting the double risks of an appointment at the Patent Office and a lodging in Talbot Road, had boldly undertaken to solve; but which must have presented even to his capacity for self-control an almost superhuman challenge. At twenty-three, he was entering that unstable phase when the body's maturity often exceeds that of the emotions, and when young men are liable to commit their worst indiscretions. At the same age, Wordsworth had already terminated his affair with Annette Vallon, Shelley had married Harriet Westbrook and run off with Mary Godwin, even Matthew Arnold had dallied somewhere in Switzerland with the mysterious "Marguerite"; but in the grip of a comparable temptation, Housman was now striving to conquer it by pretending that, under the most provocative circumstances, it did not exist. Smothered in denial and perhaps regarded as a kind of madness that he would cure by this drastic treatment, Housman's devotion was subjected to the scourge of a close and constant intimacy with its unattainable object, as he forced himself day after day to undergo a gruelling disciplinary test. But as if the habit of repression had spread rapidly and insidiously from the secrets of his heart to the smallest daily occurrence, an impenetrable silence now closed over the apartment in Talbot Road; and for the next two or three years, Housman's life became more than ever a sealed room, into which even Clemence and Laurence could not gain admission when, sometime in 1883, they also came to live in London.

Of this hermetic period, from which not a single letter has emerged until the spring of 1885, Housman contrived to account for his daily whereabouts but to leave no direct report of his experience. He could always be found, on week-days, at the Patent Office; and very often "of an evening" at the British Museum, where "I read a great deal of Greek and Latin." He continued to live at Talbot Road, to walk regularly in the parks and on Sundays to explore, with "Mo" or "Ad," the rural environs of London; but apart from the Jacksons, he cultivated no other friends, and apparently did not intermingle with theirs. It was to some extent the pinchpenny isolation imposed on a humble clerk, reinforced by that sense of anonymity which overcomes lonely people in great cities. Housman could indulge in few of the social pleasures, even if he had wanted to,

on less than £2 a week; while his menial position and dull prospects at the Patent Office only whetted his determination to
reach out for some more acceptable, some less undistinguished
means of earning a livelihood. Both his intellectual pride and
his middle-class consciousness had recently suffered, at Oxford
and in Bromsgrove, a severe set-back; but once again, in choosing how to reapply his efforts, Housman clearly did not consider, or quickly rejected, the uncertainties of a literary career.
At the age when every young writer tends to be over-confi-
dent, Housman was dubious of his own talent and realistic
about the pecuniary rewards of literature; but above all, as to
poetry, he could think of it only in terms of stripping away the
layers of insulation which encased his heart, and for that he
now felt himself certainly unprepared. Those early London
years were, on the contrary, a sedulous training in self-mastery
which allowed him no respite, and for which the nightly labours
of scholarship provided an appropriate obbligato. Between the
stern mental exercise of the British Museum and the exquisite
nervous strain of Talbot Road, therefore, Housman's leisure
was fully and alternately occupied.

CHAPTER SIX

What shall I build or write

THE young man who, shortly after his twenty-sixth birthday, broke his long silence in a letter to his step-mother was not conspicuously unlike the schoolboy who, ten years before, had assumed a debonair and facetious epistolary manner. Writing to thank her for a gift of violets and "my father for his letter," Housman went on:

> Clemence and Laurence sent me a post card with a very lovely drawing on the back, representing Cherubim and Seraphim continually crying, and an inscription in Spanish or Portuguese, I think.
>
> I saw the boat race yesterday, from the Thames boat house this time. . . . Palm branches seemed to be the commonest decoration among the lower orders. The blue which they wore was a very artful shade, which could be made out to be either Oxford or Cambridge, with equal plausibility, whichever might happen to win. . . .
>
> The juvenile son of a friend of mine at the Office has the loftiest ambition I ever heard tell of. When he goes to heaven, which he regards as a dead certainty, he wants to be *God*, and is keenly mortified to learn that it is not probable he will. However his aspirations are now turning into another channel: it has come to his knowledge, through the housemaid, that the devil has horns and a tail; and in comparison with these decorations the glories of heaven have lost their attractiveness.

Housman's salary had now risen to £137 10s. 0d. per annum, so that his life was no longer quite so narrowly circumscribed; and though he still held aloof from his family, he was at least outwardly restored to his former equability and good humour. But in the interval he had passed through one of those emotional battles which correspond to the body's warfare against some threat of infection. Faultless in his work, invariable in his habits, rather derisive in conversation and much addicted to mere reading and walking, Housman must have seemed during those early years in London not to have changed at all but simply to have become more like himself; while in reality he had been struggling to convert an impossible yet obsessive desire into a mild platonic feeling, and in the very act of consorting with Jackson, to subdue and transform the instincts of a lover. From long practice in the art of self-concealment, Housman had learned how to disarm the suspicions of his family and friends, even of Jackson himself, who were led to interpret spells of despondency and signs of tension as the natural moods of a dissatisfied clerk. For at the same time Housman was trying with an equal but overt determination to re-enter the world of classical scholarship, and on those industrious evenings at the British Museum, to prepare himself for an exacting professional career. Even before he left Bromsgrove, in fact, Housman had taken the first step towards this ultimate goal by submitting to the *Journal of Philology*, sometime in 1882, a venturesome paper on certain obscurities in the *Odes* and *Epodes* of Horace, which that august periodical had published the same year, perhaps without full cognizance of the new contributor's tender age. In the measured judgment of Mr. A. S. F. Gow, nevertheless, "it was an astonishing performance for a young man of twenty-three—astonishing both in its comparative maturity and in the extent to which it foreshadows what was to come." But as if already overwhelmed by his own rashness, and now resolved to achieve only the most unassailable reputation, Housman chose to bide his time and slowly to build up, for the next six years, a towering reserve of scholarly armament.

He wrote again to his step-mother, on June 10, 1885, describing with his accustomed sang-froid the novel experience of serving on a Coroner's jury, in the course of which:

We sat on five bodies: one laundryman who tied a hundred-weight to his neck and tipped over into the water-butt; one butcher's man who cut his throat with a rusty knife and died a week after of erysipelas (moral: use a clean knife on these occasions); one old lady who dropped down in a fit; one baby who died of convulsions; and one young woman who died of heart disease after eating spring onions for supper.

A tendency to regard laundrymen and butchers, even in the

act of suicide, as faintly laughable was one of those inborn Victorian attitudes which Housman derived from his social background, but which may have signified in his case not so much a want of humanitarian feeling as it did the tight curb of his intelligence. The schoolboy who became a deist at thirteen had evolved, by ruthless logic, into this callous young Darwinian who was, at twenty-six, no longer oppressed by the phenomenon of death, but now forced himself unflinchingly to accept it in the light of current scientific knowledge. Deprived of its religious symbolism and reduced to the mere fact of physical extinction, mortality had lost its more ominous overtones and was capable of seeming trivial or even at times grotesque, especially among the flotsam of the London underworld.

For such unlucky but as he thought predestined victims of society, with their rude manners and corrupt language, Housman had the fastidious aversion of his class, undiluted by those theories of reform and impulses of charity which already animated some of his generation. Under the dome of the Museum reading room, if his glance ever strayed now and then from the study of a Greek or Latin text, Housman might have encountered the febrile gaze of George Gissing, roaming over that "valley of the shadow of books" where he, too, sought refuge from poverty and discontent in the pages of classical literature. A tall, shabby, despondent young man of twenty-eight, Gissing had in 1885 written two of his least successful novels about the lower classes, and was himself a glaring example of the trials and vexations of Grub Street. Haunted and yet repelled by his subject, Gissing had merely rasped his nerves and suffered the gamut of hardship in his determination to portray the uncompromising sordidness of life in the slums. But without knowing or perhaps even reading him, Housman had chosen to avoid not only the pitfalls of a literary career but also the quicksands of a struggle against injustice. He was entrenched, even then, in a conservatism of spirit as well as of politics; and indeed his letter of June 10 continued, in the next paragraph, to deplore the tactics of Mr. Gladstone's Government:

> I think if there were an Inquest held on this Government of ours the verdict would have to be deliberate suicide: there does not seem to have been the least reason why they should have been beaten unless they wanted it. I should say whether they go out or not the whole affair will do a lot of damage to the Conservatives, because if they take office before the election they will have a fearful muddle to deal with, and if they do not, everyone will call them unpatriotic.

Housman was right, as it turned out, and the Government collapsed, though he did not know that on June 8, according to Sir Edward Clarke, "there were enough Liberals in the House to have given them a majority, but to some twenty-five of them a hint was given that they need not come back after dinner." By this default the Liberal ministry escaped from the embarrassment of its problems, and in the General Election of 1885 the Tories returned to power with Housman's blessing, but against the solid opposition of the agricultural vote. For every "young yeoman," lately enfranchised by the efforts of Mr. Gladstone, refused that year to "lie down," but rallied instead to the support of the party which had recognized and to some extent relieved his unhappy plight. "The social history of rural England in the nineteenth century," as Trevelyan has epitomized it, was "in many respects a chronicle of disaster"; and it was still in Housman's time a subject worthy of the sombre elegist. But though he was soon to discover the emblems of his own distress in the fate of so many country lads, Housman belonged to another class and his experience to a different world, with whose interests he did not cease to identify himself.

Of what his experience consisted during this period, Housman's occasional letters and regular occupations defined the scope if not the particulars; but certainly there was not much room for richness or variety of incident in his daily round and nightly studies. At the Patent Office he pretended to do "as little as possible," but was considered nevertheless a model of industry who might have risen by slow degrees to the highest position; and in fact, he went so far as to accept, about this time, the post of private secretary to the Comptroller, whence further advantages might have been expected to flow. But the occupational disease of the scholar—a touchy and truculent temper—had already infected Housman's once-gentle disposition, so that he could no longer restrain himself when questions were raised about the wisdom, let alone the phraseology, of certain passages in his official correspondence; and before long, by mutual consent, he returned to the lowlier but more peaceful department of trademarks, in which he was to languish undisturbed for the rest of his career in the Civil Service. Other plans, however, now consoled him, and the Patent Office had become, even as early as 1885, merely a source of livelihood and a temporary servitude whose fetters would soon be cast off. But for what proved, in the end, a longer sentence than he could then have foreseen or been able so lightly to contemplate, Housman performed his mechanical duties with his usual thoroughness, and in working hours seemed always content to be, as one of his colleagues remembered him, "a very efficient public servant."

Jackson, too, had grown restless and was looking, in a more literal sense, for some means of escape from the grindstone. A young man without the goad of a single specific talent, but with unused energies and multiple resources, he faced the choice, in his late twenties, between a comfortable prison like the Patent Office or the dangers and enticements of adventure. Dissatisfied yet uncertain, Jackson still had, to a degree not much reduced since he left Oxford, that vigour and versatility which equipped him for almost too many undertakings, none of which would be likely to exercise the full range of his powers. There were few opportunities, of the sort his expansive nature required, in Victorian London, but the Empire was a field of action created expressly by and for such eager sons of the middle class, who were seeking not only material success but some brighter, more spacious air; and in that sense the colonies began to exert their attraction, as time passed, on Jackson's mind, and to cast their shadow over Housman's future. The cosiness of Talbot Road had become as well, for both of them, an often irksome confinement, in which Housman champed against every interruption of his studies, and from which Jackson fled to livelier company. After three years of bachelor-dom, those small conflicts which strain and ruffle human inter-course were assuming, between Housman and Jackson, the kind of incompatibility that men by themselves cannot easily overcome. Pride and ambition compelled Housman to pursue an objective that was now almost within his reach, just as wishful dreams of higher achievement were driving Jackson to consider some drastic step; and even if their friendship re-mained unbroken, it was a domestic impasse, nevertheless, out of which separation seemed the only escape. Jackson still wavered and fretted, but towards the end of 1885, on his walks around London, Housman was regretfully engaged in the search for a new lodging more conducive to quietness and pure concentration.

He found it, sometime in 1886, at 17 North Road, Highgate, where he presently established himself on the ground floor of a small three-storied Georgian house (one of the few gracious dwellings that Housman ever chose to inhabit), in which he was the solitary lodger, and whose landlady gave promise of being at once superbly efficient and severely impersonal. In daylight Housman's sitting-room windows overlooked a patch of garden and, across the road, the buildings and grounds of Highgate School; while at night, behind the drawn curtains, its panelled walls enclosed an immaculate study, in which only the crackle of burning coals or a turning page broke the silence. Here, in a district still remote from the heart of London, and tucked between the open stretches of Hampstead Heath and the thickets of Highgate Wood, Housman withdrew into that monastic seclusion which from now on was to be his invariable mode of life. His step-mother and Laurence Housman were asked just once to tea at Highgate, but other invitations were not profuse and, except for the privileged "Mo" or Adalbert, no one was encouraged to intrude upon this strict regimen

now devoted, with a semi-religious zeal, to classical learning
and private meditation. Housman was barely twenty-seven,
but already an aloof and inaccessible young hermit who must
have been, in a neighbourhood haunted by the shades of
Coleridge and Keats, himself a somewhat spectral figure as he
took his exercise on misty evenings.

Having increased his expenses by removing from Talbot
Road, Housman was forced to be still more thrifty, and about
this time began to keep careful accounts in a small black note-
book, entering all his payments and purchases, along with
some occasional terse allusions of a more personal nature. It
was a record of the abstentions and economies practised by a
thousand humble clerks—those bowlered flocks in whose
company Housman travelled to and from his work each day,
and from which he was hardly distinguishable in dress and
propriety of manner. Even as to light reading, Housman had
certain tastes in common with the average man, and was
among the first to enjoy the detective story and the romantic
thriller, of which the little black notebook mentioned an early
example—*Dead Man's Rock* by Quiller-Couch—soon after its
publication. For some less apparent reason, he also listed and
must have read *Griffith Gaunt*, a voluminous old novel by
Charles Reade in which all the trappings of Victorian melo-
drama were assembled, and coincidentally one of the characters
was a country solicitor named Houseman. But these were the
intermissions of a midnight toil into which Housman threw
himself at Highgate with the persistence of one who had not
only to accomplish a purpose but to fill a void. In spite of its
unhappy associations with Oxford and with Jackson, the text
of Propertius had lured him back once more to examine and
elucidate a poet with whom he felt such a peculiar affinity;
and by now, the number of his emendations was rapidly growing into the kind of critique that would make a valid, indeed
a masterly and irrefutable contribution to the *Journal of Philology*. Still apposite to his personal life, the elegies were both a
challenge to his scholarship and a confirmation of his experi-

ence—"Here in truth," whether it be some forest scene near ancient Rome or the modern pavements of Highgate, "is a lonely and silent place where I lament." But though familiar and often impending, the mood of lamentation no longer possessed Housman as it had done five years ago, but was now kept under invincible control; while he took pains this time to enlarge his field of study, and give part of his attention to the plays of Aeschylus and Sophocles.

Thus absorbed by the minutely tortuous problems of classical scholarship, and confident of his own fast-growing abilities, Housman began to feel that deeper satisfaction which springs from doing what one likes with superlative skill; and he was thereby strengthened, during his first years at Highgate, against other sacrifices and deprivations. An evening at the Lyceum had become merely wasteful, and the luxuries of the palate were still easy to forgo; but above all, in relation to Jackson, his work now served as a comforting and dependable alternative which, in the normal course of events, he would need eventually to fall back on. Not without an element of deliberation, Housman had withdrawn to a safe distance and was loosening the ties of a friendship that already bore the faint marks of incipient discord. The experiment in Talbot Road, from which he had once hoped that some workable scheme of living might evolve, had only drifted precariously on the edge of failure, and to retire before that happened was the best chance of averting it; though by this time Housman had plainly girded himself to expect the worst and be content with a poor but unfailing substitute.

Temporarily, however, his life held more compensations and brighter prospects than he could have imagined, a few years ago, in that drab interim at Bromsgrove. He was now earning a sufficient if meagre salary; his lodging was agreeable, his privacy undisturbed and his ambition near to achievement. It was promising enough for any young man in his middle twenties, and even Housman sometimes allowed himself to show a certain lightness of heart, especially in the spring and among old friends like the Wise family. Still living at Woodchester and dispensing an effusive hospitality, they had lost none of that genial domestic air which used to gladden Housman's boyhood; and on subsequent visits, he at once reverted to a cheerful, almost prankish mood which other company seldom witnessed or induced. This teasing note had been struck as long ago as 1877, when Housman contributed some nonsense verse, in a broad vein of adolescent humour, to the Visitor's Book of Woodchester House. Apostrophizing "ecstatic" Minnie, Edie's "want of gravitation," and "Ted's moustache," the composition (in the form of a prophecy for the new year) evoked one of those intimate family parties whose jokes remain incomprehensible to the outsider; and in this rare spirit of exuberance Housman continued, even as he grew older, to record his enjoyment of a week-end at Woodchester and his affection for the only household in which he could so easily unbend. For a decade, nevertheless, his name had been missing from the Visitor's Book, until on April 7, 1887 Housman reappeared in its pages, and was moved not only to address a set of commemorative verses to E. M. W., but after his departure on April 12, to send Mrs. Wise a further instalment, describing with a lush mock-sentimentality his inconsolable journey to Paddington, where

> From attics and sky-touching flats
> Folks put out their heads through the casement
> And said, "What's that noise? Is it cats?"

> And wiping the tears from my features
> I said, in a dolorous key,
> "Go to bed, go to bed, my dear creatures,
> It is not the cats: it is me."

His return to London was in sober truth soon to be darkened by the news that emanated from Talbot Road. For not later than the spring of 1887, Jackson had met and fallen in love with a young widow, Mrs. Rosa Chambers, who from now on began to engage most of his attention, and whose figure interposed a larger shadow between the refulgent suitor and his austere bachelor friend. Even though Jackson was close at hand, still working at the Patent Office and eager to report the latest turn of his affairs, the intrusion of a third person must have had for Housman its usual insidious effect; while under the sway of this new incentive, Jackson was all the more impatient to reorganize his life, and dangerously susceptible to the most reckless plans. Then approaching twenty-eight, Jackson had good reason not to postpone, if he seriously intended to pursue, a fresh enterprise; but there was still no single preference that would help to determine, among so many potentialities, his final choice. With his Oxford laurels, to which he had recently added a Doctorate of Science and a Fellowship at University College, Jackson did not lack either high qualifications or desirable alternatives; but after six sedentary years in London, he wanted as much to escape as to succeed, and could be tempted by any project that combined an exotic change of scene with the practical means of supporting a family. Africa, Australia, Canada shimmered like a mirage through the English mist, as that sultry summer prolonged his suspense, until at last, receiving a tangible offer from the Sind College in Karachi, Jackson hungrily snatched this opportunity to go abroad even at the price of becoming a schoolmaster, and before he could safely assume the responsibilities of marriage. Filled with exciting Oriental visions, however, and assured that Mrs. Chambers would wait for him, he forthwith resigned from the Civil Service, packed his bags and precipitately sailed for India towards the end of 1887.

In spite of Housman's prior knowledge and the protective measures he had already been driven to take, the impact of this whirlwind departure was severe—a laceration of feeling akin to surgical shock. The months of preliminary adjustment to what might be in store for him did not lessen the tremors of an experience which, until it had occurred, was merely abstruse and problematical. That he must live apart from Jackson and be gradually consigned to some peripheral status, Housman had forced himself to accept, nearly two years ago; but it was a form of separation that left their friendship still constant and substantial, with all the nourishing food of propinquity. To the extent that he had cut the domestic bonds of Talbot Road, Housman had hoped at least to preserve the common ground and daily encounters of men who work together; and it was a relation built on that minimum of intercourse which had helped to sustain him at Highgate. The advent of Mrs. Chambers and the prospect of Jackson's marriage, with a corresponding loss of his intimacy, were eventualities to which Housman had already reconciled himself; but Jackson's physical disappearance, his total and conceivably permanent absence now produced a sense of desolation comparable, in Housman's life, to the death of his mother. As the ship weighed anchor and floated away, it stretched his endurance to the breaking point and in Housman's own words "tore my heart in sunder," but also gave him, unperceived at the time, the main subject and future impetus of his poetry.

In a few of those elliptical verses which Housman did not himself choose to publish, but which have since escaped from his notebooks, the scene of parting was recalled and even a scrap of imaginary dialogue set down:

> To put the world between us
>   We parted stiff and dry;
> "Good-bye," said you, "forget me."
> "I will, no fear," said I.

The pungent words expressed only what had lingered in Housman's memory, but no doubt with equal restraint and concision, as it really happened, the two young men stood erect in their starched collars and bade each other a stern farewell, both conscious of the fateful moment, yet neither betraying by an eyelid's flicker their respective agony and embarrassment. On Jackson's side, it had become not only uncomfortable to receive, but also necessary to discourage, this mute and mysterious adoration; so that among other reasons, perhaps, he welcomed exile as the most efficient and least ruthless way of resolving an awkward entanglement. Often at a loss to understand, but with exceptional tolerance for these perplexities, Jackson had contrived to support the burden of a friendship whose demands he was never quite able to meet, and which even now, within certain limits, he was trying not to destroy. The voyage to India must have seemed to him, in the light of common sense, merely a further extension of his freedom. But for Housman, no plausible interpretation could soften the blow ("Shake hands, we shall never be friends, all's over"), or misconstrue the event which now devastated his inner world; and once again, with the bitter acceptance of a man whose intensity of feeling seldom finds an outlet, he recoiled into solitude and silence.

Under the weight of that leaden winter Housman sometimes confided his distress, if only by mentioning its cause, to the diary which he had lately formed the habit of keeping as a kind of whispered and reluctant soliloquy. Such an overflow was, in a personality like Housman's, the sign of some deep cumulative pressure that on rare occasions could sweep away even his impregnable defences; and in thus articulating his emotion, he was already proceeding, tentatively and in secrecy, towards that poetic manifestation which began to unfold, several years hence, in the first pages of his note-books. But for the present, as Jackson's ship glided across the Mediterranean and down through the Canal, stopping at Pera to discharge mail for England, Housman was unable to do more than trace, over the map's barren topography, the course of his despair. With the knowledge that comes only from a trial of the spirit, he discovered in those early months of 1888 how fatally, in spite of all his efforts to detach himself, he was still subject to whatever torments and upheavals Jackson might be disposed to inflict. The cycle of Housman's boyhood appeared to be repeating itself. For just as the child's whole affection had once been centred in his mother, so the man's had been transferred and rededicated to Jackson, coiling itself around a single idealized object of devotion from which it was now all the more painfully severed, not by the agency of death, but at the

will and for the mere convenience of his beloved friend. The
amatory woes of Propertius finally conveyed their full and
sonorous meaning, in the quiet room at Highgate, as the
lessons of experience reinforced Housman's scholarship:

> Heart of stone, poised now to skim across the Phrygian waves,
> are you embarking for the shores of the Hyrcanian sea? Where are
> you flying, mad fugitive? There is no escape; go as far as Tanais, yet
> Love will track you down.[1]

Jackson did arrive safely, nevertheless, at a destination
so remote that only the immensities of interplanetary space
seemed to connect London with Karachi; and in the effort to
span this incommensurable distance, Housman's thoughts
often reverted, under the wet skies of Hampstead, to his old
penchant for astronomy. The "rainy Pleiads" provided not
only a sombre and majestic canopy for his walks, but also that
sense of a cosmic scale by which to measure the insignificance
of human affairs. But Housman could derive small comfort
just then from the contemplation of a universe which reduced
the plight of its inhabitants to that of nebulous particles. Mag-
nificently aloof, the stars hung there as if to remind him that
his throbbing consciousness would be soon extinguished in "a
foolscap of eternal shade"; and conversely that here on "the
turning globe" he was, like Empedocles, governed by some
unfathomable system which allotted to each his own ultimate
share of pain or pleasure. Tormented by such metaphysical
quandaries and yet unable to conceive another solution, Housman was chained to a purely temporal existence which became,
at times like this, all the more insupportable. For with the
spiritual deprivation of his age, Housman combined the misfortune of being entrapped by one of its particular taboos—
that repressiveness in sexual matters which condemned him to
bear in guilty self-reproach the stigma of a "nameless and
abominable" something. The decline of its religious faith had
left society clinging to its moral standards as to life-belts in a

[1] A passage (II. xxx.) whose jumbled lines Housman restored by instinct to
their natural order.

shipwreck; and for those who could not avail themselves of that support, there was neither mercy nor salvation. But more in dread of opprobrium than perdition, Housman now resolutely pledged himself never to infringe the iron code by which he was, in fact, no less bound than his contemporaries.

The single remedy at his disposal was a ruthless experiment in stifling his emotions, which Housman was to carry on implacably for the rest of his life. Adept since childhood in the practice of self-discipline, he was already well-equipped to face, at the very crest of his maturity, a prospect of almost unmitigated solitude and deliberate stultification. But as the impairment of one organ or faculty often increases the power of another, Housman's mind seemed to gain strength from his psychological disability; so that in the throes of a crippling ailment, he could still muster the perseverance to resume his work. Thus at the dismal outset of 1888, with that inveterate human tendency to count one's blessings when they are least numerous, Housman reappraised the contents of his desk and began methodically to assemble his notes on Propertius, together with any other material that might be suitable for publication. The first product of this house-cleaning—a few remarks on Isocrates and Aeschylus—appeared in the February issue of the *Classical Review*, soon to be followed by those lengthier contributions to the *Journal of Philology*—the *Emendationes Propertianae* and a searching commentary on the *Agamemnon* of Aeschylus—which Mr. Gow has called the "real harvest." They were not only models of accuracy and thoroughness, but exceptionally brilliant critiques which could not fail to produce a striking effect in philological circles; though few of the learned gentlemen who read them with mounting attention could have guessed that, behind the author's magisterial scholarship and somewhat pugnacious style, lurked a distraught young man of barely twenty-nine. The undergraduate who was so disgracefully ploughed, seven years ago, had transformed himself into a figure of incontestable authority, quite ready to compete with and even rebuke his quondam betters; while at the same time his shy, tense, introspective personality, still bleeding from recent wounds, had assumed this stern-faced disguise beneath which it would be hard to detect and implausible to surmise the dormant passion. Like Roman candles, the classical papers which spurted from Housman's hand that year celebrated both the suppression of "this cursed trouble," and the triumphant return of a prodigal student.

Most of the qualities which distinguished and sometimes marred Housman's scholarship were already evident in his early work: the lucidity of thought, range of knowledge, depth of insight and precision of method, now and then overcast by that irascible temper which took a merciless delight in exposing the mistakes and rapping the knuckles of his rivals. A long-forgotten Mr. Sidgwick, "representing, I suppose, the general opinion" in his arrant misinterpretation of a single word in the vocabulary of Aeschylus, was only the first of innumerable victims who were to feel the sting of that venomous contempt which they may have deserved but could not easily forgive. Such potential enemies were not yet awake, however, to the danger that threatened them, and indeed, so long as it struck at the minor culprits, Housman's acerbity merely helped to entertain an always quarrelsome profession. But no one could deny the logic of his arguments or the justice of his criticism, as more scathing and vituperative examples now steadily increased his reputation. Housman's chief interest and concern still apparently resided in emending Propertius, but inasmuch as "I see no hope of completing a presentable commentary within the next ten years," he chose to divert much of his effort to other tasks of a kind that would attract more immediate notice; and after the auspicious debut of 1888, a catholicity of subjects both Greek and Latin rather than a narrow concentration of aim marked his future course. Notes on the Attic dramatists, on Horace, Ovid and Miscellanea spilled forth in such abundance, during this deployment of his forces, that by inference Housman could have allowed himself no opportunity, between his daily stint at the Patent Office and his laborious evenings in Highgate, for bootless dejection and regret.

He found time, nevertheless, to continue his friendship with Adalbert Jackson, who had himself recently become a classics master and now filled a role that, in his brother's absence, no one else could so well have occupied. Having not only a natural family resemblance to "Mo," but a mind closely in tune with Housman's, Adalbert seemed to be almost providentially intended to serve as a source of comfort and alleviation in this period of Housman's life; and certainly

> that straight look, that heart of gold,
> That grace, that manhood

played some part in the remarkable efflorescence of intellectual activity which overtook Housman at a time when he had no other stimulus or consolation. One who revived the happiest of his memories, whose company he enjoyed for its own sake and with whom intimacy did not require an effort, was a triple blessing that would never be conferred on Housman again; while in addition to all this, Adalbert was, if not himself a philologist, at least conversant with the subject, and the only person in Housman's life capable of giving him just then both friendly warmth and professional encouragement. Occasional meetings and excursions with the younger Jackson must have been, therefore, one of the few pleasures to which Housman still looked forward, and which his more and more onerous working schedule did not preclude. Even his visits to Woodchester were temporarily sacrificed, as a new reign of silence and seclusion descended on Byron Cottage. But though Housman's leisure was now largely converted into a growing list of scholarly publications, two entries secreted among the memoranda of his account book recorded, on April 15, 1889, the telegraphic sentence "Swinburne 52 today," and again on September 15 the bare notation, "Walked with Add, Epping Forest." Incongruous items amid the careful tabulation of his daily expenditures, these random allusions to Poetry and

Friendship were like small but significant clues to Housman's private thoughts at the age of thirty.

Assuredly, however, the two sedate young bachelors had been discussing, under the autumnal foliage of Epping Forest, an event that was by then imminent or had already transpired. For in 1889 Jackson came home on leave, a husky bronzed figure returning, with the pioneer's look of intrepid courage, from an outpost of the Empire. His purposeful manner was, in fact, simply that of an earnest fiancé on the brink of matrimony, overlaid by the bluff tone and stalwart pose which members of the governing class tended to assume in colonial areas. As the Principal of a small college designed to educate the natives, Jackson had found, in the bizarre environment of Karachi, an occupation which not only exercised most of his talents but called forth all his ingenuity and perseverance. Reproducing on foreign soil the study halls and playing fields of an English school, it simulated the familiar tradition, the customary pattern and almost the very atmosphere in which he had grown up, yet gave him besides a vital sense of contributing to some great imperial project; and after less than two years he had persuaded himself that, if one condition could be met, his future happiness lay in carrying on this useful and patriotic work. The condition was, of course, that Mrs. Chambers would agree to share the sacrificial exile and chronic homesickness of Anglo-Indian society; but probably not without good reason to hope, Jackson had journeyed back in person to tender a proposal of marriage, and certainly soon after his arrival in England, the successful outcome of his mission would have been known to Housman. The whirl of pre-nuptial activity helped to shorten the period of strain, and before Housman's nerves could be overtaxed, the wedding itself took place, at St. Saviour's Church, Paddington, after which the unavoidable celebration did not prolong itself and the honeymoon was spent at sea, aboard one of those early P. & O. liners which transported a generation of similar couples to their global destiny.

With characteristic reluctance Housman deferred any expression of direct feeling about the subject until 1900, and even then could only begin to write that oddly tentative *Epithalamium* which he left dangling in his notebook and finally brought to completion, when it had become an ironic memento, in the last year of Jackson's life. Whatever his original sentiments may have been, Housman recalled chiefly the personal loss he had sustained, out of which he devised a marriage song that, with a singular emphasis, features not the bride's role, but her consort's. Thematically disjointed and laboriously contrived, with its mythological apparatus and its air of melancholy renunciation, the poem has preserved something of the joyless ordeal which the ceremony at St. Saviour's must have been for Housman:

> So the groomsman quits your side
> And the bridegroom seeks the bride;
> Friend and comrade yield you o'er
> To her that hardly loves you more.

It was indeed the figurative end of a relationship that would henceforth subside into a trickle of correspondence and, at still longer intervals, the spasmodic flutter of reunion, but which had already suffered its death-blow; and in this conviction Housman tried once more to cast off the spell that for so many years had possessed him. Now hardened to such losses and relinquishments, he was able without much effort to maintain the phlegmatic composure of one who has outlived the acute phase of emotional experience. But the deceptive ease with which the groomsman performed his role was not, as it must have appeared to Jackson, a welcome sign of recovery, but only a stricter enforcement of self-discipline. For Housman had learned so well how to guard his inner life that he was by this time nearly immune to outer disturbances, and registered the most severe shock, not reflexively, but in a slow, devious process of absorption. Thus belatedly, sometime in 1890, he put into words the first oblique statement of his response to

Jackson's marriage, symbolizing that traumatic episode in the solitude and despair of one who has

> lost for everlasting
> The heart out of his breast.

It was the onslaught of a wave-like poetic inspiration that for several months swept over Housman, receding finally in September with the composition of those more elaborate metaphorical verses which, under the title of *The Merry Guide*, transplanted the same theme into a pastoral setting whose "realms of woodland" and "silver waters" were haunted by the presence of an irresistible yet always elusive Mercury. Here at last by literary exorcism Jackson's image assumed a "gay delightful guise", though still equipped with his "serpent-circled wand."

On a different level Housman had received, after six years at the Patent Office, a further increment of salary which now served to ease the financial pinch; while from his Highgate study fresh commentaries and emendations continued to bombard the philological reviews. The virtuosity of his scholarship was, indeed, approaching the point where it could not much longer fail to win some academic recognition; and as the new decade opened, that was plainly the goal to which his nightly labours were directed. The earliest volume of his note-books also reposed on his desk—a large receptacle whose pages contained a random mixture of classical notes and nonsense scribblings, with an occasional effusion of poetry. But as if the incentive were exhausted, Housman wrote little or nothing more in that vein for the present.

CHAPTER SEVEN

I fetch my flute and play

EARLY in 1892, soon after Housman had passed the tenth
anniversary of his enslavement at the Patent Office, a Chair
of Greek and Latin opportunely fell vacant, upon the death of
Professor Alfred Goodwin, at University College, London. It
was the loop-hole for which Housman had so long been waiting; and though University College was not the venerable kind
of institution whose faculty he would have chosen to adorn, he
submitted his application, nevertheless, with the greatest
promptitude and in the most impressive manner. A school
of learning that was still considered, because of its comparatively recent origin, to be somewhat inferior, but which had
already begun to recruit the talents of men like W. P. Ker,
University College stood just then on the verge of a notably
luminous and expansive period. Unencumbered by tradition,
London had been the first university in England to introduce
the study of English literature, and was to blaze the trail, in
its School of Economics, for that new social doctrine which has
moulded the later course of English political history; while its
students were more varied and unconventional, if less erudite
or well-born, than those of Oxford and Cambridge. But even
though such innovations were not calculated to win Housman's
approval, they implied an official attitude that could more easily
overlook the blot on his academic record; and as if to test the
independent spirit of the authorities, Housman quite brazenly
notified them, in presenting his credentials, that he had "failed
to obtain honours in the Final School of Litterae Humaniores."
This confession, accompanied by seventeen emphatic testi-
monials from the foremost classical scholars of the day, was
bound to produce an intriguing effect which, in the event,
gained for him a unanimously affirmative verdict; and since

the dual Chair had now been converted into separate departments, one for each language, Housman received the appointment for which he had shown a slight preference—the Professorship of Latin.

In that narrowly circumscribed form of scholarship which Housman had elected to pursue, it scarcely mattered whether his subject was the literature of Greece or of Rome, or indeed what intrinsic merits any classical writer possessed, so long as the remains of his work afforded enough material for a scrupulous and painstaking reconstruction. The scholar's task was not to judge, discriminate and interpret, but merely to restore the original, even if worthless, text; and though Aeschylus had become his "favourite Greek poet," Housman felt no compunction in leaving that Athenian master to the mercy of less acute and sensitive editors, but rather considered that, in view of their insoluble problems, any further study of the seven extant plays would be superficial and unrewarding. His skill in Greek was at this time probably equal to his proficiency in Latin textual criticism, but from now on, except for random notes, his energies were devoted not only to Latin poetry, but also unfortunately to some of its least distinguished survivors. He was still occupied, however, in emending Propertius, whose art continued, with all the obscurities and corruptions which invested it, to exert an appeal that overcame the hesitancies of pure scholarship; and if Housman was already planning "to build himself a monument," Propertius seemed in those days the worthy object to which it would be dedicated.

Lesser duties began also to claim his attention, as the responsibilities of his new office loomed ahead. The professors at University College did not then enjoy the usual privileges and exemptions of their rank, but were burdened with all those menial chores of the class-room, from roll-call to the grading of papers, which Housman had rashly promised "with his best endeavours" to perform. "Much of the teaching he was required to give," as it turned out, "was elementary and he seldom had pupils who possessed a native ability for classical studies";

while on top of these vexations, he was expected to deliver a full-dress "Introductory Lecture" before the assembled faculties of Arts and Laws and of Science.

The delectable relief of escaping from the Patent Office was therefore mixed, that summer, with the tongue-tied nightmare of making a speech—something that in the end Housman forced himself to do well, but always with dread and reluctance. "Until I have broken the back of that infernal lecture," as he complained many years later, in the midst of writing *The Name and Nature of Poetry*, "I have no time for anything else"; and the labour of composing his maiden effort, not to mention the thought of reading it in public, must have been all the more hideous, as he paced the floor of his study or "sat staring in front of me and wishing for death." But no sign of discomposure was evident to the audience that awaited him on October 3, 1892. The shy slender Professor of Latin appeared, at thirty-three, slightly younger than his age, in spite of the incipient side-whiskers and drooping moustache; a carefully dressed, almost elegant figure whose gentle glance belied the firm thrust of his jaw, and who still wore the politely deferential expression of a minor civil servant. The words that issued from his mouth, in a soft unassertive voice, were nevertheless honed to a cutting edge and manipulated with the deft precision and lethal flash of daggers twirling just above the heads of his startled colleagues.

Housman had not lost that shrewd sense of how to capture his audience which used to govern his schoolboy productions, and in his present choice of theme, had cleverly picked the kind of generality that was appropriate to the occasion, yet whose treatment invited a plentiful display of his talents. "What now," he asked with an air of simple candour, "is the good which we set before us as our end when we exercise our faculties in acquiring knowledge, in learning?" What, in short, was the purpose of education?—a question to which none of his listeners could be indifferent, but about which, as he hastened to illustrate, few of them would agree. Roughly divided, then as now, between the "partisans of Science" and the "advocates of Humane Letters," they were all prone to exaggerate the benefits conferred by some "favourite study . . . the recognition of which as the aim of learning in general would increase the popularity of that study and the importance of those who profess it." Thus among the scientific faction, if not by reputable scientists themselves, it was commonly held that a subject derived its value from the degree to which it served "to equip one's self for the business of life"—an ingenuous utilitarian theory which Mr. Herbert Spencer had been one of the first to promulgate, more than thirty years ago, in his treatise on Education. By such reasoning, of course, no one would "need to pursue Science far," since in practical terms most of it did not, according to Mr. Spencer's definition, "render one efficient in producing, preparing and distributing commodities."

Having scored an easy point, Housman was now well-launched on the tide of his discourse, and after playfully dissecting the further opinions of that eminent philosopher, went on to expose, with equal relish, the pretensions of the opposite school. Whereas the doctor of science presumed to excel in the sphere of material things, the master of arts credited himself with a moral and aesthetic superiority; but "I do not believe," Housman contended, "that the proportion of the human race whose inner nature the study of the classics will specially transform and beautify is large." Indeed neither large, nor often capable of absorbing, from their intercourse with the best models, even "a good style" or "a true appreciation of literature." Those attainments seemed to exist quite apart from, though in exceptional cases they could be much enhanced by, the discipline of scholarship; and "if anyone wants convincing of the inestimable value of a classical education to those who are naturally qualified to profit by it, let him compare our two greatest poets, Shakespeare and Milton, and see what the classics did for one and what the lack of the classics did for the other."

So far Housman had contrived to provoke, without offend-

ing, the more conservative members of his audience, but the
mood of frisky defiance now overcame his discretion, and for
the next few minutes, about that name sacred to every cultured
mind, he let himself recklessly go. "Shakespeare, who at his
best is the best of all poets, at his worst is almost the worst"—
a rough untutored genius who, in spite of the "richness of his
natural endowment," could not approach the "dignity, the
sanity, the unfaltering elevation of style, the just subordination
of detail, the due adaptation of means to ends, the high respect
for his craft and for himself," which Milton alone represented
in English literature; and joining hands with Dr. Johnson and
King George III in their disdain for the Shakespearean cult,
the imprudent speaker merrily skipped along to pronounce,
upon that celebrated Latinist, Dr. Richard Bentley, the same
fearless judgment. "While he dealt with the classical poets he
was comparatively safe"; but on less familiar ground, and about
matters which required an innate poetic sensibility, even "the
greatest scholar that England or perhaps that Europe ever
bred" showed himself, as in his edition of *Paradise Lost*,
fantastically obtuse and incompetent.

Having thus impartially distributed his barbs among the
several departments of learning, and exhibited by the way his
incisive power of analysis, his urbane air of authority and his
special aversion to all forms of humbug, Housman was nearing
the point where, in order to round off and consolidate his remarks, a positive clarion note must be sounded. But if the
material advantages of more than a certain basic education
were, as he had argued, entirely negligible; and if, moreover,
few men possessed those inborn gifts which a long course of
study might help to refine; what then *was* the "good which we
set before us" in the stubborn pursuit of knowledge for its own
sake? Housman found the answer embedded, appropriately,
in the works of Aristotle, who had somewhere expressed the
conviction that everybody has "by nature a craving for knowledge," even though it may often be neglected or degraded; and
with which, Housman assured his listeners, the most enduring

if not the most perfect kind of happiness was "indissolubly bound up." The gratification of this impulse was, in fact, "part of man's duty to himself"—a virtue that arises, not from any ultimate reward or tangible profit, but merely from the exercise of his natural faculties. By the same token, one branch of knowledge, however musty and abhorrent ("say logic or mathematics or textual criticism"), could yield as much pleasure to its devotees as another, while all of them served equally to "set back the frontiers of darkness"; and with a rather sudden access of enthusiasm, Housman wound up his peroration by describing in terms of a "broad and delightful landscape," the view that unfolds before the scholar's microscopic research.

The applause that followed this cheerful and conciliatory finale overwhelmed the "tut-tuts" which, as Laurence Housman remembered the occasion, had greeted some of the earlier passages; and on the whole, amid the polite buzz of congratulation, Housman could feel sure that he had won the lasting respect of his colleagues, not many of whom would be tempted from now on to engage so dexterous an adversary. The quiet, correct, mild-looking young man had literally flowered, on the speaker's rostrum, into a pungent and forceful personality, whose characteristics still assail the reader from the printed version of his lecture. Boldness, irreverence, a gimlet penetration and a confident superiority, one would have said, were his chief attributes, mixed with a fund of acidulous humour but unrelieved by the softer emotions. It was a performance that he grew in later years to condemn as "rhetorical and not wholly sincere," but which showed the calculated disguise that he was already, in his thirties, beginning to assume. Under its immobile features, however, the mask betrayed a few signs of the wearer's defensive attitude—his over-indulgence, for example, in the kind of quotations (drawn from Solomon, Homer, Aristotle, Plato, Virgil and Dante, among others) that would help to confirm his acquaintance with the most venerable authors. As a spokesman for classical studies, Housman was perhaps more anxious to fortify his position at University

College than he would have been at Oxford or Cambridge; and his lecture reflected something of that storm-cloud which hung, even in 1892, over the disciples of humanism. But if he sounded at times unnecessarily belligerent and obtrusively well-read, the new Professor of Latin made it quite clear, nevertheless, that a man of singular parts and a scholar of the first order had arrived to bestir the academic scene.

Almost with the effect of some magical metamorphosis, Housman had changed from a bashful and obscure civil servant into this imposing figure, who was not likely to be addressed hereafter in the familiar terms which he had permitted at the Patent Office. "Dear old pal," as one of his former associates had recently written, "I'm as pleased as if I'd done something good myself"—a fraternal message that Housman prized and preserved for the rest of his life, along with the Wedgwood medallion that he had received as a farewell token of his co-workers' esteem. Touched by these mementoes, and savouring the first hours of his hard-won success, he must have felt the same temperate satisfaction which he had extolled in the closing words of his lecture, a mellow pleasure "shadowed by no fear of anxiety on the one hand or of frustration on the other." Momentarily, indeed, Housman stood on the brink of what promised to be not only a distinguished career, but also a period of emotional readjustment in which some of his melancholy and constraint might disappear. Established at last in the profession which had so lately rejected him, and now happily occupied with "those minute and pedantic studies in which I am fitted to excel," he could already enjoy a more sanguine outlook; while even casual friends had bestowed the kind of compliments that he would not have thought himself capable of inspiring. But except for Adalbert Jackson there was still no one whose company assuaged his loneliness, or in whom he was tempted to confide; and on this relationship, therefore, Housman's buoyant mood precariously depended. That furtive devotion which had been repelled or unperceived by one brother now groped its way towards the other, and taking heart again

Housman allowed himself to imagine a future not devoid of some reciprocal intimacy. Yet in the golden [light of those autumn days, and before he could share his new-found contentment with the "dear fellow" from whom it partly derived, Adalbert fell victim to one of those diseases which medical science would soon render less unavertible; and succumbing rapidly to the typhoid bacillus, the last hope of Housman's youth died in a London hospital on November 12, 1892.

This "winterfall," as Housman shudderingly evoked it in a poem written thirty years afterwards, now plunged him into the dark and forlorn condition which had so often overtaken him, but which bore this time the stamp of finality. All those climactic events—his mother's death, his "great and real troubles" at Oxford, his parting (in a bleak November, too) with Moses Jackson—which had shaped the course of Housman's life and over which he had wielded a tyrannical censorship, rose up again from his subconsciousness in a flood of uncontrollable memories; so that in mourning his present loss, he relived the most painful episodes of his past, and suffered once more a sense of being hounded by some relentless fate. One after another, those he loved had been struck down or snatched away in what seemed a spirit of capricious malevolence, and with a doom-like repetition that, in the wake of Adalbert Jackson's death, he began to regard as a fixed inevitable pattern.

For at close to thirty-four Housman was nearing the confines of middle age, with its sudden limitations and dwindling perspectives, while that mechanism by which heretofore he was able to absorb and recover from his misfortunes ceased in this emergency to operate. Always somewhat inelastic, habit-ridden and averse to change, he had become in the unremitting practice of scholarship, only more bound to his old attachments and constricted in the range of his experience. Though he had lived for ten years amid the multiple resources and distractions of London, he might have been, for all that he had gained from these opportunities, immured in a country town, and was, in fact, since his removal to Highgate, virtually cut off from new friends or pleasures. Within such a narrow compass, however, his emotions did not starve but merely redoubled their intensity, concentrating first upon Moses Jackson and then his brother an impassioned ingrown feeling that was now abruptly deprived of its single outlet and irreplaceable object. Secure in his chair of Latin, moreover, Housman could not take refuge again in the pursuit of an already half-gratified ambition. There was work enough for a lifetime, but no longer any doubt that, by dint of steady application, he would accomplish whatever task he set himself—a prospect not without its congenial and rewarding features, yet leaving him, under the pall of those winter months, profoundly disconsolate and incurably alone. To what purpose, he repeated like a catechism as each day began, did one "wash and dress and eat and drink" when even the faintest glow of human warmth had been extinguished; and it was henceforth not only in order to communicate with his fellow-men by some other means, but desperately in search of his own salvation that he more and more often resorted to the pages of his note-book.

From the blurred memory of his old age Housman recalled that "I did not begin to write poetry in earnest until the really emotional part of my life was over"; but this hiatus was, in fact, a comparatively brief interval during which the acute phase of experience that came to an end in 1892 merged almost continuously with the creative period that was already well-advanced by the last months of 1894. Roughly a hundred pages of his note-book had been filled with poetic raw material, even before he left the Patent Office, and this rate of production maintained itself or slightly increased thereafter. So that Housman had served, while he was still subject to the promptings of his heart, an extensive technical apprenticeship, without which the impulse that finally visited him would have come in vain. But if, in Housman's case, the elements indispensable to poetry were thus brought together and made ready, something more was yet required to precipitate their interaction; and such a trigger-like device was provided, at the deepest level of consciousness, by the death of Adalbert Jackson. Barely observable on the surface, but with repercussions that were soon evident in the note-book, this muffled shock set off that devious powder-train which exploded, just over two years later, in *A Shropshire Lad.*

At University College, in the meanwhile, Housman threw himself into the most trivial classroom activities, lavishing a "scrupulous care," as one of his students recalled, upon those daily exercises in Latin prose composition and extempore translation. He was a severely impersonal teacher, inflicting his censure with a brutal frankness yet forgetting, from one encounter to another, the names of his pupils—an Olympian method that especially strained the nerves of the young ladies who were just then carrying the banners of feminist emancipation. Always punctual if absent-minded, and formally dressed in a swallow-tail coat, their tormentor must have seemed a polite but merciless despot; while in his small classes there was ample time to bestow on every member a meticulous scrutiny, and since most of them were "quite unworthy" of his pains, to deliver castigations that often provoked, among the weaker sex, an outburst of tears. Thus for "about ten hours a week," Housman was engaged in the struggle to impose his own exquisite standards on a recalcitrant group, and apart from this effort which could not, as Mr. Gow has remarked, "have demanded much preparation from a scholar of Housman's calibre," he was free to carry on his real work (the further study of Propertius) undistracted by academic duties. Voluntarily, however, he not only arranged to give, each spring, a series of lectures on some phase of Latin literature, but rather surprisingly took an energetic part in the conduct of faculty affairs, and was soon acknowledged to be "the spokesman and leader of the professors." From his training in the Civil Service Housman had acquired something of that managerial technique in which the colleges were still sadly deficient. There was, even in 1893, no executive officer or separate machinery for administering the already manifold business of the University; and until this void had been filled, thanks in large part to Housman's zeal, he continued to display unwonted powers of "leadership and decisive action."

Among his colleagues Housman did not at first make any particular friends, but within a year or two he found, in the newly appointed Professor of Greek, a man both learned and sympathetic. Arthur Platt had been educated at Harrow and Cambridge, where in 1882 he failed, though less drastically than Housman had done the year before at Oxford, to obtain first class honours in the Classical Tripos; and to that distinction in common, he added an originality of mind and character that soon endeared him to the Professor of Latin. Not only a fastidious scholar who excelled in the "ascertainment of grammatical and metrical usage," but an ardent habitué of the Zoo and a literary enthusiast who "had produced a number of ingenious emendations of the corrupt text of Jane Austen, whose novels he knew almost by heart," Platt injected a note of cheerful sociability into this period of Housman's life; and if he occupied no place in those hidden recesses of the poet's consciousness, Platt was the subject, nevertheless, of a tribute in which Housman commemorated, by way of the preface to a posthumous collection of Platt's essays, his admirable qualities and "his utter unlikeness to any other creature in the world." With his insatiable curiosity and omnivorous taste that "ranged from the *Divine Comedy* to *Jorrock's Jaunts*," Platt embodied the zestful spirit of some frolicsome undergraduate, in whose company Housman caught an echo of his own student days; and it was in this vein that they conspired to relieve the tedium of departmental affairs, and even at times carried on a bantering controversy in the sober pages of the *Journal of Philology*. To Platt's influence, therefore, Housman owed much of that affable temper and comparative gusto with which he attended meetings, served on the University Council, helped to entertain the Literary Society and even submitted now and then to the ordeal of an after-dinner speech.

The outward man was already becoming, in the early nineties, a sedate professorial figure in whom it would have been difficult to recognize the incipient poet. To his students Housman would occasionally recite the less fervent works of Catullus and Ovid ("The next song is too sensuous to read here. I will omit it"), while to men like Platt, his conversation about literature might have suggested a talent for provocative criticism; but the impulse to write poetry himself seemed remote from his studious nature and chosen career, not to say his impenetrable reticence. Yet as a river steadily hews out some rocky gorge, Housman's emotions had cut a passage through which they could escape from the restrictions of a scholar's life; and now, in its narrow bed, this current began to rise and press against the system of locks and dams that held it in check. Always sensitive to the poetic art, Housman had proceeded from his youthful admiration for the English romantic school to the more austere standards of classical verse; and in the course of his studies at the British Museum he had combed through the catalogue in search of other models, enlarging still further the range of his discernment. By this time he had not only assimilated the poetry of several languages, but was in the habit of seeking in literature a vicarious outlet for his own frustration; and it was natural, therefore, that whenever this burden weighed too heavily, it should be discharged in the form of poetic driblets. But in 1893 Housman would perhaps have tried to avert, if he could have foreseen, the upsurge that presently threatened him.

The first week-end of that year, according to the Visitor's Book, Housman stayed at Woodchester House, and on his departure, composed a long impromptu farewell in the manner of Tennyson (whose Abbey funeral had been the main literary event of recent months):

> Tears, Tears, I wish you would not trickle;
>> The mess you make is past belief;
> My eyes you dim, my nose you tickle,
>> You soak my pocket handkerchief.

The high spirits of January soon gave way, however, to that

mood of despondency which, sometime in February, drove Housman to the solace of his note-book and a confessional outburst that produced, within a few weeks, "fair copies" of at least two poems, along with several pages of fragmentary lines and verses. The note-book now contained, in the form of early drafts and rough outlines, not quite one sixth of what finally emerged as *A Shropshire Lad*—the spasmodic accumulation of three or four years during which, as he added fresh material, Housman customarily revised the old. Dating inconsistently either the first or second version, and sometimes both or none at all, Housman kept only this approximate chronological record; but it was enough to indicate that his work bunched itself into fitful periods of creative activity, lasting for a matter of days or even hours, in which seldom more than a single new poem would be tentatively set down, while a previous one underwent repairs. Thus in February 1893, Housman sketched and brought near to completion those two stanzas, of an almost Chinese brevity, which might have been called "Winter Moon," (No. X in *More Poems*); he then filled a page or two with abortive efforts to develop a larger theme, and after some further scribbling at random, turned back to polish and relocate one of his old invocations to the spring landscape, originally set in the less appealing neighbourhood of "Stourbridge," but now transferred to that world of plausible yet elusive place-names where

> 'Tis time, I think, by *Wenlock* town,
> The golden broom should blow;
> The hawthorn sprinkled up and down
> Should charge the land with snow.

By such delicate adjustments a pattern of words became poetry; and having at last successfully converted the gloominess of mid-winter into this lyrical form, Housman not only desisted from writing but was temporarily relieved of his discontent.

The scholar's various quotidian occupations closed round him again, and Housman did not reopen his note-book until the following August. But in spite of a regimen that forced him "to spend much of his life," as Housman looked back on it, "in acquiring knowledge which for its own sake is not worth having and in reading books which do not in themselves deserve to be read," he contrived nevertheless to search out and absorb the kind of literature that nourishes other writers; and in fact it was apparent from his note-book that Housman had already discovered, in this phase of his apprenticeship, the models which shaped and often inspired his own style. The "chief sources of which I am conscious," he quite freely admitted in later years, "are Shakespeare's songs, the Scottish border ballads, and Heine"—an acknowledgment that did not blush to reveal his debt to these eclectic influences. Housman had probably received his first impression of Heine from Matthew Arnold's essay, and may have continued the acquaintance, on tired evenings at the Museum reading room, as a respite from the merciless pedantries of German textual criticism. There were not, certainly, many obvious points of attraction between Housman and the volatile Jewish poet. A dashing, intemperate renegade whose stormy and improvident life bore no resemblance to that of his staid Victorian admirer, Heine was an oddly foreign yet indispensable element in the growth of *A Shropshire Lad*. For by one of those far-fetched coincidences which occur in literary history, he served to provide, at the appropriate moment, just what Housman subconsciously required—a method of baring one's heart that was not merely some outworn poetic convention; and even across the frontiers of an alien culture, Heine's voice carried this valuable lesson. From the fluent strains of the *Gedichte*, his disciple learned so well how to compress emotion into a simple, melodious phrase that, for the English reader, Heine's songs seem full of lines that Housman himself might have written:

> I despaired at first, declaring
>   It could not be borne; and now—
> Now I bear it, still despairing.
>   Only never ask me how!

The best equivalent that Housman could find, in his own

language, to the morning freshness of Heine's verse was the folk-poetry which had flourished, during the late Middle Ages, in that embattled region between England and Scotland. The anonymous bards who poured into their rudimentary moulds a literature that ranged from *Chevy Chase* to *Clerk Saunders* were masters not only of the narrative art but of a subtle psychological insight; and the ballads which antiquarians had been collecting ever since preserved, as in the untarnished miniatures of some Book of Hours, the domestic scenes as well as the popular legends, the distilled composite experience of medieval country life. A kind of poetry impossible to reconstruct in the nineteenth century, this folklore had exerted, nevertheless, a compelling influence on the Victorian imagination, and was the material to which so many writers and painters harked back. It had supplied some of the favourite motifs of the Pre-Raphaelite Brotherhood, and especially in the form of the Arthurian romance had engaged the talents of Tennyson and William Morris; while even Aubrey Beardsley had, in 1893, illustrated a suitably decadent edition of the *Morte d'Arthur*. But Housman's early taste for these archaic mixtures, of which he used to copy long passages in his commonplace book, had matured into a preference for the original unadorned text; and from that multifarious Gothic revival which produced so many insipid or degenerate copies, he had gained the knowledge of just what was convertible to his own purpose. Not the mythology of the ballads but their realism was the feature of which Housman took particular note, along with that homely radiance which the story-teller cast over his subject:

> "Lie still, lie still but a little wee while,
>   Lie still but if we may;
> Gin my mother should miss us when she wakes,
>   She'll go mad ere it be day."—
>
> "Fare ye weel, my mother dear!
>   Farewell to barn and byre!
> And fare ye weel, the bonny lass
>   That kindles my mother's fire!"

It was such haunting episodes, rather than the chivalrous adventures of knighthood, that sank into Housman's memory until almost the same rhythmic phrase ("Be still, my soul, be still" or again "Farewell to barn and stack and tree") presented itself when he sought to render some coincidental aspect of his own experience. The lilting ballad metre also helped to ease the tension that underlay his poetry, while the echoes of Northumberland that often sounded across the Shropshire landscape merely gave it a timeless air; for whatever Housman borrowed was recast in his workshop and indelibly stamped with his signature.

The best of Shakespeare lay beyond Housman's reach, but the songs, which were themselves a conscious adaptation of the folk-idiom, may have pointed the way to further experiments and new incentives. Housman did not, like Shakespeare, choose to perform a brilliant improvisation on ballad themes, and he failed, oddly enough, to employ another Shakespearean device at which he might have excelled—that verbal counterpoint whereby sense alternates with nonsense in a single headlong stanza or even one somersault line:

> When birds do sing, ding a ding ding . . .

Housman's frivolous mood, however, was confined to the Visitor's Book of Woodchester House, and in so far as he drew upon the richest legacy of English literature, it was from that plaintive funeral music in *Twelfth Night* ("Come away, come away, death") or the songs of Autolycus in *The Winter's Tale*, a small if discriminating selection that answered to the severity of his taste and temperament. A poet who was straining not to emulate his masters but to relieve his unhappiness, Housman pilfered, as every honest writer does, only what was latent in himself.

The care with which Housman had studied these congenial models was already evident from his note-book, in which the first signs of their inspiriting effect began to appear as early as 1890, when his style developed from an austere economy to comparative ease and luxuriance. Housman had then written only a few poems that satisfied him, along with some of the exercises that were posthumously revealed in *More Poems*— those initial fruitless attempts to convey, in the manner of a Victorian hymn, the desolation of his heart. It was a barren didactic vein to which, after many years, he reverted with fresh determination in *Hell Gate*, but which he now luckily abandoned in favour of the ballad and the elegy. Housman was quick to solve the technical problems of his art, and could have hardly improved upon the mournful cadence of "Bring, in this timeless grave to throw," or the folk-song quality of "In summertime on Bredon," both of which were composed in this novice period; but he was still groping, as late as 1893, for an imagery less reminiscent of other poets and closer to his own specific inner world. The persistence of his effort left no doubt that Housman had elected to uncover, in some equivalent poetic form, those hidden emotions which he lacked any direct means of communicating, and whose intricacies he was forcing himself at last to explore. A stronghold which had resisted every assault yielded inch by inch to the demands of his poetry, and the voluntary if only limited process of surrender was to be, in fact, a curative treatment that took the place of what is now termed occupational therapy.

Since the entries of February 1893, Housman had made no further contributions to his notebook until, in the following August, he inscribed one of those poems ("With rue my heart is laden") which would occasionally suggest themselves, by some mysterious automatism, as he took his afternoon walks. It was in this case a message of two complete stanzas relayed apparently straight from his subconsciousness, and perhaps accompanied by other psychic "fragments" that filled the two or three successive pages; after which, in the usual sequence, he resumed the more laborious methods of a deliberate crafts-man. Between that August and the next, Housman slightly accelerated his annual rate of production, but without dating even his finished work, so that a year of some literary and considerable biographical interest was enveloped in characteristic obscurity. His outward life continued to resemble, in all its noticeable features, that of a rising young professor whose classroom hours, extra-curricular activities and always industrious application to scholarship presumably absorbed most of his energies; and though Housman had few engagements or diversions outside the University, his leisure could not have been at best very copious. The advantages that derived from a certain worldly position had given him, nevertheless, that sense of security in which even his frayed nerves tended to relax their vigilance, and as the note-book confirms, he now slipped more often into the kind of becalmed reverie by which his poetic imagination was gently spurred, like Wordsworth's, to fresh effort. The autumn of 1893 must have been such a period of "emotion recollected in tranquillity," lasting perhaps until the early months of 1894 and precipitated by the first anniversary of Adalbert Jackson's death, in whose memory Housman about this time wrote that informal if rather pedestrian monologue (No. XLII in *More Poems*) which evoked the mournful pathetic solitude of an evening at Highgate. From the rough chronology of the notebook, however, it was evident that Housman used almost invariably to interweave these expressions of personal sentiment with his better work, and in fact could only reach the upper levels of poetry by means of some preliminary descent into autobiography. So the spurt of composition which overtook him on this occasion yielded not simply one or two examples of ill-disguised reminiscence but other products of the highest quality.

Among the scraps that Housman thriftily salvaged from his moments of inspiration was an apparently trivial line, recorded in his note-book sometime that autumn or winter, which signalled the appearance of a new figure destined to assume one of the commanding roles in his poetry. "Soldier," Housman had briefly jotted down, "I wish you well"—a cryptic reference to that incident which afterwards took form in *A Shropshire Lad* (No. XXII), but which now lay for more than a year invisibly germinating. Perhaps unaware of its literary possibilities, or shy of betraying the strong emotion it aroused in him, Housman had wanted at the time merely to remind himself of some face that caught his eye, one of those glancing encounters that must often have occurred in the course of his daily exercise. The statuesque guardsmen were still a decorative feature of the London streets for which Housman had not lost his schoolboy predilection, and it was doubtless in a passing troop of these familiar giants, dramatically marching to or from their barracks in Knightsbridge (then a popular nocturnal rendezvous), that he espied the "single redcoat" whose look made so indelible an impression. England was at peace in 1894, though faintly alarmed by the rumours of a disturbance in South Africa; but Housman's sympathy for the soldier did not arise from the civilian's temporary enthusiasm for his defenders in the hour of crisis, and it had certainly no basis in a factual knowledge of the military life. The first volume of his poetry, moreover, had not only been written, but also published, before his youngest brother took part and was killed in the Boer War, so that Housman's choice of subject owed nothing to this private sorrow. It was on the contrary an attraction he had always felt towards the gallant bearing and ripe masculinity of men in uniform, now deepened by a sense of closer kinship with their unhappy lot. Even more than the farm lads for whom he nursed a romantic nostalgia, the common soldier embodied that mixture of youthful idealism and impending adversity in which Housman saw the reflection of his own experience; while if, as he must have been aware, this imaginary hero was, in fact, often susceptible to his own sex, it would have merely invested him with a further covert fascination. But the telepathic exchange that Housman cherished and commemorated was only an instant of mute recognition, flashed across impassable barriers.

Stimulated, nevertheless, by the discovery that such a powerful gust could again overtake him, Housman resumed his daydreams, along the green paths of Hampstead or behind the curtains of his study, and in the last few months of 1894 drafted nearly a dozen new poems, among them the first incomplete and fumbling version of that Jubilee salute which became the introduction to *A Shropshire Lad*. It was a prompt if still experimental development of the martial theme, whose bare suggestion had appeared so recently in his note-book; and as if grasping at once the multiple variations of which it was capable, Housman went on hastily to improvise, under the alternate titles of *Listing*, *The Queen's Shilling* or as it was finally called, *The Recruit*, a second treatment 'which included not only the brave young volunteer who will

> make the hearts of comrades
> Be heavy where you die,

but also for the first time the chiming tower of Ludlow. Thus already, with these inventions and appurtenances, Housman had assembled most of the elements—the pastoral countryside, the doomed lads, the strident bugles, the flaming beacons and the quiet churchyard—which constituted that grimly deceptive world, like an ominous Eden, where his imagination could now acclimatize itself. Hampered at first by waiting so long to learn the rudiments of his art, and then deterred by the innate reticence of his character as well as the exacting standards of his own taste, Housman had been forced to work his careful, circuitous way towards the objective which a younger writer might have reached at one bound; but he must have felt, as he was advancing towards his thirty-sixth birthday, that he had stumbled at last on that hidden spring which would henceforth release his whole poetic energy.

The impetus that, between August and December, filled more than twenty pages of his note-book had carried Housman dizzily close to the *annus mirabilis* of 1895, even though his progress may have been arrested in mid-career by what proved to be his father's ultimate collapse. For on November 27, Edward's weary sexagenarian body expired at Bromsgrove; and with his old knack for disrupting his son's peace of mind, the occasion required Housman's presence at the bedside just when he was abnormally sensitive to the kind of reminders that would emanate from Perry Hall, but above all from the cemetery at Catshill. The ghost-ridden atmosphere was bound to provoke (almost exactly on the second anniversary of Adalbert Jackson's death) Housman's gloomiest thoughts, now intensified by those repugnant mortuary arrangements which it had become his filial duty to superintend. Once again, however, the family united to preserve its customary silence in relation to Edward's misadventures; and the only public tribute to his memory appeared, succinctly and politely regretful, in the *Bromsgrove Messenger*, for December 1, 1894:

Mr. Housman had been for many years a trustee of the Bromsgrove Consolidated Charities and a member of the School of Art Committee. He was also prominently associated with the late choral and philharmonic societies. Mr. Housman held an ensign's commission in the Bromsgrove Company of Volunteers on its formation, and he was a very good shot.

Even his obituary could find nothing more to say about Edward, whose debts, follies and weaknesses were uppermost in the minds of his neighbours, and immovably enshrined in the hearts of his children.

The repercussions of this event were soon visible in the notebook, where it served indirectly to set off again, as the old year ended, that subconscious eruption which had been gathering momentum since August; and in the grip of emotions that may have been stirred but were not limited by his funerary ordeal in Bromsgrove, Housman rallied quickly and even amid the inclemencies of December was able to finish one lengthy poem (the lurid fancies of *The True Lover* in *A Shropshire Lad*), in addition to beginning another (No. XIX in *Last Poems*) whose material might seem to reflect the macabre experience he had just undergone. But a preoccupation with death was by this time so natural to Housman that perhaps no undue significance should be attributed to those lines, written not long after his own vigil "In midnights of November," and suspiciously applicable to his chronic sense of estrangement from his father:

Oh yonder faltering fingers
Are hands I used to hold;
Their false companion drowses
And leaves them in the cold.

It was in any case Housman's only problematical allusion to a relationship in which, certainly on the level of daytime reality, he had no feeling of guilt or need for atonement; and as if to underline his conviction that he was more indebted to a gifted man of letters than to a delinquent parent, Housman took the bold step of submitting to *The Academy*, as he went into ostensible mourning, a few unsigned verses in commemoration of Robert Louis Stevenson, whose premature death had lately coincided with poor Edward's.

Writing to Laurence at about the same time, Housman spared no effort, in a letter of several foolscap pages, to analyse, re-order, improve if possible and whenever necessary disembowel a collection of poems that his younger brother was threatening to publish, but himself mentioned in passing neither the loss of their father (barely two weeks after the obsequies in Broms-grove) nor his own secret literary ambition. The annoyance of one whose plans are anticipated by another may have given a slight edge to Housman's strictures, though in the main his advice showed the kind of impersonal judgment with which he regularly examined the contents of his note-book—that invaluable faculty of self-criticism which kept him, even now, from indulging the pride of authorship. His own storehouse was already crammed with enough usable or finished work from which to have assembled, in competition with Laurence, a miscellaneous volume of poetry; but as the New Year pealed its bells, Housman had rather the air of awaiting some further untapped inspiration than of reviewing his past achievements. If he did grant himself that luxury, it was to confirm the impression that he had found in recent months not only a more effective style, but a deeper poetic vein whose resources were not yet exhausted; and for whatever this might yield, he was therefore disposed to linger in a state of patient receptivity.

148

Thus, during the fog-bound germ-laden winter months of
1895, Housman proceeded so rapidly to fill his note-book that,
by the end of March, he was obliged to start a new one into
which, before the next prompt entry, he transferred an impres-
sively long index of first lines. Maintaining as well his normal
schedule of college appointments and never missing, though
often "rather out of health," his customary afternoon walks,
he was a severe thin-faced man of almost thirty-six, immersed
apparently in the quiet pursuit of study and scholarship, yet
inwardly consumed by the feverish spurts of a delirious and
overwhelming poetic afflatus. Housman remembered it as an
assault of "continuous excitement" which, "though pleasurable," had in general both "agitating and exhausting" effects
upon his nervous system; and whose origin he could only trace
dimly to some "abyss" located in "the pit of the stomach."
From this dark interior region, he alleged, "there would flow
into my mind, with sudden and unaccountable emotion," odd
scraps of verse which bore no relation to his idle thoughts as
he perambulated the streets and parklands of Hampstead; "then
there would usually be a lull of an hour or so, then perhaps the
spring would bubble up again," after which he would return
home, shaken and wearied, to commit these autonomous fragments to his note-book. The physical symptoms of a creative
seizure have seldom been more accurately described, and of that
culminating outburst, strangely enough, the most reserved of
men has left one of the most clinical reports; but Housman did
not try or even wish to unravel, beyond a certain point, the long
knotted fuse that led from the depths of his subconsciousness
to such overt manifestations. "I think," he merely noted, "that
the production of poetry is less an active than a passive and involuntary process . . . whether a natural secretion, like turpen-
tine in the fir, or a morbid secretion, like the pearl in the
oyster"; and "my own case," he affirmed with the emphasis of
a closing door, "is the latter." A poet so alert to his own performance, however, could have scarcely failed to detect, in the
material over which he exercised no deliberate control, an

obvious link with feelings that were lodged in the furthest recesses
of his heart; and in fact, as the note-books testify, Housman
was repeatedly driven to moderate, after sober reflection, the
more passionate language to which his incautious muse gave
vent. But while this demonic spirit possessed him, Housman
had neither the means nor the opportunity to restrain its
imperious dictation.

From January until May or June, the outpouring continued
to seep through Housman's defences with a tidal pressure of
emotion that transformed itself almost simultaneously into
verse, and as the spring advanced, changed its tone from wintry
discontent to a lyrical if momentary delight in the rejuvenes-
cence of nature. Housman still lapsed now and then into the
crudities of personal sentiment:

> He looked at me with eyes I thought
> I was not like to find;
> The voice he begged for pence with brought
> Another man to mind.

But most of the work produced at this time was, in view of its
impulsive and unstudied composition, remarkably flawless—
the expression of a writer who has escaped from the trammels
of his private life into the universalities of his art. Freed from
constraint yet purged of all dross, it was for Housman among
other things a process of self-revelation that did not involve
painful embarrassment or grotesque exhibitionism, though in
later years he professed to regard this divine frenzy as an attack
"of nervous travail so intense, so prostrating, that the bare
thought of a recurrence was too formidable to contemplate."
But Housman was by then ageing into tetchiness and hebetude,
a crabbed scholar whose repose would have been disturbed by
the mere recollection of such unquenchable ardour, and who
could no longer separate, among those distant memories, the
delirious upsurge of poetic inspiration from the cruel torments
which had preceded it. The experience that gave an authentic
ring to his poetry had become, in retrospect, a burden heavier
than he could again "well sustain." For in those ebullient

"early months of 1895," when Housman was already on the threshold of middle age, all the instincts of his youth combined to rebel against the pertinacity with which he had suppressed them; a rebellion deviously generated by some hurtful obsessive event in his twenties, and characterized by the bitterness, not of one long since accustomed to such tribulations, but of a young man supremely overwrought and inconsolable. The poet who lurked inside Housman's tight-reined personality and who took precedence during that phenomenal spring-time not only relived, but insistently betrayed, the anguish of spirit which had extended from his last year at Oxford to the death of Adalbert Jackson. Between those peaks of discouragement, Housman's emotional capacity had spent itself either in curbing his natural desires or in bearing the fortuitous external blows which did not fail to strike—a pincers that held its victim hopelessly subjugated yet throbbingly conscious of his frustration; and from this bondage Housman now contrived at last to deliver himself by means of his poetry. Such a release must have brought him, along with its enervating paroxysms, the tonic sense of fulfilment which he could obtain in no other way, and while the catharsis proceeded, Housman was privileged to enjoy that higher form of compensation by which suffering is so infrequently rewarded. The adversities and deprivations of the past were turning into an instrument that might serve, he could now perceive, "to harmonize the sadness of the world." But as the fountain subsided into a trickle, that summer and autumn, Housman began to feel not only the empty aftermath of his rapture, but also the great preliminary sacrifices he had been required to make for it.

CHAPTER EIGHT

To stand up straight and tread the turning mill

LIKE so many of his compatriots, Housman was addicted to reading the newspapers and especially those columns of irate correspondence to which on several occasions he could not resist the impulse to contribute his own inflammatory opinions. Thus in March 1894 he had composed a stinging letter to the Editor of the *Standard* on the subject of the depredations which "the Mayor and Commonalty and Citizens of the City of London" were inflicting on Highgate Wood—a scene once so densely "overgrown with brushwood, that if you stood in the centre you could not see the linen of the inhabitants of Archway Road hanging to dry in their back gardens. Nor could you see the advertisements of Juggins' stout and porter which surmount the front of the public house at the south corner"; but where, in addition to exposing these "bright and picturesque objects," the authorities were now engaged in clearing a view of the railway on the north and, as the writer hoped they would not neglect to do, a glimpse of the "new red-brick houses to the east," so that his "yearning gaze" would miss none "of those objects of interest which one naturally desires to see when one goes to the centre of a wood."

In the vein of Ruskin's lecture which, not many years before, had sounded excessively indignant, Housman was himself now girding, like Matthew Arnold, against the same world of Barbarians and Philistines—a world soon to be convulsed, in the spring of 1895, by the scandalous reverberations, the vindictive hysteria and moral outrage that issued from the trials of Oscar Wilde. If the gossip which already bombinated through every bar and club in London was not yet current, that preceding winter, in academic circles, it had shortly become, as Mr.

Justice Charles observed in his charge to the jury on May 1, "impossible to open a newspaper without reading some reference to this case"; and in fact, from April 5 when the ill-advised libel suit against the Marquess of Queensberry collapsed so ignominiously, until Wilde's final conviction on May 25, the press had indulged not only its lowest appetite for sensationalism but the utmost animosity towards the prisoner. Housman could not have missed, therefore, those lurid bulletins and vicious innuendoes which accompanied day by day the excoriating public spectacle at the Old Bailey; and just while he was feverishly resurrecting his own past, the pilloried figure of Oscar Wilde gripped his imagination, and the thunder of the mob which bore down upon the prostrate author filled his ears. By what now seems more than a coincidence Housman's talent freely asserted itself only at the moment when, as he must have felt, a hostile glare focussed upon the suspect moral values of literature—one further reason that may have prompted him to temper the language and obscure the implications of his poetry. But whether the hue and cry of that English man-hunt served to arouse or quench Housman's creative mood, there was no solid evidence, or at any rate none has survived, in his notebooks except those unmistakable verses,—

> Oh who is that young sinner with the handcuffs on his wrists?
> And what has he been after that they groan and shake their fists?
> And wherefore is he wearing such a conscience-stricken air?
> Oh they're taking him to prison for the colour of his hair.

Written early in the autumn of 1895, they unknowingly but almost exactly paraphrased, by some vibration of sympathy, Wilde's defence of homosexuality ("It is in this century misunderstood, so much misunderstood that it may be described as the 'Love that dare not speak its name,' and on account of it I am placed where I am now")—a defiantly incriminating speech that produced, in the dark and dismal courtroom, a spontaneous outburst of "loud applause, mingled with some hisses."

The effects of this punitive legal drama were nevertheless

insidious and far-reaching, from the sudden demise of *The Yellow Book*, whose office windows were smashed by its more violent non-readers under the misapprehension that the reprobate had been flaunting a copy at the time of his arrest, to the indecent haste with which other men of letters fled to the continent or disavowed any sense of pity for a colleague so bereft and unpopular. Thomas Hardy generously consented, but George Meredith stonily refused to sign a petition for the curtailment of Wilde's maximum sentence; and after energetic but fruitless efforts to organize some token of charity among the *Who's Who* of literary and theatrical London, even Bernard Shaw abandoned a cause that was by then irrevocably lost. But more damaging than such examples of furious vandalism and heartless prejudice were the internal injuries sustained by all those who, from motives of self-preservation or mere appeasement, submitted to the bellicose tribal mentality which took advantage of this pretext to impose its own censoriousness upon the arts. The generation that came of age in the nineties—Ernest Dowson, Richard Middleton, Aubrey Beardsley—suffered the worst consequences of being thus narrowly wedged between the permissible and the forbidden, in an airless constriction which gave so much of their work its etiolate quality, and which led in so many instances to alcoholism, suicide and premature death. Housman was luckier, to the extent that he was already habituated to the restraint of Victorian manners, and did not struggle against prohibitions to which he had long ago voluntarily subjected himself; having no taste, moreover, for those preciosities which the school of Oscar Wilde had made fashionable, and never having ventured into the precincts of Bohemia or attended those evenings of shop-talk at the Rhymers' Club, he stood untouchably apart from the coteries that were forming in the summer of 1895. Yeats was then at work in London, revolving Irish politics, theosophical speculations and a new book of verse in his mind, while poets as congenially troubled as John Davidson could have been found at the British Museum; and Francis Thompson might still be seen, a gaunt dishevelled figure adrift in the streets. But more in the spirit of Hardy, who had determined that same year, after the intolerant reception of *Jude the Obscure*, never again to write a novel, Housman withdrew into his private meditations and a startled review of the material which had been accumulating in his note-book.

He did not entirely cease, however, to add fresh poems and revise old ones, with the apparent object of setting them in order for publication; and as the summer faded into autumn, the entries multiplied in a second creative spurt almost equal to that of April and May. This recurrence may have been precipitated by the newspaper item which Housman came across, early in August, reporting the inquest on a Woolwich cadet who had shot himself at the age of eighteen and whose foresighted letter of explanation to the Coroner was quoted at length:

I wish it to be clearly understood that I am not what is commonly called "temporarily insane," and that I am putting an end to my life after several weeks of careful deliberation. I do not think that I need justify my actions to anyone but my Maker, but . . . I will state the main reasons which have determined me. The first is utter cowardice and despair. There is only one thing in this world which would make me thoroughly happy; that one thing I have no earthly hope of obtaining. The second—which I wish was the only one—is that I have absolutely ruined my own life; but I thank God that as yet, so far as I know, I have not morally injured, or "offended," as it is called in the Bible, anyone else. Now I am quite certain that I could not live another five years without doing so, and for that reason alone, even if the first did not exist, I should do what I am doing . . . At all events it is final, and consequently better than a long series of sorrows and disgraces.

The level tone, the lucid argument of this bitter *apologia* were enough, apart from the similarities to his own quondam fits of despair and suicidal unhappiness, to capture Housman's attention; and within a few days or weeks, he had produced a rough draft of that morbid elegy, with its acrid smell of gunfire and black core of nihilism, which plainly derived from the clipping that his brother found, after his death, still pressed like a dusty flower between the pages of verse it had once provoked. Thus revealingly documented, one of Housman's typical if not one of his best poems has acquired a meaning inseparable from its biographical origin. The intensity of his reaction to an episode of which he had no direct knowledge betrayed not merely his commiseration, but as the outspoken lines affirm, a sense of identity with one who had been driven (for some cause not hard to imagine, especially in the light of recent history) to such an extreme:

> Oh that was right, lad, that was brave:
> Yours was not an ill for mending,
> 'Twas best to take it to the grave.

In a more dramatic form the case evoked just that mood of self-condemnation in which, at Oxford, Housman had discovered for the first time "that one thing I have no hope of obtaining"; a disconsolate, ineradicable mood which, he had been learning ever since, clamped itself on all his prospects and achievements, but from which his poetry now insistently drew its single theme. So that, in contemplating the wilful death of a young man likewise afflicted, but so mercifully rendered "clear of danger, clean of guilt" by one courageous act of violence, Housman could not resist this appeal to his innermost feelings, and in the train of thoughts induced by the penitential agonies of Oscar Wilde, he was filled with a new urgency to relieve his oppressed conscience.

The several poems that Housman composed in August, under such gruesome auspices, displayed their topical source rather too noticeably at first, but as the impulse gathered momentum, his afternoon walks yielded further material of that purely subliminal strain from which his best work always emerged; and from September to December his note-book reflected, in the comparative absence of corrections and loose ends, the effortless renewal of his inspiration. It was a last flare-up which not only contributed substantially to the contents of *A Shropshire Lad*, but also followed the outline of a conscious editorial plan suddenly forged by the anxiety that, as he confessed in a dialogue between the "moping melancholy

mad" poet and the hypothetical reader (whose extrovert qualities were palpably drawn from a certain model), all this would
appear to be "stupid stuff." Housman was now writing with a
clear view to publication but without an experienced command
of his audience, and not unnaturally in dread of what his family
and friends, but especially Moses Jackson, might think of such
a denuding performance. The reluctant yet compulsive process
of self-exposure must have been, for one so invincibly reserved,
an exquisite torment; and as if to avoid the risk of saying too
much, as well as to provide substitutes for a number of poems
that he had already rejected on that account, Housman confined himself in the autumn of 1895 largely to those ballad or
military subjects which offered him both an emotional outlet
and a convenient disguise.

Eight or nine admirable examples of his art were thus rapidly
assembled within as many weeks, virtually completing the text
of *A Shropshire Lad*; but despite this successful outcome, the
year ended in a wave of apathy and disgust that forced itself
into those tired verses (written in December though withheld
until *Last Poems*) which proved to be Housman's temporary
swan-song.

> Let me lie abed and rest:
> Ten thousand times I've done my best
> And all's to do again . . .

he groaningly complained, not without some justification, as
the sheer labour, mental stress and nervous excitement which
had been crowded into a twelvemonth, took their toll of his
depleted energies. For in addition to the strenuous joint pursuits of a professor and a poet, Housman had found time also
to survey, in the *Classical Review*, a new edition of Propertius;
to chastise once more the early literary efforts of Laurence
Housman; and to relax for ten summer days at Woodchester
House, whose Arcadian hospitality he celebrated as usual in the
Visitor's Book. But while poetry must have claimed all
his inner thoughts, he was careful not to divulge that secret

occupation of which neither his brother nor his boyhood friends had as late as 1895 the barest inkling. Housman's double-life, in fact, had assumed proportions that were overtaxing even his powers of endurance and threatened him in December with the first symptoms of a breakdown; but opportunely this advancing state of hyperaesthesia began to arrest itself before the tension snapped, so that by the end of the month he could lay his note-book aside with a torpid yet healthy indifference.

The langour of recuperation did not keep Housman very long from the mere mechanical task of copying and arranging his poems in what then served as a presentable form of manuscript—the sixty-odd foolscap pages which bore, in that handwriting which defied the printer to mistake a word or dislodge a comma, the first definitive transcription of *A Shropshire Lad*. The principle by which Housman selected, from the jumbled contents of his note-books, this orderly sequence appeared to be more judicious than meaningful, though certainly one of its effects was the omission of any material that might betray, to the world at large, some oblique biographical reference. Housman's critical instinct happily coincided with his natural self-effacement, and now both operated not only to weed out the less perfect specimens of his work, but to impose on the remainder a formal, consistent, arbitrary design. The matrix of stifled feeling from which Housman's poetry broke forth, combined with its narrow range of experience and deliberate sameness of theme, helped to give it an effect of unity, of one pure note indefinitely sustained, that few collections of lyric verse manage to achieve; and furthermore by addressing himself not to an impersonal reader, but to "lads like me" whose present ills and nostalgic regrets equalled his own, Housman had contrived to induce as a poet the kind of quickening response that he was seldom able to provoke as a man. To these initial advantages, moreover, he brought the sensibility of one who was not only trained, but temperamentally prone, to exercise a fastidious restraint, and who had acquired an almost native taste for the refinements of classical literature; so that, in pruning his note-books, Housman could apply that strict objective discrimination which profits any fallible human endeavour.

The resulting text which had been thus overhauled by the scholar's drastic methods, satisfied even his Augustan standards, and was forthwith submitted, early in the new year, to the consideration of a publisher already favourably connected in the author's mind with Matthew Arnold and Thomas Hardy. The manuscript bore a somewhat unpromising title—*The Poems of Terence Hearsay*—which Housman may have chosen because of its mild pastoral flavour and pseudonymous concealment, but which did not in any case recommend itself to the editorial staff of Macmillan and Company, who were quick to reject the offer, apparently without comment, though as Housman believed, "on the advice of John Morley, who was their reader." Still confident of the merits, if not the commercial prospects, of his work, Housman lost no time in consulting the practical knowledge of A. W. Pollard, who had by then himself produced several books under the imprint of Kegan Paul, Trench, Trübner and Company, a dignified firm that was not averse to lending its name, but only at the poet's expense, to "prettily printed volumes of verse"; and on this rather humble basis, according to Pollard's recollection, Housman agreed to negotiate without further parley or signs of demur. Before completing the transaction, however, Pollard was happily emboldened to suggest that "*Terence* was not an attractive title, and that in the phrase 'A Shropshire Lad,' which he had used in the poem, he had a much better one." Even to this tactical revision, Housman quite readily consented, as if he would now make any sacrifice in order to expedite so urgent a matter of business; and with the same alacrity, when the publisher requested full payment in advance, he "put down £30."

In spite of their deficiencies in mechanical equipment, the typographers and bookbinders of that generation performed feats of celerity unattainable by their successors; and within a breathless period of three or four weeks, the first edition of *A Shropshire Lad* had been not only printed and bound, but distributed as well to the bookshops, the literary magazines and of course the impatient author, who professed to find its outward appearance "so extraordinarily beautiful that I cannot bear to lose sight of it by opening the book." A small slim volume priced at half a crown, it was in fact physically indistinguishable from the numerous other little books of verse that, like daffodils, graced the spring of 1896; and in a year crowded with new works by Conrad, Stevenson, Kipling, Swinburne and Henry James, it could scarcely have been expected to receive more than perfunctory notice. But in the author's family circle, as Laurence Housman recalled, it did not fail to inflict a stunning surprise upon his incredulous relatives—"Alfred has a heart," one of them blurted out, after sampling a few pages; while Laurence himself "ran around among my friends," spreading a fraternal glow of admiration. The reviews were at first somewhat less enthusiastic, and to a writer's frazzled nerves aggravatingly dilatory, so that in those early post-publication days Housman sat in fidgety suspense awaiting the public verdict, but above all some communication from one whose unliterary approval he so fearfully hoped for.

The first if not the only presentation copy of *A Shropshire Lad* that Housman inscribed to a specific person had gone forward, as fast as the postal facilities would allow, to its destination in Karachi, and was to be suitably preserved, if not closely studied, by its recipient. But the letter in which Jackson groped for words to acknowledge this eloquent gift has untraceably disappeared, though it conveyed a message that Housman, who was in the habit of keeping less valuable mementoes, would not have failed to cherish. Certainly, however, the occasion demanded that scrupulous exercise of discretion in which Jackson was already proficient, and with which he must have once again struck the right note. "My father," as Gerald Jackson has described his attitude in later years, "jokingly always professed to have a contempt for Housman's poems," and probably such was the form of badinage by means of which Jackson turned an evasion that Housman would have noticed into a retort that he could accept. But while it was reassuring that Jackson did not take offence at, or even choose to understand, certain lines applicable only to him, Housman could hardly derive from this playful obtusity much solid comfort. The struggle to articulate his feelings had brought him, on the contrary, nothing but a sense of deeper estrangement, of inveterate anti-climax, and in effect, as he now began to discover, the success of his poetry would merely serve to emphasize the paucity of his life.

On March 27, 1896, *The Times* had mentioned, briefly though promptly, a new poet whose "gift of melodious expression is genuine"; but Housman had to wait until the middle of April for more stirring words of praise. Among the several reviews which then or later commended his work in fairly lavish terms, he preferred at the time and still remembered a few weeks before his death the notice that appeared anonymously, on April 16, in a penny weekly called *The New Age*, whose radical tendencies Housman for the moment contrived to ignore. The perceptive reviewer, moreover, was less a man of letters than a member of the Fabian Society, Hubert Bland, who applied most of his energies to political reform and social criticism. He was the first, nevertheless, to recognize Housman's "heart-penetrating quality," his "individual voice," and what may have impressed the author just as much, those "narrow limits" which prevented his art from reaching the highest level, "though it comes astonishingly near." The ability thus to measure against classic standards the latest artifact was a method of appraisal that Housman valued even in relation to his own poetry, and without which more extravagant plaudits could neither flatter his vanity nor seduce his judgment. "It would be difficult," Richard Le Gallienne warmly testified in the *Star*, "to over-praise the exquisite simplicity . . . the various charms"; but the *Academy* in its turn surmounted this difficulty, on July 26, by saying that "Life, love and death make for [Mr. Housman] a trinity to be sung sweetly, purely and reverently." Such florid eulogies were calculated not only to dishearten the author but still more to repel the reader; and in fact, after the suffocating embraces of the literary press, Housman's little book sank close to oblivion, while a grim silence descended upon his prostrate muse.

These embarrassments could not of course long deter a writer already self-supporting and contemptuous of popular opinion; but they did, in Housman's case, help to reinforce the impression gained from Jackson's defensive jocularity, that one confided one's innermost self to literature at the risk of being gently ridiculed or grossly travestied. The amount of nervous tension that his poetry involved must have seemed hardly to justify, in the summer of 1896, results so disproportionate; and caring less for a bubble reputation than for peace of mind, Housman was not eager to undergo soon again the ordeal from which he had just emerged. Having involuntarily achieved, moreover, the remedial effects of transferring an exacerbation from his subconsciousness to the realm of art, Housman had lost that vital incentive without which, as he believed, "poetry was impossible." For it was not mere literary ambition but some obscure necessity which had gushed forth, a year ago, and over which the mechanism of his personality now reasserted its iron grip. Like a belated fling, Housman's poetic phase had represented in his middle age a kind of spiritual adventure and a challenge to resignation, but which left him with the sour after-taste of a futile escapade. Romantically impelled to seek in poetry a medium of unconstrained human intercourse and a substitute for the tangibilities of friendship, he was all the more disposed to feel, in the wake of Jackson's letter and the panegyrics of journalism, that it had failed to accomplish this incidental purpose; so that, with an equally romantic disillusionment, he plunged back into the makeshift occupation of a man who had no further hope of restoring his emotional life.

The alternative to which Housman determined henceforth to apply himself unreservedly was, of course, the intellectual discipline of Latin scholarship—a vocation that he had followed ever since boyhood with steady diligence and a natural aptitude, but which for several years, unlike those of comparable rank in his profession, he had subordinated to a more consuming interest. If his work had not suffered, neither had it profited from this irrelevant interlude (during which his contributions to philology were negligible); and in reverting to the pursuit of knowledge Housman chose not only to make it his rigorous primary objective, but to curtail and confine, as far as possible, those wasteful impulses which had surreptitiously debouched into his poetry. A man who, at thirty-seven, retained the physical slenderness, the nimble gait and the grave silent manner of his youth, he had also kept those ascetically studious habits which enabled him, in periods of stress, to concentrate his whole mind upon some remote abstraction. Classical learning had always been the material for this Yogi exercise, the bed of nails on which Housman sank into a forgetful and unfeeling trance; but it could not provide, especially at the peak of his maturity, the forms of experience that might have brought him less inadequate nourishment. Solitary, ratiocinative and austere, it was a calling designed to sharpen the traits and tendencies which Housman's early life had already implanted; and in fact his character would soon begin to display those ineradicable quirks which accompany the first wrinkles of middle age, though at the same time, with a sudden mellowness, he apppeared to invite more cordial relations with his immediate family.

Since the death of his father, Housman had neglected none of the responsibilities that fell upon him as the eldest son—in particular the supervision of his step-mother's affairs, which he was largely to assume for the rest of her life. Dutifully writing to, and often visiting, this aged dependent woman whose faithful services he could now undertake to repay, Housman showed himself in the unfamiliar light of an always patient and considerate benefactor. If not all his charities were recorded, certainly no urgent need presented itself to which he failed to respond; and if his manner remained somewhat forbidding even to his brothers and sisters, they could have no doubt of his unspoken loyalty. Among Edward's seven offspring, six were permanently childless and five of those unmarried, while all but three lived at a distance from each other and none was then equipped with more than sufficient means. Lacking, besides, the homestead that Perry Hall used to provide, they were still further separated by the discrepancies that were bound to arise between a medical inspector, a headmaster's wife, an infantry sergeant and a professor of Latin; so that reunions did not easily arrange themselves, and intercommunication was rather haphazard. But with Basil and his wife, who continued to dwell in the neighbourhood of Bromsgrove, Housman had very affable though infrequent encounters, at which he seemed to "enjoy amusing others with his clever nonsense"; and in the household of Mrs. Symons, who was already surrounded not only by her own four sons but the raucous population of King Edward's School at Bath, he found an equal avuncular pleasure during his intervals of holiday. Apparently Housman preferred, or was more at home with, those who led ordinary domesticated lives and who possessed the simple advantages which he so keenly missed; but even the most informal and heart-warming company did not strip away the subsurface layers of his reserve.

In spite of their accessibility in Marloes Road, where Clemence and Laurence Housman had maintained since the eighties a London residence filled with literary atmosphere, "we were," as Laurence has admitted, "the embarrassed ones" who could neither put their brother at his ease nor themselves overlook his fits of surly aversion; and with these relatives who for so long shared both the same city and many of the same interests, Housman kept in touch chiefly by correspondence, following their work with polite attention but firmly avoiding their society. Laurence Housman had ventured to publish, close on the heels of *A Shropshire Lad*, the book of poems about which his brother had already written several admonitory letters; and not to be outdone, Clemence Housman had also broken into print, late in the autumn of 1896, with a baleful Gothic

novelette called *The Were-Wolf*. Embellished with illustrations
by Laurence, who was still wavering between art and literature, these rival volumes served to gather around the name
of Housman a confusion of talents which the public could
not be expected to disentangle; and in fact, as Laurence grew
more productive, the chances of mistaken identity multiplied.
"I would far, far rather," Housman unkindly remarked at
the end of 1896, "that my verses should be attributed to you
than yours to me," but all too often, in subsequent years, he
was affronted by compliments that belonged to the rightful
author of *Gods and their Makers*, *Spikenard* and *Victoria Regina*.

If a brother and sister could not divert Housman from the
sombre meditations of scholarship, the hostesses who collect
promising writers had no hope of success, and in any case
would not have cared to repeat their invitations to one so
incorrigibly monosyllabic. The knack he had once shown for
parlour games and nonsense rhymes was now hidden from all
but a select circle, while among strangers he had developed
that "temperamental disinclination to talk for the sake of talking" which rendered his presence at the dinner table or in the
drawing room an awkward social problem. Yet Housman was
at the same time quite capable of rising to some academic
emergency, as he had done on March 22, 1895, with an impromptu but "joyous speech" that henceforth made him "the
refuge of those who had to organize" such ceremonial entertainment; and on these occasions, before an audience both
learned and attentive, he recaptured the self-assurance with
which he used to mount the platform on Prize Day. But at
Mrs. Meynell's Sunday afternoons, or in the lustier retinue of
W. E. Henley, whose cohorts were just beginning to glorify
the battlefields of the Empire, Housman was invisible if not
unknown—a morose middle-aged scholar whose poems did
not seem to fit any current classification, and who remained
indifferent to the politics of a literary career. Questioning some
initialed review that his brother had ascribed to Mrs. Meynell,
he found the style "neither sufficiently correct nor sufficiently

pretentious," and with this rather jaundiced eye Housman regarded most of the influential people who, in the late nineties, could have helped to advance his reputation.

By the end of 1896, the first edition of *A Shropshire Lad* was largely exhausted, but in view of its dwindling sale, had no prospect of an early reissue. Out of the original 500 copies, according to the publisher's records, fifty-odd were left over, even after a sizable allotment to the American market; and in fact, during the whole of 1897, the demand did not exceed this tiny surplus, while Housman's eventual profit amounted to the bare pittance of £2 5s. 3d. His former misgivings about the profession of literature were amply confirmed, though it was a period in which men of letters enjoyed both exceptional prestige and unprecedented affluence. That dying nineteenth-century world richly supported, in addition to the writers who achieved popular recognition, a host of supernumeraries who contributed to fill the massive shelves of Victorian libraries; but for the present Housman's fame depended upon a few alert and sympathetic readers, the vanguard that aids posterity by discovering, not the unmistakably great talents, but the more elusive small ones. And among this minority, as it luckily turned out, one of the most observant was a young man who was just then venturing, with modest resources but unlimited enthusiasm, to solicit the work of new authors for publication.

The nephew of a Greek scholar who had, years before, joined the Oxford examiners in "ploughing" Housman for Greats, and the son of yet another classical pedagogue who was a Fellow of Trinity College, Grant Richards had inherited none of this family appetite for learning, but on the contrary had cut short his own education, at the tender age of sixteen, to seek employment and more useful knowledge in London. Apprenticed to a company of wholesale booksellers, in the days when child labour was recompensed at the rate of £20 per annum, he had nevertheless quickly mastered the rudiments of business, and was soon acquiring a precocious taste for the amenities of urban life, along with a catholic appreciation of modern literature. Though at first difficult to gratify, these pleasures grew more tantalizing as he progressed from office boy to the editorial staff of the *Pall Mall Gazette*, where the new books and often their authors came within his reach; so that he was already, in his early twenties, not only well-versed in the gossip and manipulations of the literary market-place, but also determined to share those basic luxuries—good food and wine, the refreshment of travel—in which so many writers could then afford to indulge. A youthful connoisseur with the ambition if not yet the means to live discriminatingly, he aspired to cultivate the same epicurean standards in his literary judgment as in his wine-cellar, and thus on January 1, 1897, when the sale of *A Shropshire Lad* was beginning to drop off, he stood poised to "start as a book-publisher," in premises adjacent to the market-stalls of Covent Garden, at 9 Henrietta Street.

It was to this address, after some preliminary correspondence with the poet he coveted for his own list, that Housman was induced to come early in 1898, wearing his usual conservative but not yet unfashionable garb, and "an air of preferring to pass unnoticed through the streets." Perhaps somewhat magnified in his memory, Richards' account of this brief, impersonal interview has remained nonetheless an evocative, first-hand impression, by one who was "very used to scholars and professors," of Housman as he must have appeared, at the age of thirty-nine, to his contemporaries. Though scarcely displeased by the overtures of an eager young champion, Housman's manner was "precise . . . economical of words . . . and rather sombre"—the frosty politeness of a man whose features and conversation are stripped bare of any impulsive flicker or spontaneous irrelevance. He conformed perfectly, in his "short black coat and striped trousers," his "elastic-sided boots," his bowler and umbrella, to the standard academic dress of the period; he discussed, with the proper degree of interest but with a surprising refusal to accept royalties, the matter in hand; he confined himself to the level of a business transaction, and terminated the visit "in a quarter of an hour or less"; he was, in short, the strict late Victorian model of "respectability itself," with an almost conspicuous absence of those intimations which denote some form of poetic temperament. Such an exemplary author, who "would not hear of financial reward," but merely asked that his share of the profits should be applied "to reduce the price of subsequent editions," and who was quite satisfied to proceed without a formal contract, could only strike his publisher as a uniquely valuable acquisition; and if this remote, reticent figure who had incongruously written *A Shropshire Lad* presented certain unfathomable aspects, it was better not to incur his wrath by evincing one's curiosity. On a foundation of mutual benefit, therefore, strengthened by the latent bond which often exists between men of opposite qualities, these two, outwardly so unsuited to each other, began their long and congenial association.

For several years, however, they lingered non-committally on the verge of friendship—a thawing process of gradual acquaintance and epistolary communication during which Grant Richards (a still rather ineligible youth of twenty-six at their first meeting) made rapid strides towards his ideal of urbane worldliness; while Housman himself, in the course of his now unrelieved classical studies, found it necessary to obtain some fresh source of diversion. He had already embarked, sometime near the turn of the century, on that monumental edition of Manilius which signified his total dedication to scholarship, and of which he was preparing to publish at his own expense, in the autumn of 1902, the initial volume. "Before anything is done," he wrote to Richards, "I should be glad if you could let me have an estimate of what the printing etc., is likely to cost, as my resources are not inexhaustible"; and in the same letter, he had ventured to "drop the Mr." in his salutation, thus marking, and encouraging, a slight approach to intimacy in their relations. His publisher had earned this delicate tribute not only by issuing, in 1898 and again in 1900, two further editions of *A Shropshire Lad*, but also by retaining, despite the continued apathy of the public, his unshaken faith in the book. And if Housman was then raptly engaged with the obscurities of textual criticism, he had not lost a special fond regard for his own poetry and those few, like Richards, who persisted in admiring it. But aside from that claim on his favour, the zestful young man about town had other points of attraction to which Housman was becoming less immune. A companionable gourmet, well-stocked with anecdotes of the literary scene, Richards could provide, at lunch or dinner, the kind of entertainment that served to lift Housman out of his workaday rut, yet from which he was glad to retire afterwards into the solitude of Highgate; and with equal gratification, his publisher could take the credit of regaling one who was notoriously difficult to please. Housman's willingness, moreover, to be sociably amused was a measure of the effort he was making, in the shadow of his forties, to dispel or at least to reduce the tedium and austerity of his life.

The transition from an eruptive state of poetic feeling to the sober intellectual plane of scholarship had left a blank that Housman could not easily fill, and imposed a discipline that must have seemed, at the height of his maturity, more stringent than ever before. The classroom and the study absorbed his energies but no longer satisfied all his attainable desires. For having once known that violent but cathartic agitation which produced his poetry, Housman was unable quite so deliberately to content himself with a less intense order of experience, or to push aside the nagging sense of discomfort that afflicts those who have ceased to employ their creative talents; and in the rancour which now crept into his commentaries, as well as in the time allotted to more frivolous pursuits, Housman showed at this period the first effects of losing his only emotional outlet.

What remained to him did not lack certain minor compensations—the studious tranquillity, the pleasures of the palate, and especially the means to travel, of which Housman had promptly availed himself, in the summer of 1897, for a quick tour of the conventional sights "at Paris, Rome and Naples." His impressions were still obediently conveyed to his step-mother, the day after his return, in that dry tone reminiscent of the unexcitable schoolboy: "Notre Dame is hardly equal to WestminsterAbbey . . ." but "London has nothing at all equivalent to the Louvre." Faintly insular and always detached, it was a tone that suited the meticulously correct English gentleman who from now on, during the long vacation, habitually crossed the channel and traversed the continent, directing his attention particularly to its architectural monuments and its best restaurants. Housman had begun to refine his tastes, though in fairly strict accord with the Victorian guide-books, and upon a groundwork already so firm that he went abroad rather to verify his opinions than to enlarge his scope. Briskly inspecting the museums, examining the churches and climbing up the slopes of Vesuvius (whence he brought back a souvenir for his step-mother), Housman travelled widely in his early middle age, over most of what had been the Roman Empire and as far eastward as Constantinople, but with the jaded air of one who expects to find no refreshment. It was, in fact, too late for him to cast off those more than physical ties by which he was bound not only to his past, with its denials and restraints, but also increasingly to his professional grindstone. A few years before, perhaps, he might yet have responded, like so many English poets, to the enchantments of an Italian holiday; but in renouncing poetry for scholarship, Housman had closed himself to such aesthetic temptations, and now merely observed that "when I got into Italy it was very hot, and remained so all the while I was there." The factual, not the spiritual, aspect of things had assumed a dominant place in his consciousness, and he would speak henceforth mainly with that irascible voice which expressed both his superb command of, and his often biting contempt for, the practice of philology.

CHAPTER NINE

Forth I wander, forth I must

IN common with other men, Housman probably felt some twinges of revulsion as he passed his fortieth birthday, and was driven to ask himself what more his flagging energies and still unsatisfied hopes could be made to accomplish. About this time and in such a mood, he must have reached that all but final decision which would pervade and largely govern the rest of his life. Spurred by the ambition of one whose abilities have exceeded his opportunities, as well as by an accelerating sense of time, Housman chose the most expeditious and least fallible way to achieve, with the resources at his disposal, a position of supreme eminence. It was a choice that reflected not only his logical mind, his adamant character and his years of rigid self-discipline, but also his peculiar innate compulsion. For in struggling to overcome the handicap which set him apart from the world and deprived him of its lowlier pleasures, he was all the more fiercely determined to establish his own absolute superiority; and in a branch of learning which had grown more esoteric than philosophy or higher mathematics, he knew that he could best attain the rare sort of leadership that few might covet but certainly none would dispute. Grimly concentrating his already powerful equipment, therefore, upon this ultimate goal (a massive work of conjectural emendation), Housman had only to select the Latin author whose textual problems were numerous and intricate enough, but for a penetrating editor just barely capable of present solution; and since Propertius did not answer to the last of these drastic prerequisites, he was automatically eliminated in favour of a third-rate poet who, in the reign of Tiberius, had combined a large knowledge of ancient astronomy with a small talent for "doing sums in verse," but whose forgotten epic in five books offered an excellent target for the complete arsenal of classical learning. Thus regrettably, Manilius became the subject of that definitive recension which was to occupy Housman for so many years, and that would in the end be memorable not for its literary content but for the quality of its scholarship.

Before Housman was fully committed to this enormous task, *A Shropshire Lad* may have reached its third edition, which Grant Richards had somewhat riskily brought out early in 1900; but though it consisted of 1,000 copies, and so doubled the number already in print, the sales were encouragingly steady if still unimpressive for a book now exactly four years old. His publisher's remarkable tenacity, along with the author's persistent waiver of royalties, helped at this stage to keep alive that spark of public interest which might otherwise have died, as it often does, merely from lack of sustenance; and while Housman was turning his attention to what seemed a more profitable pursuit, his poetry was, in fact, slowly extending its influence among casual but responsive readers in England and America. Many of them were "young people of literary taste and limited means" who, like Edward Shanks, had stumbled on a "little red-covered" volume, temptingly priced at sixpence, that "came in very handy for gift-making," and coincidentally, as it were, began to capture a scattered audience of enthusiastic converts. "I wonder how you manage it," Housman had written in acknowledgment of a quarterly report that confirmed this upward trend; and though refusing either to profit from his poetry or submit to any kind of self-advertisement, he was "more than pleased," as it struck Grant Richards, by such tentative indications of popularity. A few belated reviews, in the *Manchester Guardian* and the *Athenaeum*, had also expressed their approval, but so inconspicuously that even Housman's watchfulness failed to discover one of them; and if, among these auguries, he could find some reassurance that his poetic reputation was not languishing in total neglect, it would have been difficult, nevertheless, to predict just then whether it was destined to rise or fall.

The outbreak of the Boer War, in the autumn of 1899, did not materially affect the circulation of Housman's poetry, or at once impel him, as it did Thomas Hardy, to set down his reactions to that event; though in the following February, Housman did contribute to the *Academy* a topical poem called *Illic Jacet*, dealing ostensibly with the battlefield, but written, according to his own recollection, "before 1899." In spite of himself, however, the note-book was gradually filling up again with those fragments of verse which still escaped from his subconsciousness—evidence not so much of any fresh inspiration as of a renewed pressure that, with diminishing force and at longer intervals, now spilled into variations on the familiar themes. But how slowly and spasmodically the stream flowed was deducible from the number of years Housman required, after 1895, to produce a volume of work equivalent to what he had once accomplished in as many months. Having ceased also to date occasional entries in his note-book, Housman left no further sign-posts by which the chronology of his later poems could be established; and since his own memory was either blank or unsure in these matters, the rough time-table that he afterwards drew up has remained somewhat problematical, though it was clearly subject to more frequent interruptions and lengthier delays. As a poet, in fact, Housman was slipping back to that state of dormancy from which, ten years before, he had begun to awaken; but this time, instead of repressed feeling, it was rather a condition of inertia and impoverishment. For in drawing too heavily upon the vital core of his experience, Housman had depleted his creative strength; while in resorting so much to this inner world, he had rendered himself inaccessible to any less private or merely external stimulus. With all his reserves of energy, moreover, diverted and consecrated to Manilius, only certain symbols evocative of the past could still intermittently revive his poetic impulse.

One of these symbols was personified by the young men who, at the turn of the century, offered their services and too often lost their lives on the dusty plains of South Africa. Giving the harsh stamp of reality to the dim presentiments of his Jubilee poem (written six years before the casualties and reverses of the Boer War had first shaken the self-confidence of the Empire), the hapless recruits of 1900 not only stirred Housman's former sympathies, but sent a tremor into those depths where the roots of his poetry were embedded. As the ornamental peacetime soldiers of London visibly changed into the battle-worthy Lancers and Grenadiers, soon perhaps to die in a foreign land, Housman again succumbed, if only at odd moments, to the complex nostalgia that a military parade still held for him; and thus amidst the noisy patriotism of the home front, he composed several of his finest ballads and elegies in commemoration, not so much of a literal Tommy Atkins or even a brother now engaged in combat, as of some abstract figure who epitomized in his imagination the unfulfilled, cut-off-in-its-prime spirit of youth. Nameless and unidentifiable, this fallen hero was a subject that Housman could invest with the mournful residue of his emotional capacity; and in those death-pangs of the Victorian age, he now and then found an overpowering inducement "to sit me down and weep," not only for "bones in Africa," but for himself.

It has been suggested by Mrs. Symons that such lines had, on the contrary, a "very certain connection" with specific incidents of family history, and that the poem called *Astronomy*, in particular, recorded the death in action of "our brother Herbert." Inheriting both his father's skill as a marksman and his improvident disposition, George Herbert Housman had decamped from medical school, at the age of twenty-one, to enlist in the King's Royal Rifles; and after an obscure knockabout interval of twelve years, was killed at Baakenlaage, not long before the termination of hostilities, in a final burst of reckless gallantry. That Sergeant Housman's career must have served to deepen his eldest brother's sense of involvement and at the end his compassionate feeling was an assumption the textual evidence would easily support; but that a young renegade whose misfortunes were largely self-imposed should have inspired, as Mrs.

Symons chose to believe, "many of the soldiering verses in *A Shropshire Lad* and *Last Poems*," was to credit their author with an excess of fraternal attachment, and unwarrantably to constrict his frame of reference. For the characteristic feature of Housman's poetry was its power of defining emotions peculiar to himself in terms that were just as valid for others—a transmutation that required, not the motherly sentiment that Mrs. Symons attributed to him, but the subtlest intricacies of his art. Which in turn made it equally unsafe to regard his overt subject as necessarily the real one, or to infer his whole meaning from the apparent drift of his words; but in any case the chronological sequence of his poems would have ruled out the theory that, in the almost obsessive recurrence of a theme which had promptly declared itself in his early work, Housman was concerned only with the military adventures of one who had been, during most of his life, a virtual stranger.

The sad news that reached Housman towards the end of 1901 did no doubt strike a spark once again, and quickly generate, under London's wintry sky, those sombre night-thoughts which wreathed a tribute to every anonymous veteran who had spent his courage

> For pay and medals, name and rank,
> Things that he has not found.

But with this lament for the decimating toll of heroism, Housman's poetic mood began to wane, and except for some ironic lines induced by the peace settlement, and published in *The Outlook* in the summer of 1902, his note-book contained nothing else that might be taken as a timely reference or response to the national emergency. Fraught with the nervous qualms yet detached from the physical dangers of war, it had been a season not unfavourable to literary expression—Hardy, Yeats and Kipling, for example, having published important new books while the conflict was in progress; but for Housman it had marked the decline of his talent in what should have been the most fruitful combination of circumstances. Overshadowing for the first time his private melancholy, the course of public events offered him a gamut of congenial subject matter; while in spite of the firmest resolution to stand aloof, he could not be indifferent to the fate of others who were having just then "no luck at all," and whose ordeal so keenly affected him that when some "pro-Boer Professor" disparaged the home-sick hard-pressed army in his presence, "he let his tongue curl around his unfortunate colleague" with a blast of scorching invective. Thus united in spirit with the young men who slept on desolate colonial battlefields, and perhaps also visited by those stabs of remorse which afflict the non-combatant in such a context, Housman was admirably fitted, it would have seemed, to become the valedictorian of an age whose anxious last phase coincided with the highest reach of his own sensibilities. A poet already expert in the technical manipulation of his art, he could have scarcely failed to meet, if his creative impulse had been strong enough, the challenge of this opportunity; and even without a sharper goad, he did eke out five or six brief poems that comprised a modest epitaph for the occasion. But neither intensity of feeling nor vigour of mind availed to release that subconscious mechanism which governed the ebb and flow of his poetry; so that when the historic hour struck, Housman was forced to busy himself, not with a surging Ode upon the Death of Queen Victoria, but with the minute pedestrian study of Manilius.

The second note-book which had been launched so pre-cipitately, seven years before, was completed at last in the spring of 1902—an accumulation totalling more than two hundred pages, of which about half contained material written after the appearance of *A Shropshire Lad*; but whether Hous-man paused to review this laggard if still not insubstantial achievement, he made no effort, in the midst of more pressing editorial tasks, to assemble a new collection of his verse. In-quiries on that score had already drawn a negative or at least discouraging reply: "I am afraid," Housman had informed his publisher on March 30, 1900, "there is no chance . . . yet awhile"; and though his back-log was now ample enough to have yielded a respectable second volume, other exigencies and a rival pursuit had intervened. The manuscript of the first Book of Manilius (faultlessly executed in longhand) was by this time reaching the final stage, and must have been Housman's chief concern during the festivities of that Coronation summer; for in October he despatched the "text and notes," along with the customary typographical injunctions, to a somewhat embarrassed Grant Richards, who could neither welcome nor reject this unpalatable offering. Housman was prepared, of course, to defray the full cost of production, which amounted in the end to £83 9s. and which entitled him closely to supervise every detail, from a matter of format to the usage of a semi-colon, so that the meticulous operation prolonged itself until the following June. Thus again at his own expense but with even less hope of reimbursement, a work to which Housman had applied immense knowledge, prodigious industry and masterly skill was delivered to an audience restricted in this case not only to literary circles but to that infinitesimal subdivision which alone could penetrate the arcana of his scholarship. The fretful author hastened, nevertheless, to engage the services of a press-cutting bureau, and was impatient to obtain "one of the morocco-bound copies" which had been ordered in advance for "the friend to whom the book is dedicated"; after which he entrained for the Continent to refresh himself with libations of a precious "red Hermitage" whose whereabouts in Paris he did not betray until the cache had been reduced to a few half-bottles.

The dedicatory poem, couched in Latin elegiacs, with which Housman adorned the first volume of his *Manilius* had been originally committed to his note-book at some unspecified date, but certainly before 1900; so that it must have reflected the glow of aspiration ("tactus uirtutis amore") in which he was then embarking upon a vast project that would serve as yet another wistful tribute of friendship. Openly addressed to "my comrade—M. J. Jackson," though in a language that

M   177

might elude his grasp, the twenty-eight close-packed lines recalled those nocturnal colloquies at Oxford, over which the stars had shed their brightness as they had once promisingly glittered for Manilius; and drawing ominous deductions from the example of a poet who had so narrowly escaped oblivion, Housman went on more confidently to invoke, not the immortal gods or a heedless providence, but the magic name in company with which his work was surely fated to live ("nomine sed certe vivere digna tuo"). By this graceful if transparent device which implied the opposite of what it said, Housman allowed himself to confess the hope that his own efforts would, in fact, glorify the object of his affection; and though Jackson no longer had a vital part in Housman's existence, least of all in the scholar's ambitious enterprise, it was plain that he continued unchangeably to represent a kind of mythical figure whose allurement seemed only to gather strength from so many years of separation.

The true-to-life Principal of Sind College was by this time a rather less ideal version of the young athlete who lurked in Housman's memory; erect but a little ponderous, with handlebar moustache and grizzled side-whiskers, the once casually triumphant undergraduate for whom no hurdles were insurmountable had become the stubbornly unsubmissive gentleman of middle age, bracing himself to meet not only the camera's eye but those antagonistic forces which had already made their presence felt in the trend of his affairs. Resigned to a position that afforded not much scope for new conquests yet demanded a sedulous care for the advancement of others, Jackson was further entangled by the responsibilities of a paterfamilias to whom the last of four sons had been presented in 1900; and under the weight of these burdens, to which the travail of exile in a climate so insalubrious for the Nordic constitution gave an extra rigour, he, too, was beginning more fondly to recall the past, as well as to share some of Housman's despondency about the future. But if nostalgia served to keep their old friendship alive, distance helped to prevent it from

M. J. Jackson

recovering the tone of unforced intimacy; and when Jackson did infrequently revisit his native land, at intervals of five years or more, their encounters were confined to those brief holidays, snatched from their normal pursuits, during which the most dignified of men incongruously revert to their antic youth. One such occasion, as Pollard remembered it, was enlivened by that rudimentary practical joke—the apple-pie bed—of which "I think the Professor of Latin was a fellow victim, though I'm not quite sure that he wasn't an aggressor"; but however exuberant these reunions may have been, they were calculated rather to bring back the vernal atmosphere of student days than to promote any further stage of mutual understanding.

This confirmed attachment to a person now so far removed and outwardly so different from the quondam Oxford blue was, on Housman's part, not only the aura cast by retrospect but a means of preserving some vestigial note of romance in his exiguous emotional life. That Jackson had failed, along with the majority of young men, to consummate his early promise was an observation which Housman had already, on the poetic level, shown himself to be quite capable of making; and if the contents of *A Shropshire Lad* alluded under many disguises to that once "golden friend," they had equally implied a sense of invariable disillusionment. But lacking the day-to-day proximity to Jackson that would have brought him into closer view and sharper focus, Housman could only cling to an image that, as with each meeting it grew noticeably more inappropriate, acquired nevertheless a certain fresh poignancy from these intermittent confrontations; while Jackson, too, fell unconsciously into the habit of assuming in Housman's company the buoyant manner of his better days.

The wrench of parting did not, after such cursory renewals, any longer induce that nervous agitation which used to disturb Housman's walks, but now instead merely rippled the surface of those memories out of which his poetry had once been goaded to emerge. The comings and goings, at intervals so widely spaced and across gaps so impossible to fill, of a rather

179

portly colonial schoolmaster, encumbered by his attendant family, alien background and other hindrances to easy intercourse, could not have much more than a sedative effect on the imagination of one who was hoarding the remnants of twenty years ago; yet if only it had been more continuous, Jackson's physical presence might have broken the spell which, by almost unbridgeable exile, he still inadvertently retained the power to cast over Housman's life. But with its roots fastened to his character like barnacles, the spell had outlasted its potency, and was now perversely sustained by his determination not only to repel the encroachment of some alternative experience, but to draw from the bitter dregs of his past an irrefutable lesson; one to which, moreover, the course of events had recently given yet further support and heavier emphasis.

Aside from the obloquy that invested the name of Oscar Wilde (to whom, after his release from Reading gaol, Housman had been moved to send a complimentary copy of *A Shropshire Lad*, from which the ex-inmate soon took a leaf), other spasms of literary censorship and moral coercion had punctuated the silence over Hampstead: a twice-imposed prison term, with additional fines, for Zola's impenitent English publisher, followed by the all but forcible suppression of Hardy's later novels, and in 1898 by the abortive though severely admonitory trial of the scapegoat Secretary of the Legitimation League, for "having unlawfully and wickedly published and sold, and caused to be procured and to be sold, a wicked, bawdy, and scandalous, and obscene book called *Studies in the Psychology of Sex*, Vol. I, Sexual Inversion." A work then barely known to the laity, and designed as the corner-stone of an elaborate scientific treatise, it became the convenient pretext for a legal assault, not upon the practice but the mere clinical discussion of what the courts, along with the arbiters of Victorian society, held to be unspeakably "evil ways." The author was himself a young doctor with no personal involvement, or even specific data, in his subject, one of those pioneers who are innocently drawn to explore some forbidden territory; and in fact it was only by accident that, embarking on a project of much wider scope, he devoted himself first to this invidious marginalia. For at the suggestion of a "critic and historian" who had already "printed privately two small books dealing with the matter," and who could not only provide valuable documentary evidence but also lend a name "of recognized distinction" to the title-page, the adventurous beginner had consented to initiate the *Studies* with such a challenging salvo; and but for that ill-conceived introduction, the whole enterprise might have served a more useful than controversial purpose. As it was, however, John Addington Symonds "died suddenly in Rome" before Volume One could be issued or his name associated with it; and taking alarm at the contents of an earlier German edition, his literary executor hastened to intercept, until all signs of collaboration were removed, the launching in England of that untimely tract on which Havelock Ellis built his fame.

The difficulties that attended its publication must have been a source of lively gossip among literary circles in London; and it was therefore with a natural surprise that, several years later, Grant Richards found himself dining by appointment with Housman, not only in debonair style at the Café Royal, but in the company of Horatio Brown, who had figured, as the behind-the-scenes guardian, in that recent notorious affair. An old and trusty friend of John Addington Symonds, with whom he had travelled and corresponded since 1872, Brown was now one of those learned men of leisure supported either by a college fellowship or independent means, and in his case further enriched by a house in Venice, where he had become a leader of the English colony as well as an expert on Italian art and history. Doubtless in the course of a summer visit Housman had met him there, at some Anglo-Venetian social event or assemblage of scholars, and was merely repaying, at the Café Royal, Brown's previous hospitality; but as the acquaintance had been thus encouraged to ripen, it could be reasonably assumed that Housman was by this time familiar with the surreptitious expurgation, and might even have been allowed to peruse the unobtainable *erotica*, of which Brown had in fact confiscated the entire first printing. But certainly the public outcry and prompt retribution that marked the incident would have lost none of their effect upon a bystander already driven to commiserate with Oscar Wilde and the unfortunate Woolwich cadet—an effect calculated, just then, to narrow the single aperture through which Housman's inner feelings were allowed to peer out, and to invest those feelings with a still muddier reprobation.

Whether Housman did or not lay hands on the dark secrets of Volume One, it could offer him, among its thirty-odd case histories, no exact parallel with his own affliction—an evidently rare type (the self-condemned invert who betrays no sign) of a disorder that in all its forms was estimated to beset "slightly over two per cent" of the population; while the access of knowledge and easement of conscience that it might have brought him at an earlier age had come, in his maturity, as the needless probing of an old wound. Like so many campaigns of reform, the *Studies in the Psychology of Sex* had merely drawn attention to, without suggesting a remedy for, the victims of a current social prudishness; and indeed the victims themselves were made to suffer more keenly because of that wishful propaganda on their behalf. But least of all for the clandestine minority to which Housman belonged was it possible, by compiling facts or advocating tolerance, to speed the millennium. What had been a pious Victorian conspiracy of suppression and silence became, in the nineties, a wavecrest of unholy moral vigilance, under which the pangs of illicit love must have been tormentingly accentuated. It was, for Housman as well, a decade that not only invited but amplified that sense of ominous predestination, of "injustice done," to which he had already so often adapted himself and so instinctively given expression in his poetry. Thus once again, without engaging but rather as if in retreat from a superior force, he drew back, this time irrevocably, into a fastness which no one else could enter and henceforth nothing could disturb.

Housman stood, then, at the point where natural ability combines with sustained effort to yield, in middle life, the best results; and certainly in terms of professional distinction upheld by the solid achievements of a notable scholarship, he had reached all but the highest eminence. His edition of Juvenal, interrupting for a few years the laborious preliminaries to the second volume of Manilius, came out in 1905; his contributions ranging from a note on Sidonius Apollinaris to remarks about Virgil and Calpurnius, invigorated almost every issue of the *Classical Review*; while at University College he continued not only to drill his classes but, whenever duty called, to attend dinners or conferences and obligingly to perform the most uncongenial tasks. On five or six occasions, in spite of the "awful job" such pronouncements entailed for him, Housman was induced to read, before the College Literary Society, papers on the Victorian poets—Tennyson, Matthew Arnold, Swinburne—and more whimsical subjects like Erasmus Darwin and the Spasmodic School; but though entertainingly pungent, they did not conform to that infallible standard which he demanded of himself, and were expressly forbidden to be published even after his death. "Do not tell me," he retorted, "that there is much more vanity than modesty in this, because I know it already." But carrying this neurasthenic distrust of posterity a step further, he defiantly tore up, in the course of delivering it, the text of another speech to which the sponsor was accustomed to lay claim; so that only hearsay evidence has remained of these reckless words and casual judgments which might have helped to soften the austere dignity of his reputation.

Yet in that sanctum of his privacy to which almost nobody was admitted, Housman's sombre disposition had begun a little to mellow under the influence of his rising prestige and growing financial security. Kindlier if not more accessible to his friends and relations, he must have seemed to them, as the Edwardian reign diffused its blandness, a figure comfortably but incurably aloof in his monastic solitude. Still resident in the same lodgings at Highgate, where even his protective landlady sometimes wished for a stray visitor, Housman would less unwillingly emerge, from now on, either to sign the Visitor's Book at Woodchester House (where he spent, at least once a year, long amiable holidays), or to indulge his palate and entertain his guests at the Café Royal. A restaurant that contrived to maintain a Parisian cuisine in the heart of London, and whose clientele gave it the raffish elegance of a picture by Toulouse-Lautrec, this haunt of artists and men about town was to become, rather unexpectedly, Housman's favourite resort. "Will you dine with me at the Café Royal at 7:45" (or "lunch at 1:30"), he wrote repeatedly to Grant Richards, and often to Arthur Platt, Horatio Brown, Laurence Housman, William Rothenstein or to G. H. Vize ("collector of antiquities and china, once champion heavyweight boxer etc."), juggling these names in rotation at the little dinners which he planned with a gustatory discernment that commanded the respect of the "white-haired and priest-like *sommelier*." A sedate and punctilious host presiding at one of the quieter tables in that galleried cosmopolitan rendezvous, Housman made it a substitute for the club he did not belong to, and a vantage-point from which, in brief snatches, he could observe the ways of the world. But if he allowed himself these infrequent costly diversions, he was careful as a rule to practise the small econo_mies of one who had known impoverishment, always buying the cheapest paper-bound editions of the English novelists and thriftily saving up for his annual tour of the continent. So that by this budgetary method he could afford to travel, in the summer of 1904, via the "expensive" Orient Express to Constantinople; a year hence he was roaming through France and Italy; in the spring of 1907 he went to Paris; and once again was "going abroad," in the summer of 1908, "for about a month."

From a life so well-ordered, so much to his personal taste and now so little clouded by uncertainties or disappointments, it was natural to assume that Housman had entered a phase which, if less inviting to the muse of poetry, would at any rate colour and enrich the fruits of his intellectual prime; and in fact he did continue to scale the peaks of scholarship, but with an air of increasing rancour and hostility. "I suppose," the reviewer of his Juvenal had remarked, "it is useless to express a wish that Mr. Housman would cease to speak about veteran scholars of eminence in that fashion"—a scornful, acidulous fashion which more and more gratuitously displayed itself, at every opportunity, in those devastating commentaries with which he raked the field of philology. Housman was, of course, often justified and nearly always right; while in defence of his vituperations, as a colleague has tried sympathetically to argue, "the neglect and misrepresentation of Housman's earlier work by certain scholars, especially in Germany, had been little less than scandalous." The splenetic tone of his classical papers, however, antedated this provocation by several years and was not confined to those who had ignored or disparaged him, but heaped itself indiscriminately upon offenders of all ranks, nationalities and degrees of guilt. Doubtless what Mr. Gow called his "love of truth"—an implacable unyielding element in his work—was at the root of Housman's critical intemperance, but noticeably it gained momentum as his own position grew more immune to revenge; and if, in this period, the product of his invective still lacked its finest edge, he was merely storing up, until he could safely give free rein to, a murderous animosity.

For the pages of his note-book (always the repository of his innermost thoughts) were now frequently diverted to the compilation of waspish epigrams and demolishing phrases—a malevolent catalogue of quips and insults directed at no specific target but kept in readiness for a suitable occasion. In dramatic contrast to the material which surrounded it, this patch of aconite and deadly nightshade betrayed the presence, among those budding rose-beds, of a spirit torn between contrary impulses, and on its reverse side hardly to be described, as his brother sought charitably to do, in terms of "jolly ferocity." Whatever streaks of malice or sadism may have lurked in Housman's character, they did not conspire to produce a "jolly" effect, and his unkindest cuts had at least the merit of being delivered with a blunt effrontery. "Nature, not content with denying to Mr. X the faculty of thought, has endowed him with the faculty of writing"—such hypothetical blasts, conceived without apparent object or motive, were designed not only to impale their future victims but to relieve some inward grievance; while even upon the doddering heads of septuagenarian poets whom he had once revered, Housman's acrimony sometimes overflowed. The origins of his embitterment lay, coiled and sibilant, beneath the rigour of his self-control; but were not these furtive jibes at a nameless scholar's "versatile incapacity" or at a garrulous Swinburne who "has now said not only all he has to say about everything, but all he has to say about nothing"; were these poison darts not also an extension of the cankerous irascibility which must have animated them?

As a poet of advancing years, who had virtually retired more than a decade ago, Housman was further embarrassed and exasperated by the steady increase of his popularity. Edition after edition of *A Shropshire Lad*, issued in pocket size and at ever-diminishing prices, had both enlarged its circle of readers and in their wake brought a constant solicitation from composers, anthologists or those who merely collect autographs. The ubiquitous little book which threatened to rival the success of *The Rubáiyát* or *Poems of Passion* became, for its author, not only an irksome responsibility but even more a baneful reminder that his poetic reputation was outdistancing his ability to sustain it. Capricious and erratic at best ("Poetry is either easy or impossible," he claimed in self-defence), the muse had lately all but deserted him, just when his audience at home and in America had begun to grow in sympathy as well as in numbers. The young musicians who found their impetus in English folk-song were naturally drawn to the lyric simplicity of his verse; the literary generation that would some day comprise the Georgians was equally attracted to a poet so devoid of the tendentious Victorian manner; and in fact, between the nineties and the outbreak of the Great War, Housman's voice conveyed, by historical accident but with a delicate precision, that note of lingering yet apprehensive quietude which marked the turn of the century. Thus rendered famous in spite of himself, but without present means to support the role, Housman could have barely escaped, on his now fruitless afternoon walks, the pangs of one who has lost his creative faculty.

But if, wishfully or unconsciously, Housman nursed the desire to resume a more active part in the world of letters, and if, in dealing with literary business, he conducted himself with all the touchy egoism of a professional writer ("I have just noticed a trifling misprint," he cautioned Grant Richards in the summer of 1907 and less gently, a fortnight later, "Pray who gave Mr. E. Thomas leave to print two of my inspired lays"), he was at the same time drifting further away from a sense of identification with the contemporary scene—its works of art, above all. The taste formed by Perry Hall (exquisite though it was in some areas) had remained aesthetically so dormant that neither the galleries in Venice where "the painter best represented is that lurid and theatrical Tintoret, whom I avoid" nor a private view of the Lane collection could raise its level; while correspondence with and favours granted to Vaughan Williams, John Ireland and Charles Butterworth, among the composers who applied their talents to his poetry, only provoked the remark that "I never hear the music, so I do not suffer." Even Housman's reading, apart from what duty prescribed, showed a frivolous and haphazard inclination to be entertained by current literature, but to neglect its more valuable properties—the poetry of Yeats, for example. Liberally supplied with new books from his publisher's list, Housman was guided and perhaps too much influenced by that arbitrary selection; though he did at times register a strong personal bias. The novels of John Galsworthy, in particular, had some infectious pollen to which he was acutely susceptible and could not be exposed without violent emissions ("How not to write" and "You liar!") flung into the margins of his

paper-bound copies. But as if normally affected by total indifference to his surroundings, he preserved in his daily affairs
a look of such remote detachment that, on his moving from
Highgate to the suburban outpost of Pinner, it was said, falsely
but credibly, that some loquacious passenger had accosted him
in the "train to Gower Street," thereby rendering that means of
transport forever unsafe.

At Pinner where he lived for six years, under the care of that
same invaluable landlady whose domestic accomplishments had
in fact enticed him to follow her from Highgate to 1, Yar-
borough Villas, he withdrew into a still deeper cranny of retirement and seclusion. If the laurels were now all metaphorically
"cut," they flourished here, nonetheless, in the shrubberies
and hedges that coiled like green boas around the solid Victorian architecture; while a hush of impeccability pervaded these
rural fringes of the great city, in which Housman was doubly
insured against the curiosity of his neighbours. A setting whose
nocturnal dullness invited thoughts of violence, it drove
Housman, like so many of its residents, to the refuge of
detective fiction; and his relish for this new intellectual game,
over which the Master of Baker Street himself was then
presiding, may have been the chief boon that life in Pinner
bestowed. But even the art of imaginary homicide had in those
days an appeal divorced from psychological or political
realities; and for Housman as for other addicts it supplied
not only a sedentary pastime but a vicarious primordial throb
in what seemed the almost oppressive security of the nineteen
hundreds.

Few were granted the privilege, and none has recorded the
experience, of visiting the recluse at Pinner, where conditions
favoured that mordant aloofness by which Housman incarcer-
ated himself as firmly as all strangers were excluded. Thicken-
ing around him and accompanied in middle age by an overt
dislike of women (except those few with whom he was already
acquainted), it might have been attributed simply to his monastic habits and impenetrable reserve. But though comparatively

detached and remote, his life involved participation enough, on
some levels, to have rubbed off these anti-social tendencies.
Not only as a professor accustomed to wield authority in the
class-room and the faculty meeting, but as a poet steadily pursued, if seldom captured, by his admirers, Housman contrived
to hold, in the midst of solitude, a considerable intercourse with
the world; and would even at times voluntarily undergo some
trial beyond the call of duty. The after-dinner speech was one
of those challenging tasks which he pretended to evade but did
not often refuse; and from the elocutionary skill he so grudgingly acquired, it could be surmised that his loneliness as well
as his vanity enjoyed a brief triumph in these performances.
As the dominant yet deprecating figure who occupies the platform or the Chair, Housman must have appeared to his best
advantage; whereas in less formal converse, but especially
among the sex with whom it is more difficult to remain impersonal, he preferred to wrap himself in that sullen cloak of
silence which now forbiddingly enveloped him and could no
longer be removed at will.

Towards young men if towards no other category of intruders Housman was apt to display a certain lenience that was,
for him, almost welcoming, but which recoiled with a snap
unless the circumstances proved to be, as they seldom were,
exceptionally propitious. Such an abortive episode of dire
misunderstanding was reported, from the young man's point
of view, by Richard Middleton, who had never met but was
eagerly awaiting, on a sunlit November day in 1910, "the
author of that book of poems which I have admired so long."
Then a somewhat florid specimen of Bohemian manners, with
a "huge felt hat" and "an enormous black beard," Middleton
was the sort of apparition calculated to alarm Housman at first
sight and, in the still more opprobrious company of Frank
Harris, to endanger this impromptu luncheon which had been
conceived, by men who were adept in doing rather blatantly
what they pleased, as a simple device both to pay their respects
and to gratify their curiosity. That Housman had accepted on

the spur of the moment such a reckless invitation seemed a not unpromising sign; but as it turned out, the result surpassed the worst that might have been predicted:

It is perhaps foolish to expect men of talent to be either very handsome or very ugly, but I confess that I was disappointed with my first impression of the poet. He looked elderly and insignificant and suggested in some subtle way an undertaker's mute, the kind of man who wears black kid-gloves too long in the fingers, and generally has a cold in the head. I thought, however, that his eyes might be rather fine in repose, but the whole body and speech of the man were twittering with nervousness, and he affected me like an actor in a cinematograph picture. All Nature is the friend of the shy man, and behind this superficial unease we divined qualities of enthusiasm and amiability that would no doubt be patent when this overwhelming timidity had passed away.

Looking back, it seems to me that we all worked rather hard to set the man at his ease and find him worthy of his own work. We told him stories, we found mutual friends, we encouraged him to talk, we sympathized with him over his luckless environment, and when called upon we praised and quoted his poetry without stint; but still he fluttered like a bird caught in a snare. He took his food without enjoyment, the sunny wine of France did not warm him a degree. We piped to him his own tunes, all the tunes of the world, and yet he would not dance. It was not that he was embarrassed by our compliments; he took them for his due, as a poet should. But he seemed to think that our enthusiasm must have a sinister motive, that it was impossible that any one should have discrimination enough to wish to meet the author of his book for the book's sake. Nevertheless, being optimists in matters of art, our faith in the man held true; if only we could persuade him to drop the mask of his nervousness we thought——

At the end of lunch we succeeded, and then I think we were all sorry. He stood there leaning gently against the table, while soured vanity spoke with a stammering tongue. It seemed that our little luncheon-party was a conspiracy to persuade him to publish some of his poems in the editor's paper, and therefore he found it necessary to be rude. Had his suspicions been true, a more modest man might have thought such a plot pardonable, or even rather flattering. But the terms in which our poet expressed himself placed him beyond argument or sympathy. We shook hands and said good-bye, and he went away out of our world of sunshine.

On Housman's side, the fiasco was barely mentioned once to Grant Richards, who perceived that "he did not care to talk of it" again; and thereafter its effects, so much more wounding for Housman than for his interlocutors, were automatically secreted within himself—one further accession to that store of rancid memories. An awkward scene that could have been turned, with a lighter touch, into harmless comedy, it had persisted in becoming one of those occasions-that-go-wrong, trivial in themselves, which end in something never to be rectified or undone; and in fact, not only for Housman but for Middleton, who was destined a few years later to commit suicide, its shadow extended beyond the limits of that single unhappy encounter. As if caught in a travesty of themselves, both were compelled to act out, in deadly earnest and regardless of the consequences, a vicious misrepresentation; while for Housman besides, this deplorable tantrum flashed a warning of some internal strain which had begun to corrode his temper, a morbidity unnoticed or disregarded by his friends, but which did once again vent itself, to the dismay of another innocent trespasser, with the same "curl of lip and look crowded with venom." Under the threat of these bilious attacks, moreover, Housman grew from now on more disposed to repel the homage that so many would have tendered him.

Soon after the "little luncheon-party," of which Frank Harris must have been quick to circulate a derisive anecdote among his cronies, the scholar's hopes were opportunely renewed by the death, in December 1910, of the incumbent Kennedy Professor of Latin at Cambridge. This empty chair with its lustre and dignity now presented, from the crepuscular purlieus of Gower Street, a temptation that lacked only the ultimate charm, for a prodigal son, of its Oxford equivalent; and though alleging his reluctance to stand, Housman did not reject the suggestion when it came, but launched his campaign with that deceptive and elaborate strategy which precedes the battle for such a coveted academic post. "His election was not inevitable," Mr. Gow has recalled; and Grant Richards heard from his uncle that "He's the man for the place, of course, but he's been too rude to the men he didn't like." That within a month, nevertheless, the palm of victory did fall to Housman was both a tribute conferred upon his merits and a prize wrested from his enemies; but as they congratulated him, no doubt the losers were already girding themselves for the Jovian thunderbolts to come. In temporary magnanimity, however, the winner bade farewell to University College by delivering one of his brightest after-dinner speeches and neatest epigrams. Glass in hand he remarked that "Cambridge has seen Wordsworth drunk, and Porson sober. Now I am a greater scholar than Wordsworth, and a greater poet than Porson; so I fall betwixt and between" —a position that he dramatized, one likes to think, by a playful stagger.

With less modest satisfaction Housman might have reviewed, at this close of another chapter, the progress that linked the outcast Oxonian who had arrived at Paddington twenty-eight years before with the eminent man of learning now so sweetly avenged by Cambridge; and if, in a harsh light, he could sometimes look "elderly and insignificant," his features might also reflect, with the mercurial transitions of middle age, a distinguished meditative gravity. Averse to sittings and plainly one of those refractory subjects unable to strike a natural pose before the easel or the camera, Housman could not yet altogether conceal, from the quick insights of photography, that weary sadness which accompanied, in the early months of 1911, the proud flush of success. It was an elusive glance that, in spite of the down-curled moustache and clamped jaw, betrayed something more akin to the regretful poet than to the choleric pedant; a face of which the set mouth and inflexible chin were defiantly at odds with the sombre introspective eyes. But these lurking traces of a gentle melancholy did not interfere with his energetic preparations for removal to Trinity College (at which, as the delectable plum on his cake, he had been granted a fellowship); and in fact, during his final months at Pinner, Housman superimposed upon his regular schedule not only the intrepid labour of completing the Second Book of Manilius, but the painful task of composing a new Inaugural Lecture, which he delivered well in advance, on May 9, to a solemnly gowned and ceremonious assemblage in the Senate House. Before and after that harrowing but triumphant ordeal, he made room for two short recuperative trips to Paris along with a Bank Holiday week-end in Woodchester; maintaining through it all an imperturbable nonchalance that, in response to queries, would admit to be "mostly satisfied" by the prospect of joining the "Wine and the Garden Committees." Thus on the far side of fifty and crowned with the laurels of scholarship, Housman was approaching what should be not merely a relative contentment but a sunset oasis—the goal for which he had been so long and relentlessly striving.

CHAPTER TEN

We now to peace and darkness

In the group of "younger scholars" to which Andrew Gow belonged at Cambridge, Housman's literary gift served to enhance his philological reputation, and he was a sort of dual celebrity whose advent they regarded with "general delight." But in other circles, too, and even on some levels of under-graduate society he commanded, as the author of *A Shropshire Lad*, more than the respectful attention that would have greeted the Kennedy Professor of Latin—a curiosity whetted by the severe pedantic tone of the Inaugural Lecture and now focused, in the autumn of 1911, upon this notable if rather colourless recruit who was forbiddingly "slow to overcome an initial mis-trust of our intentions." Not unfamiliar with many of the high tables and common rooms where he had been, during recent years, an occasional visitor, Housman found himself among either old acquaintances or potential friends who combined to make him welcome; while in addition to the grace of its bridges and buildings, the ritual and serenity of its life (infused with so much adolescent vigour), the University offered him the boon of a spiritual birthplace which had accumulated no ineradicable memories.

The palatial Renaissance courtyards and spell-bound Gothic vistas must have seemed to reflect, in those last pre-war days, an outer world not conspicuously more turbulent, but only less perfect. The not-yet-doomed generation of 1914 was drifting innocently along the peaceful Cam, or striving to grasp the fruits of irrelevant knowledge; and in their book-lined rooms the Fellows and Tutors, men whose learning ranged through all the arts and sciences, were diligently if helplessly at work. It was just then a galaxy of scintillating minds—Whitehead, Bertrand Russell, Lowes Dickinson, G. E. Moore—which, in spite of the havoc that was about to descend, left their imprint upon the survivors; a school from which equally brilliant disciples—E. M. Forster, Lytton Strachey, J. M. Keynes and the future arbiters of Bloomsbury—drew their inspiration. But the crannies of an edifice so ancient housed also the dusty rubble of its long history: an effluvium so pervasive that, in the summer of 1911, one of the newer dons felt obliged to discard the illusion that "people here lived in an intellectual atmosphere. They do not—they live in affairs and gossip." At Trinity the atmosphere was more serious, though not perhaps less opaque, under the influence of an aged Master who stoutly "maintained that Thackeray [an alumnus of 1833] had no conception of the best type of English gentleman" and who still "expressed unqualified horror" at the contents of *Vanity Fair*. Beyond the majestic college gateway, nevertheless, Housman entered a scene both architecturally resplendent and humanly rich in the idiosyncrasies of a semi-monastic, time-encrusted institution.

The biggest and wealthiest of the colleges, extending spaciously round a cobblestone square that might have served by itself as the nucleus of a Tudor village, Trinity had overflowed even this manorial domain, during the nineteenth century, into a sort of Victorian tenement wedged between two narrow arteries of traffic; and here, whether by choice or assignment but in any case without objection, Housman established himself in the dark honeycomb of Whewell's Court. "Up two flights" of staircase K, his quarters overlooked on one side the busy intersection of Sinclair Street and Jesus Lane, and on the other a shadowy enclosure adorned by the seated bronze figure of a Grecian youth whose naked form was at certain hours touched by sunlight. Few locations in Cambridge and none at Trinity could have taken less advantage of the amenities that everywhere presented themselves; and of course within his own four walls Housman did nothing to improve the appearance of a dismally uninviting apartment. Though convenient to his lecture room and dining hall, it was an abode that possessed no attraction other than bookshelves and solitude. For he had been quick to discourage, by his withering unsociability, all but the most persistent overtures, and to throw up that prickly "barrier of reserve" across which not many dared to stretch a hand. "Seldom visiting and seldom visited," Housman was in fact resuming, amidst the muffled shouts and bangs of a college dormitory, the pattern of his life at Highgate and Pinner—a cenobite's retirement broken only, as in London, by the diversions of an epicure; and it was at these ritual banquets of the Family, an oddly misnamed club of congenital bachelors who assembled twice a month religiously to invoke the blessings of the domestic kitchen, that he would sometimes "pour out" not merely "anecdote and reminiscence with a felicity and economy of language which made him an admirable raconteur," but also "silvery bursts of laughter."

If these convivial gatherings had to some extent replaced the fastidious little dinner parties at the Café Royal, his nightly presence at the crowded high table of his college did not, as his landlady had fondly hoped it might, draw him out of that monosyllabic detachment which his once-rebuffed colleagues had soon learned to accept, but which unwary guests tried to breach at their peril. "Knowing my brother Laurence," he replied to one of these conversational gambits, "is no introduction to *me*"; and though he was beginning to select, among the resident Fellows, two or three favourites, Housman seldom adjourned to that upstairs common room, hung with the portraits of Trinity's pantheon, where the traditional port might have loosened his tongue. Crotchetiness was the academic prerogative of which Housman freely availed himself, and whose exhibition may have seemed less flagrant in such a hotbed of eccentricity, but whose practice now all the more insidiously gripped his character because he was never made to suffer the social penalty for his churlish manners. The refusal to salute, in the gregarious streets of Cambridge, some familiar passer-by was one of those discourtesies which no one resented or challenged, while even through a jostle of University faces Housman continued to march as impersonally as in the traffic of London, glassy-eyed but always noting with scientific exactitude the daily advance of the seasons. "The lilacs," he could authoritatively predict, "usually come into bloom on May 7th,"—a calculation that resulted from the Selbornesque diary he had kept "for twenty years or so from 1887 onward"; but human feelings had been relegated to almost inaccessible depths.

Beyond these long somnambulistic walks which might exceed a distance of several miles, Housman was not strenuously occupied with the cares of his new office; and having already consigned to oblivion the script of his Inaugural Lecture, on the flimsy pretext that he had neglected to verify a reference to one of Shelley's minor poems, he could find nothing seriously to complain of. His Cambridge duties were both "vaguely defined" and, by comparison with the classroom drill he was used to, agreeable to perform. He was required now and then to assist in grading the candidates for medals and scholarships —an examination that he conducted with the harsh scruples of those who have once failed themselves; but he was otherwise at liberty to promote "the advancement of knowledge" according to his own inclinations and "to give lectures" upon whatever lacunae of his subject might engage his attention. Interpreting this mandate with the same conscientious severity that he so unsparingly applied elsewhere, Housman launched at once into a course of lectures on Persius, delivered twice a week in that first Michaelmas term, and he thereafter never missed, except during spells of illness, this regular self-imposed schedule. The attendance at his lectures was not "very numerous," partly because of the fearsome technicalities inherent in his material, and partly because Housman's mode of presentation did not help to ingratiate his audience—"a neat erect figure entering the room punctually at five minutes past the hour and disposing his notes on the desk, an icy silence while some embarrassed late-comer hurried to his place, and then the level impassive voice . . . austere both in matter and in manner." Surrounding himself with an air so grimly professorial and cultivating no further acquaintance with his students, Housman became rapidly more unapproachable at Cambridge than he had been among the eighty-nine dogged but grateful novices of Gower Street who had, on the occasion of his departure, conveyed their sense of "our debt to you" in a testimonial scroll and a silver tankard. Even some of those now best-equipped to profit from his instruction "shrank from the intellectual effort" as well as the inhuman aridity of the experience; though if a remarkably bold or ingenuous undergraduate ventured to call in Whewell's Court, he was received with a kindness precisely measured to outlast the interview but not to encourage its repetition.

As a teacher concerned for so many years in shaping the minds of young men, Housman's outward indifference to their other needs (of which he could be least of all unaware) would have been singular enough; but as a poet who continued nostalgically to cherish the memory of his own youth, attaching a transcendent value to that distraught phase of immaturity, it was an omission that implied something more than the process of growing old. Among the resolute band of his current and former students, there must have been some who might have enlisted his sympathy or won his friendship; but neither at University College nor at Cambridge did Housman allow himself to display, by those gentle pats which he could have so easily bestowed, the faintest personal regard for "all this note-less number"; while at the same time, as we know, his feelings could be warmly provoked by those anonymous soldiers and mythical country lads with whom he had no relations at all. Such a studied avoidance on the one hand, and such emotional susceptibility on the other, did not consort naturally together; and indeed were only explicable on the grounds that he would not risk, in his encounters with possible rivals of or later substitutes for the Jackson brothers, a recurrence of that desire which he had so implacably subdued. It was a corollary of Housman's private struggle against his own impulses that he must punish others by averting himself from the temptation

they embodied; a relentless course of abstention which pro-
hibited all chances of entanglement, and which may have been
reinforced, just then, by the latest news from Karachi.

After his long term of colonial service, rewarded only by the
claustrophobic tedium of exile, Jackson had begun once again
to think of some fresh alternative to the climatically enervating,
psychologically stagnant confines of the Sind College; and perhaps further goaded by the success which had recently overtaken his old friend, he too, before the end of 1911, uprooted
his family and restlessly migrated to the damp northern latitude
of British Columbia. In contrast with the usual homeward-
bound refugee from the Empire, Jackson had preferred to
invest his savings, not in the comforts of an English villa, but
in the hardships of a Canadian farm; and at the age of fifty-
three, it was unlikely that he would muster the energy for yet
another transplantation, or even for many more journeys and
reunions. Certainly the ultimate effects of his choice were not
lost upon Housman, whose sequestered academic life now held
no prospect of that Odyssean culmination of which, hitherto,
he could indulge the patient hope; and suffering this disap-
pointment in the hour of his triumph, he was not only listless
with regret for what-might-have-been, but more prone to withdraw, in his first winter at Cambridge, from the pleasures that
were left to him. However rich in consolations and harmoni-
ously designed for a man of his temperament, the place was
already becoming, as he laconically described it to Grant
Richards, "an asylum in more senses than one"; while at
Aldergrove, in the far-distant hinterland of Vancouver, Jackson applied himself to the robust exercise of his not yet flaccid
muscles.

In a spirit thus overcast by yearnings of which no one would
have suspected the Kennedy Professor, Housman spent the
beginning of his Cambridge period and the last mellow pre-
war years. They were, except for the publication of *Manilius II*,
several holiday trips to the continent and one of his few appearances in literary society, a rather humdrum interval that gained

its precious aroma only in retrospect. Wearing a look of "depression and indifferent health" (probably attributable in part to the ravages of "so many College feasts"), Housman had weakened enough to let himself be lured by Wilfrid Meynell, in the late autumn of 1911, to attend a small week-end party at the country house of Wilfrid Scawen Blunt. Exotically colourful even at the age of seventy-one, this retired diplomat, veteran traveller and still active poet, who presided over a Sussex manor with the flamboyant style of an Arab chieftain, was hardly the sort of host to put Housman at his ease; and especially amid the further embarrassments of a "poetical evening" at which Meynell declaimed, "with a running commentary," the whole sonorous text of *Modern Love*. Cornered but unmoved by this "excellent entertainment" which had been arranged to provoke his emulation, the speechless guest firmly declined to read a medley of his own poems, or to admit the occurrence "of any episode in his life which suggested their gruesome character"; and when the subject was dropped at last, in the face of an author so perverse that he would neither recite nor talk about himself, the stubborn paragon gratefully joined in "telling ghost stories" for the duration of his visit. "Nevertheless," Blunt conditionally reported in his diary, "I like him," though the acquaintance did not renew itself on either side, and Housman was not often again corralled by lion-hunters.

Returning from such timid ventures into the halls of fame, he must have been more thankful to enter that "asylum" of oddities where his own quirks did not stand out, and where a mall circle was becoming inured to the rigours of his conversation. Housman's friends at Cambridge were chosen, like the bottles in his wine-cellar, for their subtle bouquet and rare vintage, but excepting Andrew Gow, none of them had the durable qualities of his favourite Burgundy, or was decanted for daily use. This convenient young tutor who shared his classical knowledge and surpassed his range of aesthetic sensibility offered him, as Housman soon recognized, something more than fluent table-talk; and between them a spontaneous respect, fostered by the Scotsman's patient enterprise, grew eventually into a staunch attachment. Other meetings at the high table also flowered into cordial if less intimate relations with G. T. Lapsley, the correspondent of Henry James and Edith Wharton (whose Paris garden "Monsieur Oozman" himself called one summer day to inspect), and some deeper accord with R. V. Laurence, the Junior Bursar of Trinity; while in heterogeneous company or at the Family's revels, Housman indulged a preference for that local brand of champagne— Arthur Christopher Benson, whose bubbling repartee was "by far the best he had ever known." The son of an archbishop, the prolific author of popular *belles-lettres*, and the most indefatigable diner-out in college society, Benson combined all these hereditary advantages and graceful talents with some devouring neurosis that lurked just under the bland surface of his life, a manic oscillation that swung him from the peaks of rosy optimism to "the desert and the dimness" which threatened at every moment to engulf his exuberant activities. Outwardly so untouched by adversity, he waged a frantic inner struggle, not unlike Housman's, against those waves of desperation which broke at intervals over both of them, and whose invisible shadow may have drawn them together.

But from the published record of Benson's voracious sociability the Kennedy Professor was conspicuous by his absence, and in fact, whenever he could, Housman escaped from Cambridge to Paris or to Venice—the sybaritic haunts where he liked incongruously to cultivate his few solitary amusements. A more and more discriminating gastronome as well as faithful student of architecture, he would map out his itinerary in accordance with these joint objectives; while as an avid pioneer motorist, he was in the habit of renting a car and chauffeur at some convenient headquarters, from which he could proceed with leisurely comfort to explore both the neighbouring monuments and the regional cooking. It was such a methodical tour that, in the spring of 1914, marked Housman's farewell excursion to the soon-to-be-redevastated battleground of France—a southward journey, overhung by the judas trees "in very magnificent bloom," through the dusty towns of Provence, stopping to view the Roman theatres and aqueducts, the medieval fortresses, or to consume "much bouillabaisse." His impressions were crisply summarized ("The Gourmet's Guide on Marseilles," he chided, "is full of blunders") for the benefit of his publisher, who had become, since the death of his step-mother, the chief recipient of Housman's travel notes; but there was by then no one else to whom he might have addressed these lonely observations on food and wine. His unspent reserves of small talk were thus poured into a correspondence of which every scrap was ironically salvaged for posterity; but not surprisingly, in that postal dialogue with Grant Richards, he failed to discuss topics of a more than ephemeral nature, and even when it befell, he did not mention the outbreak of war.

In previous years Housman had been accustomed to stay at Woodchester House during August, but like so many things the Visitor's Book had abruptly terminated in 1914, and his movements that summer were uncharted; though he was back at Trinity in September, whence he patriotically despatched the sum of £100 "to help in equipping three nephews who had joined the Army" and "all the rest of his bank balance" as a contribution to the Chancellor of the Exchequer. Impulsive and unsolicited, these acts of generosity were the financial tokens of that instant feeling with which he had, ever since boyhood, responded to the appeal of military sacrifice and of panoplied young men; but on the poetic levels of his con-sciousness, Housman was not this time spurred to reopen his note-books, despite the presence at Cambridge of "20,000 sol-diers, 500 of them billeted in the building in which I write," and so far as he gave expression to his mood the war years passed from the airy confidence of 1915 ("now is my chance," to see the Riviera, "when the worst classes who infest it are away") to the numb tenacity that preceded the armistice. Pro-gressing into his late fifties as the foundations of his world literally "fled," Housman was no longer able easily to grasp an experience whose magnitude only shattered and stupefied those who were enduring it at first hand. To some extent he lived, or persuaded Grant Richards that he did, "as if there were no war," and with a natural conservation of his waning energies applied himself to that immaculate scholarship which served, in the midst of such a holocaust, to preserve not only his sanity but the values that were being so furiously obliterated. He continued stubbornly to lecture on Horace and Catullus while the battle raged at Vimy and Verdun; he published the third book of Manilius—a fragile tower rising out of the debris—in 1916; he travelled as much as the restrictions imposed by "mines or torpedoes" would permit, making a tour of the cathedral towns when "the War Office does not view with favour my proposed escape to France" in 1917, and once or twice even submitting to be "crowded into a small and ancient cottage" in Cornwall, where he took part affably with the obstreperous Richards household in their games and picnics. But seldom visibly did a revulsion against the carnage that daily mounted not far off break through his phlegmatic composure, and even then without irresistible force; so that, after one of his nephews was killed in Flanders, it was a copy of *Illic Jacet* and not a new poem that Housman inscribed for Mrs. Symons in order "to harmonize the sadness of the world."

Middle age did evidently wither, in Housman's case, that pliant spirit which enabled Thomas Hardy, on the verge of eighty, to recover his poetic impulse; though perhaps, too, the austerities of self-discipline and scholastic life had begun to harden, like a premature arterio-sclerosis, those veins that "leapt once with dancing fires." Neglected and disused for so long, the apparatus of Housman's art was simply rusting away —an intricate manipulative skill which he had, for more than a decade, almost totally ceased to practise and which now resembled, in the closed pages of his note-books, a derelict workshop; while instead of exercising his talent, he was idly absorbed by the typographical errata, the minutest blemish ("there should be a colon after *town*," he was already protesting, a fortnight after the guns fell silent) in the text of a book written more than twenty years before. Under the diligent supervision of its faithful impresario, *A Shropshire Lad* had lately reached the summit of its popularity and was, in the very thick of the war, several times reprinted in varieties of format and numerically enlarged editions; yet Housman still profusely complained not only of the invariable "mistakes," but about raising the price from sixpence to a shilling, which "therefore diminishes my chances of the advertisement to which I am always looking forward"—some authentic report of a soldier whose life had been saved by the little bullet-proof volume in his breast-pocket. This ghoulish desire (shared with, and perhaps borrowed from, Walt Whitman) was indeed eventually fulfilled, and the account of such an incident remained, among the author's papers, as the tangible souvenir of a curious day-dream. But if Housman did often seem to be fanatically obsessed by his own literary image, an editorial Narcissus wielding his blue pencil with a zest that even the vainest of writers could not so tirelessly maintain, it was not merely from egoistic pleasure or pedantic habit, but rather because, in jealously tending that bare sheaf of poems whose every syllable he must have known by heart, he was preserving to the last drop a precious elixir and a thread, not yet altogether broken, of personal communication. Who could say, however, that a poet reduced to such expedients would somewhere again find a mysterious improbable stimulus?

The angel of peace brought Housman no considerable alleviations except the greater freedom of action which he was prompt to celebrate, in the summer of 1919, by revisiting France and motoring in state through the aromatic vineyards of Brive. It was a reward conferred upon himself for "my sacrifices . . . during the war" as well as his labours of the past year. For on August 29 he had "sent Manilius IV" to Grant Richards, thus achieving the penultimate stage of that Roman excavation. But the irksome correction of proofs still awaited his return and was not finally discharged, complete with notes and index, until the following May; after which he conceived, as a triumphal flourish, the bold plan of embarking for Paris in September "by Air Express." The sense of dangerous, almost suicidal risk which then attached to this mode of travel gave the project, now that his masterpiece had been deposited like an incubus at the printer's, an extra fillip and "my inclination . . . is confirmed by the crash they had yesterday, which will make them careful." Soaring dizzily as the time approached, Housman's spirits became so ebullient that he permitted himself to contemplate a still more daring enterprise, and on the brink of one reckless adventure, he staggered his publisher by formulating this hypothetical question: "Suppose I produced a new volume of poetry, in what part of the year ought it to be published, and how long would it take after the MS. left my hands?" But though it was the first whisper of that announcement for which Grant Richards had been so interminably waiting, he was too "nervous," when they dined together the night before Housman's departure, to pursue a subject overshadowed just then by the fearful prospect of the next morning; and until reassured by a postcard from Paris, he did not hope for any extension of the poet's career.

A stern-faced elderly passenger who must have looked, among the sartorial fashions and hectic manners of 1920, disconcertingly reminiscent of a gas-lit horse-drawn era, Housman enjoyed nonetheless his baptismal flight, refusing to wear his life-belt or to stuff his ears with cotton-wool; and peering bravely from the diaphanous windblown aircraft whose gyrations "sometimes imitated a ship at sea" as they produced the same nauseating tremors, he determined willy-nilly that he was "never going by any other route in future." With a penchant for the speediest engines of transport, however, he combined an equal aversion to less perilous facilities of the machine age, and resolutely held out against not only the modern bath and telephone, but even softer collars and more comfortable shoes. Abetted perhaps by the normal quixotry of his profession, though in his earlier days Housman paid some attention to his wardrobe, this indifference to changing styles had assumed the defiant air of a pose that expects not to be ignored; and if his anachronism of dress and sedate deportment now seemed almost flauntingly Victorian, it may have been half-consciously a means of attracting the notice he pretended to shun. For by this time Housman was, and felt himself to be, not without high claims to recognition in both academic and literary circles. But as a poet voluntarily withdrawn from his contemporaries, and a scholar openly disdainful of *his*, he left himself no recourse to those who might have flattered his self-esteem; yet with that "horror of being known to like being known" which he nursed in secret with T. E. Lawrence, his dissimulating modesty only conspired, as did Lawrence's, to defeat its purpose, and led him to adopt those very stratagems —the cult of inaccessibility, the distinctive garb, the enigmatic silence—which helped to provoke the greediest notoriety. "Tell him," the would-be recluse growled in reply to some indirect appeal for an interview, "that the wish to include a glimpse of my personality . . . is low, unworthy and American," though "of course . . . I should not turn him out, as I only do that to newspaper reporters"; while by such teasing methods Housman contrived at once to court and repulse many of his admirers who, if they persevered, were seldom denied a moderate request. But especially in relation to Grant Richards, these vagaries of Housman's temperament were given full rein, alternately shedding reprimands and smiles upon the loyal servitor who performed with equal agility the functions of a publisher, a friend and if need be a court jester.

The all but final instalment of Manilius appeared in the autumn of 1920, with the label "stuck on upside down" but no serious derangement of the contents; and having passed this critical test, Richards could begin to anticipate that "almost promised manuscript" which would lend such a rare distinction to his spring list. "Knowing my poet," however, he refrained from any premature inquiries until the New Year, and was then greeted by one of those irate missives with which Housman used to pounce upon some quite unintentional offence:

My new book [he curtly rejoined] does not exist and possibly never may. Neither your traveller nor anybody else must be told that it is even contemplated. What I asked you was a question inspired by an unusually bright and sanguine mood, which has not at present been justified.

That was all; and if such extreme touchiness in respect to the delicate, subjective matters evidently interwoven with his poetry was a characteristic trait, it was unlike Housman, nevertheless, to have betrayed in advance a design so contingent upon his private feelings. Inadvertently, four months ago, the half-formed resolution must have slipped out, and was now circling back to plague him with an awkward reminder of that momentary euphoria to which there might have been, as he vanished into the clouds, no terrestrial aftermath. But though Housman had then clearly wanted and rashly committed himself to invoke his muse again, the effort must have temporarily failed or the results proved so far unsatisfactory; and while awaiting something else requisite to the spiritual history of *Last Poems*, he could only languish in a state of irritable suspension.

The dashed hopes with which Grant Richards had been left to console himself at the beginning of 1921 were as suddenly and unaccountably lifted on April 9, 1922, when out of the blue Housman wrote that "It is now practically certain that I shall have a volume of poems ready for the autumn"—a forecast which could not, this time, be open to doubt or recantation; and in fact the elusive manuscript itself arrived not long afterwards in St. Martin's Street, where it was received with a breathless urgency. "Rather shorter than *A Shropshire Lad*"— it contained forty-one poems and would make a slender book of about sixty pages—the text had been drafted as meticulously as ever by hand, and was attended by the ceremonial hush in which, two generations before, the poetry of Tennyson must have been awesomely unveiled. Rumour and speculation had preceded it; a taut expectancy followed the bare three lines of preliminary advertisement that were inserted, at the author's dictation, in *The Times Literary Supplement*. For despite his minimal contribution to literature, and perhaps even because of his long abstemious retirement, Housman stood just then poised upon that enviable crest of a writer's career, when his utterance is charged with almost oracular import. A figure of mystery and one of those ancestral voices to which old and young both sometimes consent to defer, the poet enjoyed a brief unchallenged supremacy; while in wry subjection to his *alter ego*, the scholar prepared to endure this limelit interlude ("Silence may now be broken," he advised, several weeks before the date of publication, "as I am now safely away from Cambridge and out of humanity's reach"). But the habit of assuming incontestable authority in academic circles so nearly overcame the queasy palpitations of authorship that Housman, upheld by the rapturous verdict of his publisher, bore himself that anxious summer with an outwardly impassive aloofness to the fate of his book. Retreating to Woodchester, he perambulated the countryside wearing "a cloth cap, a hard starched collar and stiff, correct tie"—the caricature of an elderly professor on holiday, beneath whose unromantic appearance an artist's eye could still detect "a frustrated and sombre twist," but no flicker of the rejuvenescent poet abiding the verdict of a new literary generation. What would it say, that world of English letters, already besieged if not yet conquered by the forces of rebellion, and in 1922 divided among hostile internecine factions to none of which Housman belonged? But as if looking down from Olympus he was able indifferently to regard the mud-soaked battles of other books like *Ulysses*, that outrageous masterpiece "which I have scrambled and waded through," he deigned to observe, "and found one or two half-pages amusing."

The roots of his own work lay so far back in a period antecedent to the birth of James Joyce that Housman could be excused, if not defended, for a lack of prompt sympathy with aesthetic principles which violated not only the conventions of his art, but all the repressive moral standards by which he lived; and especially when, at the brink of old age, the last, unhoped-for chapter of his experience had just been so compactly rendered. Both in choosing a title (against the plea of Grant Richards) as well as in the wording of a prefatory note, Housman clearly meant beforehand to announce the delivery of a swan-song that would have, he firmly promised, no Swinburnian echoes; and indeed the sparseness along with the redundancy of the poems themselves would have sufficed to establish the point that "I can no longer expect to be revisited by the continuous excitement" of *A Shropshire Lad.* Still exquisitely fashioned and miraculously indistinguishable from his earlier verse, the new poems, of which all but a handful were indeed simply crumbs garnered from his note-book, had for an audience bereft or disorientated by war the attraction of *memorabilia* that seemed to make literary time reverse itself and indisputably to show that familiar patterns had not lost their intrinsic value. But though gratifying to his vanity no less than to his readers, all this was hardly enough to set the complex and reluctant mechanism of Housman's poetry in motion again; nor was it easy to understand why he had delayed so long or elected just then to belabour his creative energies. And furthermore, what impulse could have moved him to persist in a mistimed experiment that was at first so fruitless?

Between the winter of 1921 when his "bright and sanguine mood . . . had not been justified," and the spring of 1922 when the existence of *Last Poems* was "practically certain," Housman had not only revised or elaborated the best material in his notebooks, but had composed in addition a small batch of new verse, most of which he specifically assigned to the early days of that April which inaugurated his sixty-third year. It was the season whose "things in bloom" and playful weather always held for him a lyrical charm, but which now smote his heart with a jolting impact not felt since the delirious intensities of

1895; and as before, he would have said, the strange flurry arose from that "morbid secretion" which by some accidental or cumulative pressure was impelled once more to discharge itself. Evidently preceded, however, by the struggles which had threatened for a twelvemonth to obstruct it, the process was a laggard rather than a spontaneous one that must have required, for its climactic phase, some aggressive external prod; and about this time, as it happened, the kind of message that would be sure to cause such an emotional disturbance may have reached Housman from Vancouver. Striving manfully on that remote frontier to cultivate his farm and to educate his boys (one of whom had lately been killed in a bicycle collision), Jackson was being driven to overtax his strength at an age when the sturdiest bodies are liable to collapse; and by 1922, he had already begun to manifest the symptoms of a disorder that was to grant him no reprieve. Thus overshadowed by the presentiment if not the knowledge of his own impending death, he would have been likely to seek consolation from the friend whose tenderness had come at last to seem not unacceptable; and receiving a signal at once so urgent yet so conclusive, Housman could reply, at a distance of ten thousand miles, with nothing more efficacious than a gift of words drawn from his almost, but not quite, exhausted supply.

The poetry that issued from this dark reservoir was, in spite of the Cambridge gardens flowering around it, rather bleak than vernal in spirit, and not surprisingly, in view of the anxieties which provoked it, a sombre restatement of habitual themes—the meditations of one who, for so many afternoons, had taken a solitary walk; but there were none of those enrichments and accretions which the passage of time might have been expected to yield. Borrowing from Heine in one case and in others from the ballad repertory, the author of the latest poems formed himself upon the same literary models and adopted or reverted to the guise of a personality which had changed, through the epochal intervening years, hardly at all; whereas in fact Housman had grown more to resemble a corrosively exasperated satirist than a poet of this gentle dolorous vein, by whom the scholar's pedantries and phobias were all suddenly forgotten. In his poetic imagination, on the contrary, that other side of the coin lay uppermost and the travail of young soldiers was still an obsessive fantasy, recurring ten times as the subject of a "sumless tale of sorrow" which unfolded on every page and which haunted not only the military graveyard but the rural landscape and even the circumambient universe; while the grim sequence was carefully modulated to produce, as in *A Shropshire Lad*, the unity of some ill-omened but representative saga. A text that deserved the music of the *Winterreise*, it was marred only by that faint note of self-parody (No. X, for example)[1] or that funeral wreath (No. XVIII) too plainly addressed to the memory of Adalbert Jackson, odd blemishes which Housman's censorial eye did not always eradicate. But these were flaws barely to obtrude themselves from a work that combined such rigorous craftsmanship with such inveterate self-discipline, over which unmistakably hovered that flighty demon Euterpe, the lyric muse. "Once again," as *The Times* declared in a premature review on October 17, 1922, "has the classical tradition told in the making of an English poet," and to the credit of public taste during the next three months this austere indigo-blue volume of marmoreal verse (priced at five shillings) enjoyed not only a round of discriminating critical applause but a whirlwind success.

The day of publication was not "an available date" for Housman to dine in London, but was spent quietly at Cambridge, collecting early notices for inclusion with an autographed copy which he forwarded at once to the hospital bed in Vancouver where, more than ever impatient with literature, Jackson might have turned the pages inattentively, but could not overlook, from "a fellow who thinks more of you than anything in the world," the blunt protestation that "you are largely responsible for my writing poetry and you ought to take the consequences." A list of other privileged recipients, to the number

[1] First deplored by Mr. Walter de la Mare in his introduction to *Love: An Anthology*.

of thirty-three, had already been transmitted to Grant Richards, and their letters of more than polite acknowledgment now began to shower like autumn leaves—encomiums among which Housman took the trouble to preserve those from such nodding acquaintances as Gilbert Murray and Sir James Frazer, though again fortuitously or deliberately none from Jackson has survived. The consensus of praise which the "press-cutting agency sends me, with due delay," together with this swollen fan-mail helped to relieve the pangs that beset, like the twinges of an exposed nerve, the writer's (and above all Housman's) emergence into book-form; though once more, by contending that his talent was not merely unimpaired but had even surpassed itself, his friends and critics too warmly hailed an effort whose merits he knew to be derived from the past and now linked with events drawing inexorably to an end. If the literary fame that perversely celebrated this private dejection had to some extent already "interposed between me and the hard ground" what felt like a soft "mattress," it did not modify his rule against inscribing for others the poetry which belonged exclusively to one; or inveigle Housman into the wide discussion and festive celebration which his verse provoked.

The press-cutting agency must have kept him, as the days passed, more liberally supplied with material augmented from America, where *Last Poems* appeared in November with the same happy results and from whose coffers he was now "prepared to receive royalty" at the rate of fifteen per cent. On every side these graceful tropes carved from a substance like granite rewon his old and captured new readers; but the feature that intrigued the more judicious of them by its novelty was that latest, longest and certainly grimmest of Housman's poems —*Hell Gate*, whose portals verging on "the slimepit and the mire" yawned at the inhabitants of the Jazz Age. Adumbrated, many years before, with a few tentative lines in his note-book and then rushed to completion in the spring of 1922, it had, against the customary pastoral background of his poetry, the phantasmagorical effect of a nightmare whose frantic symbol-

POST CARD

Grant Richards, Esq.
8 St Martin's Street
Leicester Square
W. C. 2.

No, don't put in an errata slip. The blunder will probably enhance the value of the 1st edition in the eyes of biblio-philes, an idiotic class.

Yrs

A. E. Housman

14 Oct. 1922   Trin. Coll. Camb.

Postcard to Grant Richards

ism could not easily be deciphered; and indeed, with its lurid setting and ghostly protagonist, its visionary reunion among the shades of an Inferno guarded not by Charon but that sentinel "Trim and burning" in his transparent disguise, the work contained as much psychiatric as literary significance:

> Tyranny and terror flown
> Left a pair of friends alone,
> And beneath the nether sky
> All that stirred was he and I.

But if such brief passages lent themselves to an obvious biographical interpretation, the rest of this "dusk and mute" allegory failed to escape from the labyrinthine coils of Housman's subconsciousness; and what seemed then a promising late development of style was in fact one of his earliest inventions (of which several other examples were exhumed in *More Poems*), a stern lugubrious vein which blended the pieties of youthful romanticism with those of the Victorian hymn-book, and which might, but for a happier choice, have prevailed over the lyric mode that drew out another side of his character. Relishing this inadvertent mystery which even *The Times* did not presume to unravel, and having safely entrusted the key to Jackson's care (if he were still able to assimilate more of the "stupid stuff"), the author himself devoured in silence the breakfast of laudatory speculation with which the daily post now regaled him.

During the week before the publication of *Last Poems*, a noteworthy but unsuspected American visitor had "chased his retreating tall, thin grey figure and cotton umbrella for about half a mile through the streets of Cambridge," but had "caught just a glimpse of his face, a nice face" doubtless wrapped in that look of abstraction which ignored all human obstacles in his path. "They say nobody ever sees him," Miss Millay went on to report, deferentially accepting what she must have been told by those who themselves lacked the means to obtain an introduction; and though Housman allegedly "got more enjoyment from Millay than from either Robinson or Frost," an

213

encounter with his glamorous disciple was fated to be one of those might-have-beens which tempt yet defy the imagination. But if his nerves would have been unequal just then to receiving a caller so demurely feminine, they were soon further strained by the trials of becoming a best-seller whose circulation, as Grant Richards proudly tabulated it, had "reached twenty-one thousand!" within three months; and from such acclaim, with its unwarranted demands and excessive interruptions, Housman now had a legitimate reason to defend himself. For was he not still the Kennedy Professor whose duties, he must have felt, required even stricter observance after this culpable literary fling, and whose reputation could no longer afford to neglect the mountainous labours of scholarship; while in the irreducible activities of his Cambridge life, Housman's social circle had already widened to the limits of his tolerance for company and of his leisure for distraction. But apart from the Trinity neighbours with whom he dined conveniently every night, Housman's friends were neither numerous nor pressing enough to exact more than perfunctory attention—a group satisfied to meet whenever it suited him and among whom none was admitted to his innermost confidence, though perhaps the most nearly successful, in Housman's later days, was Dr. Percy Withers.

The first impression of "an agreeable man," luckily produced by this middle-aged medical officer whom Housman had befriended in the gloomy summer of 1917, contrived miraculously to outlast not only a special war-time appeal but the persistently "renewed importunities" which few others would have dared more than once to make; and with his engaging boldness helped along by his natural sympathy Dr. Withers had soon established himself in a relation that, for one trained to diagnose the ills of the body, could have drawn from his unwitting patient some expert scientific deductions. But the professional doctor was, in Housman's presence, more often replaced by the literary amateur, seeking rather to exalt than to examine the poet's character, and what might have been a

unique advantage for clinical study lost itself in random Bos-
wellian observations. Of Housman's external appearance—
"his erect soldier-like figure" still preserved in his sixties by
that astonishing "pair of dumb bells" which "lay on the floor
beside his chair"; and of "the struggle I found it to keep conversation going" long after the awkward stages of a new
acquaintance had been passed; of all the deterrents one faced
in knowing Housman, and the compensations that might be
gathered from the experience, Dr. Withers' anecdotal scrapbook has proved to be, nevertheless, one of the most useful.
For with an evident sincerity of purpose that disarmed his
fractious subject, this inquisitive but forgivable admirer would
now and then overstep those bounds of discretion which older
friends might have wished, but none had ever summoned the
courage, to exceed; and in thus venturing so far, as with his
stethoscope in hand, the doctor was allowed to touch, if not
explore, certain vulnerable spots which always betrayed themselves by "a voice striving ineffectually for composure" or by
an equally violent facial tremor. But while these audacities
obviously sometimes hit their mark, they did not in the end
produce, aside from such wincing spasms, very definitive revela-
tions; and in fact the valuable result of Dr. Withers' colloquies
was not the secrets they divulged but those grimaces "wrought
and flushed in torment" which could be so readily induced by
his questions.

The topics that Dr. Withers learned not to raise without
cautious preparation, and which never failed to provoke a
sharp recoil, were Housman's poetry ("an intolerable memory
lived over again," as it seemed, each time he was reminded of
that emotional onslaught) and his attachment to "three friends"
of whom he named, with more guile than frankness, only Miss
Becker. It was a subterfuge that easily misled the doctor's
romantic thoughts into a bypath which ended nowhere; for
whatever Housman's feelings may once have been for the
motherly governess who had so many years before rescued him
from despair, he did not, in the course of all his later travels,

desire their reunion enough to visit her homeland, and now could scarcely pretend to be cherishing, for this object of schoolboy sentiment, a life-long passion. The "three friends" had, in truth, never been more than two, and of those but one distantly survived when Dr. Withers began to prod for information; while the ungovernable tic that used to greet his innocent queries must have been painfully accentuated, early in 1923, by the bulletins from Jackson's sickbed. That imagery of the "clenched" lightning and the ominously chiming clock which the poet had contrived with such dramatic effect must have been just then a literal rendition of the suspense in which Housman awaited, day by day, the imminent letter, the disastrous telegram; and when it came—Jackson's final salute from the hospital where he was dying in the throes of a stomach cancer—the "figure tense and bolt upright as though in an extremity" which Dr. Withers had espied on lesser occasions must have been a counterpart of the unseen transfixity in which Housman endured this aching blow. But the records of that year made no allusion to an event that was only afterwards traceable in the poignant document which his brother found among Housman's relics: "an envelope endorsed, 'Mo's last letter,' " whose faltering pencilled contents had been, with the devotion accorded to some irreplaceable memento, carefully inked over, "the better to preserve it." Yet even this vestige, so affectionately treasured while Housman lived, has been subsequently lost or conveniently mislaid by Jackson's heirs.

The death, officially registered at Vancouver on January 14, 1923, of Moses John Jackson in his sixty-fourth year also marked or coincided with the virtual termination of Housman's literary life, and thereafter, as if entombed by a landslide, his note-books were all but sealed forever, though he did just once more (sometime in 1925) compose a few valedictory lines to serve, in already calm anticipation, as the posthumous dirge for his own funeral. It was the beginning of a finale that did not lack notable accomplishments, and might have seemed the enviable old age of one whose intellectual powers were undiminished, whose health was to be for another decade still vigorous, whose means were more than adequate to his needs, and whose deserved renown brought him the warming praise of younger people; yet Housman wished and "reiterated in latter years like an obsession," as it struck Dr. Withers, "that death might come suddenly." There was in fact but one remaining task to which he felt himself committed—the last volume of his Manilius; and as so many times before, the onerous discipline of textual criticism saved him once again from the clutches of despondency. But a decelerating tempo of work forced him to admit, by the end of 1925, that "the 5th book of Manilius is not likely to be published before 1929," and it was eventually delayed until 1930, capping then with meticulous perfection what had become a monument of incomparable skill and thankless labour.

As the clock now mechanically ticked on, the scholar's apartment was filled with that contemplative silence in which, each morning, his manservant had been trained to present himself on tiptoe, receiving his orders by written memoranda (so that the concentration of thought might not for a moment be interrupted), and then proceeding to bring up the specified bottle of wine for lunch, or maybe to replenish the supply of wing collars and elastic-sided boots, always exactly duplicating the old ones. Over the fireplace, alongside the green turtle's shell that was a souvenir of some Lucullian repast, hung that still more unexpected photograph of the St. John's crew which Housman, if asked by incredulous callers, would identify in a choked voice; while round about books covered the walls and piled themselves on the solid Victorian tables, where stray copies of *Trent's Last Case* or *Du Côté de chez Swann* might temporarily belie the monastic atmosphere. Here too, in 1926, unflinchingly and almost resentfully, with a look of grim sufferance, Housman posed for the drawing, by Francis Dodd, which caught, in the estimation of Mr. Gow, "the best likeness" of his contemporaneous features. Authoritative, glowering, impregnable, it was the face before which scholars and students were accustomed to quail, but from whose cold eyes most literary pilgrims retired in hasty defeat; and this ogreish misanthropic glare was indeed the mask behind which Housman chose habitually to conceal himself, repelling intruders with the frozen scowl of a Chinese dragon and emitting, when roused to ire, streams of that inky poison which stained so many of his philological papers.

Under such hostile flourishes, however, he was not yet immune to the afflictions of others, and in that same year performed, at the age of sixty-seven, a strenuous errand of mercy that carried him precipitately to Venice, "where my poor gondolier says he is dying and wants to see me again." Formed during Housman's first trip to Italy in 1900, this acquaintance of a kind that travellers casually strike up but as inevitably break off had ripened nevertheless into something more, and was in several respects intriguing as well as unprecedented. Housman did not at best make friends easily, but almost never outside his own social or intellectual class, and not often among those younger than himself (he had been forty-one when his gondolier was twenty-three); nor was he prone to assist beggars merely because of their picturesqueness. Yet for one who had from the outset complained of hopeless family burdens and who was clearly doomed to propel his interminable misfortunes along those romantic waterways, Housman felt an attraction which not even the spell cast by moonlit Venetian canals could suffice to explain; while on later visits no disillusionment followed, no mounting demands for charity went unheeded, and in the last emergency Housman still impulsively responded with "all provision," as he told Dr. Withers, "for the man's comfort." Such a protracted idyll might have seemed less innocently altruistic if Housman had not, when it began, quite openly written to his step-mother about the charms of a gondolier "who has had one eye kicked out by a horse," and with the same unblushing candour twice again, as they occurred, mentioned these rendezvous to Mrs. Symons. But though the key to Housman's emotional life always lay somewhere in his poetry, the mystery was in this case wrapped in a salute (No. XLIV in *More Poems*) which refused to convey more than the toll of its iron bell, and which he did not himself think worthy of publication:

> Andrea, fare you well;
> Venice, farewell to thee.
> The tower that stood and fell
> Is not rebuilt in me.

Clanging heavily, it commemorated a series of episodes for which the appropriate words could never be found.

Housman returned on June 26 from the dazzle of Italian sunlight to the sepulchral quietude of Whewell's Court and the pallid labours of scholarship, perhaps enlivened that summer by several new accessions to the catalogue he was compiling— a sort of *index non expurgatorius* of the most indecorous passages in Latin literature. Assembling this bombshell must have gleefully occupied him for many summers; and exploding at last in 1931, it was plainly the result of extensive research and a calculated defiance of the proprieties, though aimed at the smallest possible target. It had proved to be no less unprintable in England, however, and only after numerous rejections saw the light in a more daring German periodical called *Hermes*. Bluntly entitled *Praefanda* (or Dirty Words), the joke consisted of an eleven-page discourse revolving, with a solemn pedantry, around those naughty but not uncommon Latinisms from which respectable modern scholars had until then primly averted their eyes, and which are still omitted in some editions even today. Culled from the works of Martial, Suetonius, Seneca and Catullus, among others, these ancient obscenities were bound to ignite the fires of common-room gossip, but signally not to relax the censorship against which, if anything, they were directed; while because of Housman's ill-judged approach to the problem, his own motives appeared not only suspect but almost incriminating. The case might have been argued, with so much better effect, by a more circuitous method and under some other pretext, like the one he himself had already provided in a lecture on *The Application of Thought to Textual Criticism*, which inferred that the members of the Classical Association were "not willing to look all the facts in the face"—a human propensity which led straight, as he could then have implied without offence, to the prurient suppression of such tid-bits. Whereas, behind the lewd gesture of *Praefanda*, Housman had elected rather to shock than to persuade his audience, and in a manner that not simply fanned its opposition but reflected adversely upon himself. But perhaps the surreptitious concealment of this erotica would have been worse than his flagrant indiscretion; and certainly it betrayed, at the age of seventy-two, a venerable gusto along with a still defiant, if incurably warped, antagonism to the profession of which he had become at once the greatest living ornament and the most unsparing gadfly.

For poetry, on the other hand, he never lost the kind of ardour that responds to a natural, an irresistible preference; and though literary criticism was one of its branches for which he always claimed to have "no talent," he could not refuse, in spite of the "anxiety and depression" it would sorely inflict, the honour of being asked to give, in the late spring of 1933, the Leslie Stephen Lecture—a distinction annually conferred upon some eligible man of letters. Until then, Housman had stubbornly rejected all the citations and degrees, including even the royal Order of Merit, which had offered themselves, and he was now on the threshold of his seventy-fifth year, with its physical downgrade and lethargy of spirit; but this not-likely-to-recur chance of making a last, categorical pronouncement —on a theme so vitally related to his own life—overcame every scruple and was embraced with a groan of determination. Between March and May, in that season which perennially revived his dormant poetic faculties, the trials and torments of composition assailed him anew as the inexorable hour drew near, and the fluent-sounding phrases which, "at 5 o'clock on May 9," echoed through the Senate House had cost him "a great deal of trouble" that partly robbed the occasion of its zest if not its triumph. For the speaker's gracious performance (so unlike the scholar's) was hailed not only by its auditors but on the morning after by a "longish 'leader' " in *The Times*; while the printed version repeated both in England and America a success which the few dissenting voices here and there only helped to promote. That his effort commanded so much respect might have assured him that his words contained some approximation to veracity; but on such a perilous subject, he could not forget, the danger of misapprehension haunted every statement, and therefore, as he gruffly declared when it was over, "I don't like the lecture."

Under its euphonious and rather sweeping title, *The Name and Nature of Poetry* soon acquired, from the tone of its reception, weightier values than Housman had intended it to possess, and has suffered, as one of his least substantial literary works, from being elevated to a position it did not claim or deserve. Unable to believe that a scholar so crushingly authoritative might descend to a more informal plane, his readers appraised too highly these late and somewhat tenuous "Observations on the Art of English Poesy," in which Housman had the temerity to advance opinions by then so conservative that they sounded radical, and thus inadvertently "upset," as Mr. Ezra Pound was pleased to note, "a lot of the Cambridge critics." Quite as oblivious of their existence as of their disapproval, the Kennedy Professor was in all honesty revealing the zigzag development of his personal taste and, so far as he dared, the process by which he had himself become a poet. It was the unrepentant credo of one who, inside his conventional Victorian shell, had remained immutably governed by his own intuitions; and this form of solitary independence, of eccentric detachment, now led him to the same conclusion reached long ago by Emily Dickinson: "If I feel physically as if the top of my head were taken off, I know *that* is poetry." A test that relied so much upon *whose* head was tingling, it failed even Housman at several stages in the history of English literature, and could neither justify nor dispel his temperamental aversion to certain styles and periods. From the convolutions of meta-physical verse to the couplets of Dryden and Pope, he con-fessed, no shivers ran down *his* spine, and hence no qualities of the first order could be ascribed to those currently fashionable schools; while there was "no single indication," as Mr. Pound went on more bitterly to remark, "that Mr. Housman was aware of the world of my contemporaries," and indeed the source from which most of his quotations came was, oddly enough, the Bible.

What his judgment of other poetry may have lacked, how-ever, was promisingly if not richly supplied by those brief autobiographical passages which related how "this stuff"—the bulk of *A Shropshire Lad*—was conceived during his aimless afternoon walks, under the sedative influence of "a pint of beer." The minor details of that mysterious eruption could not have been more accurately or frankly described—"I happen to remember distinctly the genesis of the piece which stands last in my first volume. Two of the stanzas, I do not say which, came into my head, just as they are printed, while I was crossing the corner of Hampstead Heath between the Spaniards Inn and the footpath to Temple Fortune. A third stanza came with a little coaxing after tea. One more was needed, but it did not come"; and there, having installed a plaque of the kind that marks the site where some historical incident has occurred, Housman abruptly closed his report on the verge of that "abyss" from which, as he darkly hinted, not only his own but all true poetry was conjured up in a manner akin to the irrational procedure of one who, by the manipulations of a witch-hazel rod, divines the subterranean tributaries of a water-course.

It was the significance Housman attached to this impene-trable element in his art that "upset a lot of the Cambridge critics"—those young, scientifically-equipped theoreticians who, like Mr. I. A. Richards, were trying to rescue literature from just that kind of subjective hocus-pocus to which the Kennedy Professor now seemed mischievously bent on restor-ing it; and certainly, under an air of specious diffidence, *The*

Name and Nature of Poetry did encourage the view that no inquiry could hope to discover the origins of "something in man which is obscure and latent, something older than the present organization of his nature." Housman was explaining how an often meaningless line by Blake ("for me the most poetical of all poets") could so violently quicken his pulse-beat; but in proclaiming himself "not equal to" some further definition of this "unreasonable excitement," and in appearing to suggest, moreover, that the best gauge of poetic merit was a "constriction of the throat" or a "precipitation of water to the eyes" (the ingenuous belief of one who had first attended the cinema in 1930), he unwisely reduced this imponderable subject to a deceptive ease. Perhaps within the space of an hour, he could have done no more; and yet a tantalizing sense of all that Housman left consciously unsaid hung over his lecture as over his poetry, the residue not of those extraneous factors which every artist strives to keep out, but of something missing from and indispensable to his work. Here, too late and in the wrong place (for who could bare his soul in the Senate House?) he must have felt slipping from his grasp the writer's precious though painful heritage—that never-ending but always persistent struggle towards clarification; and with the self-knowledge by which he was still so much oppressed yet of which he could impart so little, Housman retired that afternoon to his now irretrievably silent death-watch.

Not only disconsolate in spirit but also physically unwell, Housman showed, when his publisher "walked round to his rooms" after the lecture, the marks of an "evident fatigue" from which he did not again recover; and writing to Laurence in the middle of June, he confided the first appearance of troublesome coronary symptoms which recently "sent me to bed for a week in a nursing home." He was able later that summer to undertake a "disagreeable tour in France," but relapsed on his return and was vainly urged by Grant Richards to seek rooms better appointed and more accessible for a frail septuagenarian. Still bounding up his forty-four stair-steps "two at a time," after the exertion of his daily cross-country walks, he began to suffer besides from that irrepressible impatience which goads the victims of heart disease to overtax themselves; while in the dank recesses of Whewell's Court he continued to live without the barest of modern conveniences. Noticing in himself, moreover, the stertorous tell-tale signs of Cheyne-Stokes respiration which he recalled from the death-scene of *Clayhanger*, Housman's thoughts now focused more intently upon the dread of pain and the wish for a sudden cessation. (He had already signed, on November 17, 1932, that controversial Last Will and Testament which bequeathed to others so many decisions that he alone could resolve.) But his seventy-fifth and then his seventy-sixth birthdays passed, bringing only more debility and "shortness of breath," though in the summer of 1935 he rallied enough for a last flight "through the tempestuous air" back and forth to France. In need of occasional injections of morphine, yet persevering that Michaelmas term (his twenty-fifth at Cambridge) with a course on Ovid, he plainly could not be allowed any longer to make the dangerous ascent of Staircase K, and while he took refuge once more in the nursing home, his books and chattels, like the numbered stones of a dismantled edifice, were carefully removed to a ground-floor suite on the Great Court of Trinity. But his enjoyment of this location was temporary and did not relieve the panting effort to keep up, with "invincible determination," his regular tasks. It was, for those who attended his lectures on Horace in the early spring of 1936, the spectacle of a powerful, relentless mind battling with a weak and decadent body until, one April day, Housman did not, "punctually at five minutes past the hour," shuffle his notes and break the "icy silence." Lying then on his deathbed and imploring his doctor to hasten the end, he "talked quite a lot" to that most intimate of strangers and with the gesture of one who has finally discarded all pretence, "held my hand for nearly half an hour." He died soon afterwards, on April 30, 1936, and wore in absolute repose a look of "proud challenge."

Bibliography and Notes

The main sources to which the text refers are designated by the following abbreviations in parenthesis.

The Collected Poems of A. E. Housman. Jonathan Cape.
  A Shropshire Lad. (ASL)
  Last Poems. (LP)
  More Poems. (MP)
  Additional Poems. (AP)
The Name and Nature of Poetry, by A. E. Housman. Cambridge
  University Press. (N&N)
Introductory Lecture, by A. E. Housman. Cambridge University
  Press. (IL)
Recollections of A. E. Housman, A Supplement to the *Bromsgrovian.*
  (*Bromsgrovian*)
A. E. Housman, A Sketch, by A. S. F. Gow. Cambridge University
  Press. (Gow)
A. E. H. Some Poems, Some Letters and a Personal Memoir, by
  Laurence Housman. Jonathan Cape. (AEH)
The Unexpected Years, by Laurence Housman. Jonathan Cape. (UY)
Housman, 1897–1936, by Grant Richards. Oxford University Press.
  (GR)

Other titles are listed in the notes as they occur; and to avoid the use of distracting symbols or footnotes in the text, quotations are identified by their closing words, under the chapter and page where they are found.

CHAPTER I

17, "of England"—Housman family records (in the possession
    of N. V. H. Symons)
20, "of mind"—*Life and Remains of the Rev. Robert Housman,* by
    Robert Fletcher Housman (New York 1846) p. 6
20, "as mine"—ASL, No. LI
21, "every particular"—*Life and Remains* p. 10
24, "his heart"—*Ibid.* p. 140
25, "way, William"—Housman family records
25, "will perish"—*Life and Remains* p. 283
26, "scientific character"—*Ibid.* p. 284
26, "trembling hope"—*Ibid.* pp. 223–4
31, "parish priest"—*Bromsgrovian* p. 10

32, "of England"—*An Account of Roman Antiquities discovered at Woodchester*, by Samuel Lysons
32, "and hamlets"—ASL, No. XLII
33, "came across"—GR p. 270
33, "regenerated Jane"—"Memories of A. E. Housman," by Mrs. E. W. Symons. (*The Edwardian*, King Edward's School, Bath. Vol. 17, No. 3, Sept. 1936)
34, "was unacquainted"—*Life and Remains* p. 104
34, "was right"—*Ibid.* p. 85
34, "fellow man"—ASL, No. XLI
34, "was Lancashire"—GR p. 269

CHAPTER II

38, "of birth"—MP, No. XXV
39, "a legacy"—AEH pp. 279–86
39, "the house"—GR p. 270
41, "good-night"—UY p. 24
43, "her inside"—"Memories of Housman," by Mrs. E. W. Symons
44, "die for"—LP, No. XXXII
45, "and affecting"—*Life and Remains* p. 320
45, "avoid troubles"—*Bromsgrovian* p. 8
46, "the town"—*Bromsgrove School*. A brochure published by the Bromsgrove School Bookshop
47, "grown-up person"—AEH p. 24
51, "hearse and spade"—ASL, No. XXVIII
51, "bed of mould"—ASL, No. XXX

CHAPTER III

53, "pulling faces" et seq.—Unpublished notes by Mrs. Symons (in the possession of N. V. H. Symons)
53, "to cry"—GR p. 289
54, "and butter"—UY p. 22
55, "western brookland"—ASL, No. LII
56, "poetic emotion"—*Memoirs of Mark Pattison* p. 34
56, "broad glade"—*Memories and Opinions*, by Quiller-Couch p. 53
57, "coming death"—AEH pp. 33–4
58, "all this"—*Bromsgrovian* p. 16
58, "rigid discipline"—Unpublished notes by Mrs. Symons
59, "comfortable friendships"—AEH p. 25
59, "Farnese Mercury" et seq.—AEH p. 26
61, "your room"—AEH p. 27
61, "his 'opes"—Unpublished notes by Mrs. Symons

62, "financial difficulties"—*Ibid.*
63, "like him"—AEH p. 35
64, "the classics"—AEH p. 36
64, "of Catullus"—*The Times* obituary, Dec. 17, 1922
65, "on life"—*Ibid.*
65, "open countenance"—*Bromsgrovian* p. 20
66, "Shropshire Lad"—*Bromsgrovian* p. 15
66, "of means"—GR, Introduction p. xiv
67, "passed on"—*Bromsgrovian* p. 21
67, "troubled depths"—*Ibid.* p. 23
69, "and hills" et seq.—*Ibid.* p. 23

CHAPTER IV

70, "brickish skirt"—*Poems of Gerard Manley Hopkins* ("Duns
        Scotus's Oxford")
71, "other things"—AEH pp. 40–1
71, "on me"—GR p. 304
72, "original ways" et seq.—Testimonial by T. H. Warren,
        Pres. Magdalen Coll. Oxford, submitted to University
        of London
73, "telling them"—*Bromsgrovian* p. 30
74, "empty benches"—AEH pp. 42–3
74, "to students"—Abbott and Campbell, *Life of Benjamin
        Jowett*, Vol. II, p. 155
75, "great dislike"—*Ibid.* Vol. II, p. 186
75, "of scholarship"—Gow p. 5
76, "a genius"—*Bromsgrovian* p. 31
76, "quietly happy"—*Ibid.* p. 30
78, "thought away"—MP, No. XXXI
79, "never made"—LP, No. XII
80, "growing taciturnity"—*Bromsgrovian* p. 24
80, "the prophets"—*Ibid.* p. 30
81, "novel popular"—*A Pair of Blue Eyes* p. 186
82, "a makeshift"—*Ibid.* p. 155
83, "by thee"—*Elegies of Propertius* (Loeb Classical Library) p. 51
84, "the audience"—*Bromsgrovian* p. 30
85, "we did"—*Ibid.* p. 24
86, "no votes!"—AEH p. 52
86, "the college"—*Bromsgrovian* p. 30
87, "been doing?" et seq.—*Ibid.* p. 31
88, "or follies"—*Ibid.* p. 24
89, "never extinguished"—*Elegies of Propertius* p. 71
90, "in love"—Emendationes Propertianae, *Journal of Philology*,
        Vol. XVI, 1888

90, "questions set"—Gow p. 7
91, "sleep sound"—MP, No. XLVIII

CHAPTER V

93, "any answers"—*Bromsgrovian* p. 32
93, "and scrappy"—GR p. 322
94, "and lasting"—GR, Introduction p. xv
94, "of reserve"—*Ibid.*
94, "of concentration"—AEH p. 60
95, "exasperating strain"—*Ibid.* p. 61
96, "dancing, drinking"—ASL, No. XLIX
96, "could know"—ASL, No. XXIII
96, "in vain"—MP, No. XXVII
99, "grew older"—UY p. 84
99, "of Worcestershire"—*Ibid.* p. 83
101, "easy education"—*Ibid.* p. 85
102, "as we were"—*Ibid.* Preface p. v
102, "forsaken west"—ASL, No. XXXVII
103, "grasp to"—*Ibid.*
106, "and Latin"—GR p. 270

CHAPTER VI

108, "their attractiveness"—AEH pp. 128-9
109, "to come"—Gow p. 11
109, "for supper"—AEH p. 130
111, "them unpatriotic"—*Ibid.* pp. 130-1
111, "after dinner"—Sir Edward Clarke: *Story of My Life* p. 240
111, "as possible"—Gow p. 10
112, "public servant"—*Ibid.*
115, "I lament"—*Elegies of Propertius* p. 49
116, "it is me"—Visitor's Book (in the possession of Mr. H. B. Collamore)
118, "sunder"—AP, No. VII
118, "said I"—MP, No. XXXI
119, "all's over"—MP, No. XXX
120, "track you down"—*Elegies of Propertius* p. 153
120, "and abominable"—AP, No. XVIII
122, "cursed trouble"—MP, No. XXI
122, "general opinion"—*Journal of Philology*, Vol. XVI, No. 31 (1888)
122, "next ten years"—Gow p. 12
123, "that manhood"—MP, No. XLII
125, "loves you more"—LP, No. XXIV
126, "his breast"—ASL, No. XIV

CHAPTER VII

127, "Litterae Humaniores"—Gow p. 14
128, "favourite Greek poet"—*Ibid.* p. 15
128, "a monument"—*Ibid.* p. 15
128, "best endeavours" et seq.—*Ibid.* p. 17
129, "anything else"—GR p. 275
129, "wishing for death"—AEH p. 109
129, "in learning?" et seq.—IL
132, "not wholly sincere"—GR p. 303
133, "something good myself"—AEH p. 93
134, "dear fellow"—MP, No. XLII
134, "winterfall"—LP, No. XX
136, "scrupulous care"—*Man's Unconquerable Mind*, by R. W. Chambers p. 369
136, "Housman's calibre"—Gow p. 17
137, "decisive action"—GR p. 439
137, "by heart"—*Man's Unconquerable Mind* p. 361
137, "Jorrock's Jaunts"—*Ibid.* p. 364
138, "omit it"—GR p. 331
139, "with snow"—ASL, No. XXXIX
140, "to be read"—Gow p. 15
140, "and Heine"—GR p. 270
140, "ask me how"—*Poems of Heinrich Heine.* Translated by Louis Untermeyer
141, "my mother's fire!"—*Oxford Book of Ballads* pp. 136–8
148, "in the cold"—LP, No. XIX
149, "pit of the stomach" et seq.—N&N pp. 48–50
150, "to contemplate"—GR p. 391
151, "the world"—*Bromsgrovian* p. 29

CHAPTER VIII

152, "south corner" et seq.—AEH pp. 73–4
153, "to this case"—*Trials of Oscar Wilde* (British Notable Trials) p. 254
153, "where I am now"—*Trials of Oscar Wilde* p. 236
155, "and disgraces"—AEH p. 104
156, "to the grave"—ASL, No. XLIV
157, "melancholy mad"—ASL, No. LXII
157, "to do again"—LP No. XI
159, "better one"—*Bromsgrovian* p. 32
159, "put down £30"—*Ibid.*
160, "opening the book"—AEH p. 83
160, "among my friends"—*Ibid.* p. 80
160, "for Housman's poems"—Letter from Dr. Jackson to the author

164, "clever nonsense"—AEH p. 96
164, "embarrassed ones"—*Ibid.* p. 95
165, "than yours to me"—*Ibid.* p. 77
165, "sake of talking"—*Ibid.* p. 95
165, "had to organize"—*Man's Unconquerable Mind* p. 374
166, "sufficiently pretentious"—AEH p. 166
167, "through the streets" et seq.—GR pp. 29–31
168, "are not inexhaustible"—*Ibid.* pp. 47–8
170, "the Louvre"—AEH p. 134
170, "I was there"—*Ibid.*

CHAPTER IX

171, "doing sums in verse"—Gow p. 13
172, "limited means" et seq.—GR p. 34
174, "down and weep"—LP XVII
174, "certain connection"—*Bromsgrovian* p. 26
175, "has not found"—LP, No. XVII
176, "unfortunate colleague"—*Man's Unconquerable Mind* p. 378
177, "yet awhile"—GR p. 46
177, "is dedicated"—*Ibid.* p. 56
179, "an aggressor"—*Bromsgrovian* p. 33
180, "Sexual Inversion"—Foreword by Havelock Ellis, p. xvii
181, "with the matter"—*Ibid.* p. xi
183, "know it already"—Gow p. 22
184, "heavy-weight boxer etc."—GR p. 124
184, "priest-like sommelier"—*Ibid.* p. 40
185, "in that fashion"—Review of Housman's *Juvenal*, by W. M.
     Lindsay, *The Classical Review*, Dec. 1905
185, "less than scandalous"—Gow p. 29
186, "faculty of writing"—AEH p. 89
186, "about nothing"—*Ibid.*
187, "trifling misprint"—GR p. 76
187, "whom I avoid"—AEH p. 141
189, "admired so long"—*Monologues*, by Richard Middleton
     p. 222
189, "enormous black beard"—*Richard Middleton*, by Henry
     Savage p. 47
190, "world of sunshine"—*Monologues* p. 219
190, "talk of it"—GR p. 95
191, "crowded with venom"—*A Buried Life*, by Percy Withers
     p. 120
191, "he didn't like"—GR p. 98
192, "betwixt and between"—Unpublished letter by R. W.
     Chambers
193, "Garden Committees"—*Ibid.* p. 99

Bibliography and Notes

CHAPTER X

194, "our intentions"—Gow p. 48
195, "and gossip"—*Diary of A. C. Benson*, July 19, 1911
195, "English gentleman"—*The Harrow Life of Henry Montagu Butler* p. 328
196, "seldom visited"—Gow p. 51
196, "bursts of laughter"—*Ibid.* p. 50
196, "to *me*"—AEH p. 91
197, "from 1887 onward"—*A Buried Life* p. 30
197, "vaguely defined" et seq.—Gow pp. 42-3
198, "noteless number"—MP, No. XX
200, "depression and indifferent health" et seq.—*My Diaries*, by W. S. Blunt p. 287
201, "ever known"—*A Buried Life* p. 35
201, "and the dimness"—*Diary of A. C. Benson* p. 175
202, "magnificent bloom" et seq.—GR p. 123
202, "his bank balance"—*Bromsgrovian* p. 26
202, "are away"—GR p. 127
203, "to France"—*Ibid.* p. 158
203, "of the world"—*Bromsgrovian* p. 29
204, "after *town*"—GR p. 161
205, "make them careful"—*Ibid.* p. 175
205, "left my hands"—*Ibid.* p. 178
205, "in future"—AEH p. 147
206, "like being known"—AEH p. 99
206, "newspaper reporters"—GR p. 187
207, "been justified"—*Ibid.* p. 184
208, "humanity's reach"—*Ibid.* p. 199
208, "correct tie"—*Since Fifty*, by William Rothenstein p. 5
208, "half-pages amusing"—GR p. 197
209, "continuous excitement"—LP, Foreword
211, "tale of sorrow"—LP, No. XXXIV
211, "take the consequences"—Quoted in a letter from Dr. Jackson to the author
212, "the hard ground"—AEH p. 198
213, "a nice face" et seq.—*Letters of E. St. Vincent Millay* p. 161
213, "Robinson or Frost"—"Housman as a Conversationalist" by Cyril Clemens. *Mark Twain Quarterly*, Winter 1936
214, "an agreeable man"—GR p. 158
215, "keep conversation going"—*A Buried Life* p. 52
216, "to preserve it"—AEH p. 62
217, "might come suddenly"—GR p. 391
217, "before 1929"—*Ibid.* p. 215
218, "see me again"—AEH p. 150
218, "the man's comfort"—GR p. 395
218, "by a horse"—AEH p. 142

219, "rebuilt in me"—MP, No. XLIV
220, "on May 9"—GR p. 275
221, "don't like the lecture"—*Ibid.*
221, "Cambridge critics"—*Polite Essays*, by Ezra Pound p. 17
221, "*that* is poetry"—*Emily Dickinson*, by Richard Chase p. 184
222, "of beer" et seq.—N&N pp. 49-50
223, "of his nature"—N&N p. 46
223, "evident fatigue"—GR p. 275
223, "in a nursing home"—AEH p. 186
224, "through the tempestuous air"—GR p. 281
224, "nearly half an hour"—AEH p. 121
224, "proud challenge"—*Bromsgrovian* p. 65

Index

Index

Thackeray, W. M., 195
Thompson, Francis, 154
Times, The, 161, 211, 213, 221
Times Literary Supplement, The, 208
Tintoretto, 187
Toulouse-Lautrec, 184

Valley House, 36, 37, 38
Virgil, 132, 183
Vize, G. H., 184

Wharton, Edith, 201
Whitman, Walt, 204
Wilberforce, William, 24
Wilde, Oscar, 152, 153, 154, 156, 180, 182

Williams, John (grandfather), 31, 32, 33, 36
Williams, Sarah Jane (*see* Mrs. Edward Housman)
Wise family, 47, 116; Mrs. Wise, 48, 49, 50, 51, 59, 61, 116; Edith, 50, 51, 61, 62, 116; Minnie, 116; Theodore, 51, 116
Withers, Dr. Percy, 214–16, 217
Woodchester, 31, 32, 50, 51, 103, 116, 123, 184, 193, 202
Wordsworth, William, 106, 144

Yeats, W. B., 154, 175, 187
Yellow Book, The, 154

Zola, 180